Social Partnership and Governance Under Crises

Carol Nelson
University of the West Indies, Jamaica

A volume in the Advances in Public Policy and Administration (APPA) Book Series

Published in the United States of America by
IGI Global
Information Science Reference (an imprint of IGI Global)
701 E. Chocolate Avenue
Hershey PA, USA 17033
Tel: 717-533-8845
Fax: 717-533-8661
E-mail: cust@igi-global.com
Web site: http://www.igi-global.com

Library of Congress Cataloging-in-Publication Data

Names: Nelson, Carol, 1960- author.
Title: Social partnership and governance under crises / by Carol Nelson.
Description: Hershey : Information Science Reference, [2019]
Identifiers: LCCN 2018059003| ISBN 9781522589617 (hardcover) | ISBN 9781522589624 (ebook) | ISBN 9781522591931 (softcover)
Subjects: LCSH: Public administration--Jamaica. | Jamaica--Social policy | Jamaica--Economic policy. | Industrial relations--Jamaica. | Jamaica--Politics and government.
Classification: LCC JF1525.P6 N45 2019 | DDC 320.6097292--dc23 LC record available at https://lccn.loc.gov/2018059003

This book is published in the IGI Global book series Advances in Public Policy and Administration (APPA) (ISSN: 2475-6644; eISSN: 2475-6652)

British Cataloguing in Publication Data
A Cataloguing in Publication record for this book is available from the British Library.

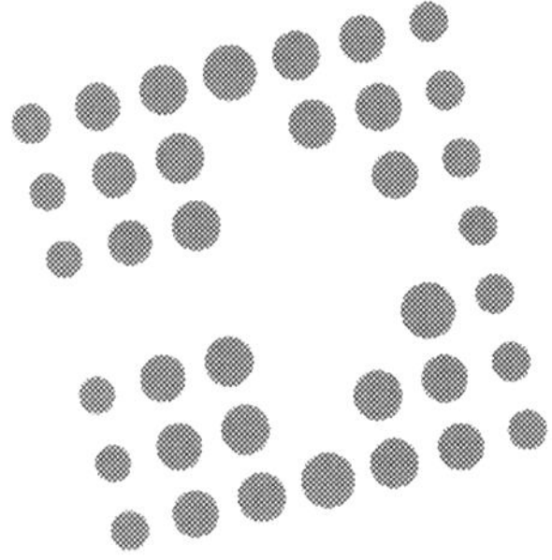

Advances in Public Policy and Administration (APPA) Book Series

ISSN:2475-6644
EISSN:2475-6652

MISSION

Proper management of the public sphere is necessary in order to maintain order in modern society. Research developments in the field of public policy and administration can assist in uncovering the latest tools, practices, and methodologies for governing societies around the world.

The **Advances in Public Policy and Administration (APPA) Book Series** aims to publish scholarly publications focused on topics pertaining to the governance of the public domain. APPA's focus on timely topics relating to government, public funding, politics, public safety, policy, and law enforcement is particularly relevant to academicians, government officials, and upper-level students seeking the most up-to-date research in their field.

COVERAGE

- Government
- Law Enforcement
- Political Economy
- Politics
- Public Administration
- Public Funding
- Public Policy
- Resource Allocation
- Urban Planning

IGI Global is currently accepting manuscripts for publication within this series. To submit a proposal for a volume in this series, please contact our Acquisition Editors at Acquisitions@igi-global.com or visit: http://www.igi-global.com/publish/.

The Advances in Public Policy and Administration (APPA) Book Series (ISSN 2475-6644) is published by IGI Global, 701 E. Chocolate Avenue, Hershey, PA 17033-1240, USA, www.igi-global.com. This series is composed of titles available for purchase individually; each title is edited to be contextually exclusive from any other title within the series. For pricing and ordering information please visit http://www.igi-global.com/book-series/advances-public-policy-administration/97862. Postmaster: Send all address changes to above address.

Titles in this Series

For a list of additional titles in this series, please visit:
https://www.igi-global.com/book-series/advances-public-policy-administration/97862

Building a Sustainable Transportation Infrastructure for Long-Term Econmic Growth
Olga V. Smirnova (East Carolina University, USA)
Engineering Science Reference • ©2019 • 309pp • H/C (ISBN: 9781522573968) • US $195.00

Industrial and Urban Growth Policies at the Sub-National, National, and Global Levels
Umar G. Benna (Benna Associates, Nigeria)
Information Science Reference • ©2019 • 418pp • H/C (ISBN: 9781522576259) • US $205.00

Analytics, Operations, and Strategic Decision Making in the Public Sector
Gerald William Evans (University of Louisville, USA) William E. Biles (University of Louisville, USA) and Ki-Hwan G. Bae (University of Louisville, USA)
Information Science Reference • ©2019 • 441pp • H/C (ISBN: 9781522575917) • US $215.00

Social Jurisprudence in the Changing of Social Norms Emerging Research and...
Karla L. Drenner (Purdue University Global, USA)
Information Science Reference • ©2019 • 174pp • H/C (ISBN: 9781522579618) • US $135.00

Capital Management and Budgeting in the Public Sector
Arwiphawee Srithongrung (University of Illinois at Springfield, USA) Natalia B. Ermasova (Governors State University, USA) and Juita-Elena (Wie) Yusuf (Old Dominion University, USA)
Business Science Reference • ©2019 • 379pp • H/C (ISBN: 9781522573296) • US $225.00

Handbook of Research on Advocacy, Promotion, and Public Programming for Memory...
Patrick Ngulube (University of South Africa, South Africa)
Information Science Reference • ©2019 • 453pp • H/C (ISBN: 9781522574293) • US $265.00

For an entire list of titles in this series, please visit:
https://www.igi-global.com/book-series/advances-public-policy-administration/97862

701 East Chocolate Avenue, Hershey, PA 17033, USA
Tel: 717-533-8845 x100 • Fax: 717-533-8661
E-Mail: cust@igi-global.com • www.igi-global.com

Table of Contents

Preface

INTRODUCTION

The word "crisis" evokes diverse imageries of danger, disaster, things falling apart or a feeling of a culmination, a forced point of turning, or an unavoidable decision that has to be made. Crises have been etched into the fabric of the 21st century, from which no country has been exempt, emanating from diverse domains and revealing themselves in times of intense difficulty, danger or challenge. The problematique of crisis compels governments and policymakers to consider change and to entertain new modalities and relationships for self-preservation in the new, emerging dispensation.

Governance and accepted practices and institutions long established, undergo change and compromise in the process of entertaining new power sharing arrangements, instigated by crisis, with a view to regain stability. In terms of governance, former combatants become strange bedfellows in tacit arrangements brokered in convergence around the Accord in mutual reciprocity, minimizing the risk of loss while those on the periphery are networked in.

Social partnership has emerged, in several contexts globally, as a governance response to crisis and the potential fragmentation of the established status quo, which compels the networking and coming together of diverse societal actors, seeking to minimize potential losses and maximize mutual gains.

Against the background of pending macroeconomic crisis, the case of the Public Sector Memorandum of Understanding or 'MOU' social partnership agreement, forged between the Government of Jamaica and the Jamaica Confederation of Trade Unions (JCTU) reflected such a governance response to crisis.

The crisis was rooted in the ballooning of the public sector wage bill which had the potential to exacerbate and derail the Government's macroeconomic efforts at fiscal stabilization.

This exploration differs from others researching social partnership agreements by using Actor Network Theory's (ANT) relational approach to explore the development of social partnership between traditional adversaries, in the context of the small island developing state of Jamaica. With respect to Jamaica, several authors (Brewster, 2007; Brown, 2002) posit that the society is undergirded by an environment of low social capital. This deficit arguably, has flavoured Jamaica's social partnership experience limiting them to bipartite arrangements being forged out of crisis, where the case of the Public Sector Memorandum of Understanding (MOU) is no different, emerging as a governance response to crisis

ANT's unique ontology and value lies in its focus on network interaction, as compared to other network related approaches. Activity Theory, pivots around the developmental tasks and Structuration Theory does not have the unique facility to include and recognize agency in non-human objects. While Diffusion Theory, oscillates around innovations as being central to it, excluding relational issues of power and the political.

Firstly, by 'following the actors', in ANT and the moments of *problematization, interessement, enrollment* and *mobilization,* involved in 'translation, the research undertaken, sought to deconstruct network connectivity and the power relations of the actor network, created by utilizing the unique ontology of Actor Network Theory, which affords the conceptualization of the MOU as an equal actor in the network. As an actor the MOU is conferred equity with other actors, vesting it with a discourse of its own. Secondly, Critical Discourse Analysis (CDA) is combined concomitantly, with ANT, to explore the networked connectivity in actor networks, through their interaction and the context of the discourses of the actors involved during the implementation of the Agreement. Within the 'black box' of MOU network relations, Norman Fairclough's Critical Discourse Analysis approach was used, analyzing discourses, linking 'socio cognitive 'dimensions of text production and interpretation' (Fairclough 1993, p. 80) with social analyses of the context of the actors, furthering the relational analysis of the networks. The probing of the actors' discourses and practices with CDA, enables the impenetrable black box of network interaction to become penetrable and is demystified.

These networks deconstructed and revelations of operation have implications for network relations, the practice of power and the implementation of public policy and industrial relations.

The discourses and discoursal relations of and between the actors in social partnership arrangements were explored through Critical Discourse

Analysis (CDA) bringing to the fore their importance in determining the degree of connectivity that undergirds the fulfilment and implementation of agreements and which signal the effectiveness of the outcomes and delivery of commitments.

Challenges were embedded in the development of the network of relations that converged to undergird the MOU actor network to make the Agreement hold. The implementation of the MOU Agreement, born out of mutual need, had implications for the discourse and practice of the partners to the accord, giving rise to discoursal contests between the diverse parties, inherent in the process of convergence in actor networks.

Challenges were revealed in the contests between the 'new' MOU discourse and traditional discourses of the actors. Evidence of changing discourses such as, genre mixing of entrepreneurialism within public sector modernization and their institutionalization, were explored, locating '*power in discourse and power over discourse*' (Fairclough 2003, p. 205). The analysis of discourse provided a tool for multilayered analyses to take into account a specific outcome of a process not only in terms of goal achievement but also factoring the social, thereby enhancing the future legitimacy of certain policy options (Roozendaal, 2002, p.33). This may engender new insight as to the actual 'on the ground' inner outworking of social phenomenon- agreements, relationships and policy initiatives, as these methods seeks to identify the key variables or hidden elements which inhibit effectiveness and what can be mitigated to improve results and deliver more successful governance outcomes.

In terms of the utility of ANT and CDA, the text of agreements, could form a basis for their application, where 'actants' are ascribed their own discourse and practice. Through the exploration of network relations and discoursal interactions surrounding their implementation, one could ascertain the implications for the inculcation of 'Treaty discourse' within contexts- cultural, political and the institutional fabric of governance regimes. Specific issues embedded in discourse may come to the fore to reveal the hidden deterrents to the transformational outcomes desired within and between partners, as envisioned in the texts of the agreement.

The book contributes to industrial relations and social partnership literature as well as gives insight into the inner workings of networks and their value in the implementation of policy and governance frameworks. It also gives a glimpse of the nature of interactions and furthers an understanding of the connectedness and underlying interactions within different types of multilevel network relations that can determine the success or failure of agreements being implemented. ANT retains its relevance and flavour, by constructing and holding equivalence between actors - animate and inanimate - that are reconfigured and negotiated in terms of significance, power and agency.

Convergence, apart from the meaning within ANT's construct, relates to the idea of actors coming together or pivoting around a central objective in response to a common issue or consensus object, forming, in this case a social partnership agreement – for reasons of self -interest to, not always maximize gains, but also to minimize the risk of loss.

Agreements become much more than just the paper they are written on to capture an appreciation of how parties must undergo change, or adjustment in – identity", "relational" and "ideational" functions (Fairclough, 1992) -in response to the language, discourse and practice of participants in an agreement that reconstructs their accepted norms- of discourse, practice- and processes that have become intrinsic to and characteristic of their networks.

These established network characteristics are altered or subsumed to give agreements 'life' and meaning in the space of flows being assimilated into their new connectivity and new networks to support 'social identities, subject positions and relationships between people and systems of knowledge and belief.' (Fairclough, 1992, p.193)

The book captures the inner workings of the MOU social partnership captured in discourse and text and relates how the MOU was used to configure new modalities of governance and relations within actor networks of the public sector, trade unions and industrial relations.

Challenge for leadership, political, public or private, policymakers and public officials faced with the problem of multifaceted crisis, resides in taking decisions that configure governance and present new ways of operating that, hopefully, can still facilitate the retention of the existing social relations. In the context of brokering new arrangements, networks of relations are formed that involves partnering or creating or renewing relationships with commensurate degrees of power sharing which are unavoidable, but critical in responding to the new dynamic.

For public sector officials, part of the challenge is in mobilization and responding to imperatives of the political directorate and policymakers treating with crisis in order to operationalize decisions and dictates. These may be, both formal and informal, that ultimately engenders contest within their domain and discourse practice to achieve the desired result. Driven by the intention to address the crisis condition there is the recognition that these inevitably spillover into adjoining societal networks of relations and domain with reciprocity. The value of discourse in navigating multiple interests- in terms of analyses of language, culture and practice- in partnership arrangements are highlighted.

The importance for entities that adopt governance and participatory mechanisms with multilevel actors, inclusive of engendering diversity in participatory governance regimes are brought to the fore.

For policymakers and labour practitioners an alternative, discoursal perspective for evaluating social partnership processes is presented. Albeit, not only in terms of the norms, benefits, costs and outcomes, but by an appreciation of and the value gained from unearthing the inner working of relationships, practices and power, albeit from the context of the network relations and implementation of a social partnership agreement.

For students and researchers, the approach of leveraging ANT and CDA presents an alternative ontological framework of analysis for agreements or networks where inanimate subjects can be observed as engendering dynamic 'network relations.' Audiences that frame policies and agreements to implement across diverse multilevel networks of interests, power and capacity, such as in industrial Relations fields, labour related and corporate governance spheres may also find resonance, in strengthening an understanding the role of and interplay of discourse, identity and social practices oftentimes backgrounded in navigating such accords.

The MOU social partnership agreement is presented as an agent of discoursal change, possessing its own discourse, and in turn having implications in the context of the accord, for the traditional discourse and practice of the public sector, trade unions and the practice of industrial relations. As an alternative 'lens' of analysis, discourse and texts is also advocated for social studies differing from the institutional, socio economic, political and trade related frames, emphasizing instead, networks of interaction, systems, social action, processes, structures (Waller, 2006) and discourse practice.

That the MOU came to fruition, is significant when one understands the limited success of the social partnership experiences specific to Jamaica, due in part to the legacy of political divisiveness and bipartisanship which permeates the institutional fabric of society and around which societal discourse subtly pivots.

What was also brought to the fore is the nature of the interactions within actor network relations and the need to analyze the mechanics of them, the dynamics of their cycle of formation - cohesion, divergence, convergence and reformulation. Both enable an understanding of the hidden mechanics and intricacies of power relations as revealed through actor network linkages and the deconstruction of text and discourse. Together, they enable an appreciation for the complexity of network interaction, hidden in the pages of agreements and texts, which arise as an outcome of implementation and decision making linked to processes of governance. To arise to the challenges of behavioural change conditioned by agreements and texts, that heterogeneous actors must negotiate and embrace together, metering their individualities and raison d'etre in contributing to balance needed and obligations to a framework of text, of governance and overall good governance.

Social partnership as a mode of governance has been recognized as a governance response to crisis, reflected in agreements created in terms of text and commitments as dictated by the consensus of the partners to the process. Social partnership can also be considered, through the lens of "symmetry' and the unique ontology of Actor Network Theory, as being an equal actor or player with other actors, both animate and inanimate. Hence the agreement in text "comes to life' by possessing its own discourse, agency and power, initiating change in discursive terms in other actors, replacing their discourse with its own. Its own-way of thinking interpreting speaking genre and styles interdiscursivity and new relations of power.

Consequently, there is a recognition that:

The strategy for partnership governance has a significantly discursive character – it includes a particular discourse of governance (which the word "governance" is a part of), as well as narratives of past and present issues and problems of governance, and imaginaries for their solution. Actually, the situation is more complicated because the move towards partnership governance is controversial – for instance with respect to whether partnerships are really between equals – and there is a proliferation of strategies, discourses and narratives. (Fairclough, 2005, p. 2)

ORGANIZATION OF THE BOOK

The book is organized into 10 chapters of which a brief synopsis of each follows:

The Introduction

Globalization and governance perspectives are presents contextualize social partnership as a governance response. Thereafter the Jamaican context from which a governance response was crafted in the form of the Public Sector Memorandum of Understanding between the Government of Jamaica and the Jamaica Confederation of Trade Unions in 2004 is explained and chronicled. The qualitative research design, steps and approach taken to explore the MOU social partnership agreement, its text and discourse and governance outcomes, are discussed. The theoretical tool and methodological lens of analysis of Actor Network Theory (ANT) and Norman Fairclough's Critical Discourse Analysis (CDA respectively, are explained and their utility presented. In order to unearth the social realities and interpretations of the MOU experience and perspectives, diverse data sources were collected for use and in triangulation.

Chapter 1: Context – Globalization, Crisis, and the Public Sector Memorandum of Understanding (MOU)

Explores elements of globalization and governance and forms presented in the context of globalization. Crisis is highlighted and the elements that inform it. Characteristics of the Jamaican economy weakened by attempts to integrate into the global political economy and the context of crisis that obtained, contextualizing the crisis event that triggered negotiations leading to the creation of the Public Sector Memorandum of Understanding Agreement (MOU) between the Government of Jamaica and the trade unions. Characteristics of Government as an actor and the drivers of the dialogue are positioned with insight provided into the key concerns held by the Partners to the accord, influencing the type of inclusions in the text of the MOU in terms of the principles, provisions, processes and policies.

Chapter 2: Social Partnership

constitutes a conceptual review of social partnership, its epistemology and etymological foundations and contributary themes such as social dialogue, partnership and their relationship with social partnership. The partnership dialogue is embedded within the epistemology, discourse and practice of the International Labour Organization (ILO) whose models are promulgated and institutionalized from the perspective of global governance. The influence of the ILO and its networked policy coherence with other global governance institutions around social dialogue and its capture of the social dialogue discourse and practice.

Chapter 3: Social Partnership – Global Expressions

Linked to the former chapter which precipitates, an exploration of the phenomenon of social partnerships arrangements in various regions of the world, there is reflection on the common denominator of crisis, the different ways and context from which these arrangements have emerged and are represented. The characteristics of power sharing by the actors and how societies are reflected in the modalities of governance responding to various societal crisis or threats. The value and benefit of social partnership as a governance response that incorporates multiple stakeholders in societal adjustment to minimize the effect of crisis conditions is outlined, as well as recommendations for effective social dialogue.

Chapter 4: Social Partnership – Jamaican Expressions

Social partnership arrangements and synopses of efforts made by Jamaica to establish social partnership governance mechanisms are discussed. Highlighted for compare the Social Partnership Agreements of Barbados which are tri-partite and extensive and a bi-partite accord as exhibited in the context of the Jamaican Bauxite Industry and another embryonic initiative in Jamaica, at that time such as the Partnership for Progress (PFP). Reflections on the limited application of ILO concepts to Third World contexts and challenges to the further institutionalization of ILO norms.

Chapter 5: Actor Network Theory (ANT)

Reviews the origin and theoretical framework of Actor Network Theory (ANT), its conceptual components and epistemological worldview that converges around network relations. ANT's unique ontology confers subjects, social actors, animate and inanimate objects with equity and the status of being an actant or actor. Through the sociology of translation which consists of four moments- *problematization, interessement, enrollment* and *mobilization*, actors are networked in chains of association. Furthermore, ANT explains the mechanics of network convergence and the changing power relations that occur as a result with implications for governance and equity. Attributes, supporting its unique ontology and epistemology are discussed, as when applied to the MOU, enables the MOU Agreement to be conceptualized as a heterogeneous actor. An exploration is made of ANT's application to various fields of study including its strengths and weaknesses and relevance.

Chapter 6: Convergence – Actor Network Theory (ANT) and Critical Discourse Analysis (CDA)

This Chapter "follows the actors" (Latour, 1987, p. 176) to explore the mechanics of the formation of the MOU actor network of relations. Using the participant data and texts to trace the chronology of the formation of the social partnership agreement, its dimensions as it develops and how the actor network is derived. The chronology illuminates why and how associations between actors were created, what factors mobilized these heterogeneous actors to come together, how their functions were ascribed and how stability or a 'black box' status was achieved for the MOU actor network. The MOU emerges as an actor, with its own discourse having attained a 'black box' or "macro social status' composed of all the other actor networks and the relations that it controls for itself. Key elements of Norman Fairclough's Critical Discourse Analysis (CDA) methodology (1992) are highlighted distinguishing it from just the study of language text, to the study of text, language and their manifestation in the realm of the social. Fairclough's analyses include the properties of text, their production, distribution and consumption, the socio-cognitive processes of producing and interpreting them. The Chapter examines the language and text of the provisions of the MOU Agreement from the lens of CDA, foregrounding the intertextual and discursive linkages with other text and discourse. The value of the inclusion of discourse as a moment in the MOU actor network to facilitate an exploration of the connections between actor networks of the MOU is posited.

Chapter 7: MOU Convergence – Public Sector Discourse and Practice

Historical attributes and elements contributing to the traditional public sector discourse and practice are explored. The implementation of the MOU discourse and practice resulted in contests in the black box of network interaction as the culture and practice of the public sector was challenged with elements of the new MOU discourse. Structural and institutional responses required due to the MOU Provisions operandi led public sector managers to respond reluctantly at times to the new requirements and specific action being taken to remedy deficiencies. The analysis of the discourses revealed contests between the actors in the network and within their constituencies, from deep within the black box of network relations played out in the realm of discourse, throughout the MOU network. The nature and extent of diffusion and inculcation of the new discourse within the network of relations of actors within the public sector was a function of the effectiveness of the *enrollment* of public sector management juxtaposed with modalities of resistance from within the context of a Westminsterial construct that had conditioned attitudes and responses to the new discourse.

Chapter 8: MOU Convergence – Trade Union Discourse and Practice

The elevation of the trade unions to leadership on the Monitoring Committee subordinated the relative power position of public sector management under the new MOU discourse, reflected in how rigorous the convergence process became. Public sector management were reticent to accept the new position of the trade unions afforded by the new discourse, their increased advocacy and heightened inclusion within policymaking fora. Elements of the trade union movement's, discourse practice, culture and social relations became contested as against the requirements and elements of the MOU discourse as revealed in text and data. Additionally, in the context of traditional trade union practice, there were contests as the trade unions participated at the seat of power on the Monitoring Committee in terms of leadership and decision making. This managerial interface created issues in the union constituency whereby there was a feeling of betrayal and mistrust as the union leaders 'boxed and danced' (Huzzard et.al., 2004) allegedly, taking on a more managerial stance and conciliatory dialogue.

Chapter 9: MOU Convergence – Governance, Institutions, Discourse

The institution of governance of the MOU, the Monitoring Committee enabled the trade unions to access relations and networks beyond their traditional spheres. Empowered by MOU discourse there were implications for the practice of power within the Monitoring Committee, network of relations, between constituents within traditional network relations and other actors outside of the MOU actor network. Challenges arise when the leadership of the Monitoring Committee blurred the political divide in the practice of the power of governance

Chapter 10: Reflections: Social Partnership and Governance Under Crisis

Chapter 10 reflects upon the MOU actor network implications for the Partners and issues for consideration in brokering such arrangements. Finally, I reflect on the usefulness of ANT as a framework to explore the mechanics of power and networks and the value of CDA as a methodology for analyzing the discourse moment in network connectivity arguing for the inclusion of discourse as an additional moment in ANT.

REFERENCES

Brewster, H. (2007). *Understanding development challenges of the Caribbean*. Prepared for World Bank Forum for parliamentarians on Shaping A Trade Agenda to Promote Regional Integration and Competitiveness for CARICOM, St. Lucia.

Brown, D. (2002). The private sector as a social partnership: the Barbados model. In R. D. Selwyn & A. M. Bissessar (Eds.), *Governance in the Caribbean. Sir Arthur Lewis Institute of Social and Economic Studies (SALISES)*. University of the West Indies.

Fairclough, N. (1992). *Discourse and Social Change*. Cambridge, UK: Polity Press.

Fairclough, N. (2003). *Analysing discourse: Textual analysis for social research*. Psychology Press. doi:10.4324/9780203697078

Fairclough, N. (2005, May). Governance, partnership and participation: cooperation and conflict. Conference of the International Association for Dialogue Analysis, Bucharest, Romania.

Huzzard, T., Gregory, D., & Scott, R. (2004). Strategic unionism and partnership: boxing or dancing? In Book of Abstracts (p. 135). Academic Press.

Latour, B. (1987). *Science in action: How to follow scientists and engineers through society*. Cambridge, MA: Harvard University Press.

Rogers, E. M. (2003). *Diffusion of innovations* (5th ed.). New York: Free Press.

Van Roozendaal, G. (2002). *Trade unions and global governance: the debate on a social clause*. Psychology Press.

Waller, L. G. (2006). Introducing Fairclough's critical discourse analysis methodology for analyzing Caribbean social problems: Going beyond systems, resources, social action, social practices and forces of structure or lack thereof as units of analysis. *The Journal of Diplomatic Language*, *3*(1), 5.

Introduction

BACKGROUND

Governance is the creation of structure or order not externally imposed but arises as a result of the interaction of a multiplicity of the governing actors and does not rest upon recourse to authority or government sanctions (Kooiman,1993). Governance, as complex structures processes and issues, describes and prescribes power arrangements in society which embrace and transcends government (Munroe, 2000), and which signifies the dynamics of interaction and interrelationship, which in turn interfaces with other centres of authority and contenders as adversaries or partners in the distribution and exercise of power. With respect to the contemporary Caribbean, government was to be conceptualized as a 'hub in a network of social power partners engaged in the process of continuing interaction, for the purpose of policy' (Dumas, 1975 p. 79).

Governments, on the other hand, have become nodes of communication and decision-making, constantly interacting with concerned groups (Hertin, et.al., 2000) and as a governance response, social partnerships emerge as an outcome of such interaction.

Social partnership which is one of the subjects of this book, is understood not only as an agreement in terms of text and commitments as dictated by consensus of the partners to the process . Social partnerships involve the convergence of parties to formulate a joint response to an agreed challenge to ensure mutual benefit or minimize the risk of loss which has umbilical linkages to the discourse of industrial and labour relations and related global discourses. This exploration differs from others by leveraging Actor Network Theory and a relational approach to the development of social partnership combined with Critical Discourse Analysis (CDA) meythodology.

Capturing the events leading up to the formation of the Public Sector Memorandum of Understanding Agreement, (2004-2006) or 'MOU" of

Jamaica, this book unravels how the Agreement was created and how the network of relations sustained it and a degree of longevity, as an enduring social partnership agreement on the Jamaican governance landscape. Key 'moments' are highlighted within the history of Jamaica, a small Caribbean state and the crisis conditions that prevailed, arguably from a historical and political context, that backgrounded the emergence and development of the 'MOU' (2004-2006) social partnership agreement.

The context was the immediate macroeconomic environment, as on the eve of the creation of the MOU itself. These concerns were of focus, precipitating and fuelling the dialogue, the negotiations and deriving the text of inclusions and accompanying discourse and the text of the Agreement itself. The commitments agreed within the Agreement conferred obligations upon the Partners. In order to explore these implications, it was opined that the conceptualizations and approaches involved in the leveraging of Actor Network Theory or 'ANT' and Critical Discourse Analysis or 'CDA' would be insightful. There are several concepts and themes that will be discussed in the text.

As a theoretical mechanism to analyse networks Actor Network Theory (ANT), was used to explore the emergence of this social partnership and to trace the chronology of the development of the MOU actor network. Actor Network Theory (ANT) has a unique ontology, being termed a distinctive approach to social theory (Law, 2007) as actors or actants in the network are conceptualized as being heterogeneous, unique in incorporation and considered as equals, both the human and non-human actants (Michael, 1996) and possess symmetry in the formation of chains of associations (Law, 1991a; Latour, 1991). According to Latour (1986) one of the proponents, ANT as an approach to social theory has no 'social' dimension, but rather 'the social' is always already 'technical' just as the 'technical' is always already 'social,' (Couldry, 2008) as we are 'faced with chains which are associations of humans and the non-humans.' (Latour, 1991). ANT entails the interweaving of the technical and human (Callon, 1991) and convergence (Bowker & Leigh Star, 1996) has produced 'hybrids' or 'imbroglios of human and non-human' (Michael, 2000) that populate and proliferate (Law & Hassard, 1999) within the structures of everyday life. Thereby suggesting that society, organizations, agents and machines are all effects generated in patterned networks of diverse and not simply human, material. (Law, 2007).

ANT's unique ontology confers an 'actor' status to the MOU Agreement which affords an explanation as to the mechanics of the MOU's network relations are assembled being "a social construction of social relations" (Lowe,

2001, p. 345) and the dynamics within the network. ANT's 'radical' ontology affords the MOU Agreement text, an inanimate object, with an actor status in the network of relations, having its own identity, discourse and a status of equity with other actors. Within ANT constructs, the MOU Agreement becomes an actor seeking to build its own actor network by incorporating other actors and their related networks, through the process of the sociology of translation (Callon, 1986; Latour, 1996; Law & Hassard, 1999). Translation consists of four (4) moments- *problematization, interessement, enrollment and mobilization,* to create the MOU actor network of relations. Once the network has been formed and the actors and their respective networks converge and are complicit to the point where they become dynamically positioned and interconnected within the MOU actor network, the MOU then emerges as a macro social actor in terms of power relations. If the network becomes stabilized, reflected by the cessation of controversy and the acceptance of common (MOU) social meanings and discourse, demonstrated in ways of acting by the actors, then the MOU actor network achieves the 'black box' configuration. This signifies that relative positions are established, and an active state of equilibrium is achieved between the actor networks and 'black box' stability

Actor networks possess an inherent dynamism and constant fluidity due to the heterogeneity of the actors in the MOU actor-network whereby actors can, over time, still converge or diverge, reflected in shifting alliances (Williams-Jones & Graham, 2003; Callon, 1986) and even realignment.

The MOU Agreement seeks to establish MOU discourse, as the dominant discourse to be inculcated throughout the MOU actor network in relation to the Partners and other actor networks of the Agreement.

The text of the Agreement provides an MOU discourse, which has the intent to permeate or be inscribed within the actor networks being assimilated into the MOU actor network, through translation involving processes of negotiation, alignment and inscription of the actors.

To probe the nature of the connectivity of discourse between the actors within the MOU actor network and the modalities of the equilibrium of the black box of relations created, Norman Fairclough's Critical Discourse Analysis (CDA) methodology, provides for such an exploration, and an appreciation of the diverse perspectives surrounding discourse and related concepts- of text, language, and discourse.

Text, for example, is defined as a communicative event by Titscher, et.al. (2000) and consists of material objects as an outcome of representational practices, using a variety of signifying actors which contribute individually to the specific meaning of text (Kress & Van Leeuwen, 1996). Text refers to any product whether written or spoken that is simultaneously constituting and representing, relations and identities (Fairclough, 1992). Language is conceptualized as a form of social practice and there is a reciprocity of influence between language and social structure (Fairclough, 1989; Van Dijk, 1993; Wodak, 1989). The boundaries of social life result in different domains for the social use of language that has formative and transformative effects on culture and society and relations of power (Fairclough, 2003). Language is conceptualized as a form of social practice and attempts to make human beings aware of the reciprocal influences of language and social structure of which they are normally unaware (Fairclough 1989; Van Dijk 1993; Wodak 1989). The concept of social practice facilitates the oscillation between the perspective of social structure, social action and agency (Chouliaraki & Fairclough, 1999).

The meaning of discourse, following Foucauldian tradition (Jorgenson & Phillips, 2002) views discourse as systems of knowledge (Wodak & Meyer, 2009; Gee, 1996; Fairclough, 2001) which informs the social and constituted power. Harvey (1996) echoes similar views by focusing on how words and actions frame and represent spaces based on power relations (Richardson & Jensen, 2003). Habermas (1984) regarded discourse as communicative action and as ideological practice while Thompson (1984) related structures of discourse with structures of society (Van Dijk, 2001). These perspectives have synergies with Frow (1985) for whom the discursive, socially constructs and distinguishes reality and the symbolic.

Norman Fairclough's Critical Discourse Analysis

On account of using discourse as the unit of analysis, Norman Fairclough's approach to CDA was deemed the more appropriate methodology, to deconstruct and explore in depth the discourses surrounding the MOU as an actor network. Its usefulness partly rests in being able to facilitate 'multiple points of analytic entry' (Pennycook, 2001, p. 79) into texts and their contexts as well being a vehicle to investigate, describe, interpret and explain in depth, the patterns within the moments of interactions within the study.

The diverse perspectives which converge within the conceptualizations of Critical Discourse Analysis (CDA), as espoused by Norman Fairclough, holding to the Foucauldian tradition and steeped within Critical Theory are contemplated. Tenets of CDA, related themes - text, language and discourse

- are discussed and utilized to traverse the Provisions within the text of the MOU Agreement itself.

In the study of discourse, every text is seen as being embedded in a context which in turn, requires the study of differential relations to the social, political or other context from which the basis of interpretation is derived (Titscher, et.al., 2000, p. 24). Fairclough and Chouliaraki (1999) also emphasize that the analysis of a particular discourse, as a piece of discursive practice, focuses upon text production, consumption and distribution. These social processes require embedding in the economic, political and institutional contexts from within which the discourse originated and which may explain the social constructions of responses in text production.). Based on these conceptualizations, Fairclough (1992) espouses the use of texts as units of analyses and forms of social activity within the operations in the network that can reveal relations of power. In the process of analyzing discourse and the influences involved in the production and consumption of language, verbally and in text, there is an intrinsic connection between how language is used in its context - historical, cultural, political and social, in time and space - the nature of the social interaction and how this in turn influences social relations, practices - discourse.

Research Design

The epistemological approach, for the qualitative study, was interpretive and maintained an emphasis on socially constructed meaning, where knowledge is socially constructed, and reality emerges from interpretation. Maxwell's (1996, p.5) Interactive model was strategic, to anchor the inter relations of the processes of the exploratory study such as coding of data from notes, observations or interviews, recording reflections, data sorting for patterns, themes, differences, key features, themes etc.

An adaptation of the Conceptual Framework (Miles & Huberman, 1994) served to guide the exploratory research methodology in terms of the deconstruction and identification of the translation of interests within the actor network and black box through the exploration of discourse as text.

The methodology used was CDA, along with employing appropriate techniques such as Constant Comparative Methods (Strauss & Corbin, 1990), Case Study techniques (Yin, 1994, 2002) and various matrices ((Miles & Huberman, 1994) that assist the data, as discourse, to be analyzed. The findings from the analyses were validated through triangulation with data from the multiple data sources

Activities Involved in CDA

Sampling

Several activities to carry out the analytical procedures of CDA were undertaken, in terms of selecting a sample of individuals for the research based on their relevance to the study, and using cases that would provide the greatest in-depth information about the phenomenon under investigation (Patton, 1990). As an informal sampling frame, it is dependent on the 'expert judgment" or resources of the researcher in choice, as ''particular settings, persons, or events are deliberately selected for the important information they can provide that cannot be gotten as well from other choices' (Teddlie & Fu, 2007).

Purposive sampling and snowball techniques (Patton, 1990) were used to locate a 'highly specific' (Neumann, 2006, p. 222) sample possessing experience and information.

The issue of size can be deemed contentious depending on a number of factors. For Kvale (1996) and Merriam (1998), sample size depends on the questions being asked, the data being gathered, the analysis in progress and resources you have to support the study, and one had to 'seek out groups, settings, and individuals where ...the processes being studied are most likely to occur' (Denzin & Lincoln, 1994, p. 202). In this case, the size of the sample may be considered small, but it represented a significant proportion (more than 60%) of the total population of persons directly involved in the creation and development of the MOU. The informants selected consisted of persons who were the closest to the development of the MOU Agreement, in terms of the initial discussions, the negotiation process, who determined the provisions and inclusions within the text of the Agreement and whose discourse drew upon other fields and discourses. These individuals themselves were a part of other networks and practices which in turn influenced and were interwoven into the modalities of the text and process. Patton (1990, p. 186) suggests the establishment of a minimum sample size contingent upon the informants required to provide comprehensive coverage of the phenomenon, according to the purpose of the study. In this circumstance, sampling was driven to the point of redundancy (Lincoln & Guba, 1985, p. 202) whereby no new information was forthcoming from the informants as a saturation point was reached (Strauss & Corbin, 1998; Lincoln & Guba, 1985).

In terms of how representative, the sample was, one primary objective was to gain insight and ideas about the phenomenon, from the informants' perspective. According to Guba (1985), questions about appropriate sample size have less to do with actual numbers of participants or cases and much more with the quality and depth of information elicited through the research process. As mentioned earlier the sampling decision was based upon involvement with the MOU first-hand namely members of the negotiating team, drafters of the text of the Agreement, implementers of the provisions as well as related projects in the ministries and core members of the Monitoring Committee (MC).

The participants were involved with the MOU Agreement from its developmental stages to implementation, eventually engrafting those on the periphery into the network of relations.

Some of the informants worked across areas, e.g. some members of the Monitoring Committee, technical advisers, assigned as negotiators representing their particular interest group- Union or Government, thereby playing dual roles and hence bringing wider experience and informational sources as well as yielding multiple interpretative stances in their discourse.

Where there emerged "regularities' (Lincoln & Guba,1985) and homogeneity of perspectives in several areas, with a reduction in the diversity, depth and quality of the additional information gleaned with each successive interview, it was deemed necessary to probe beyond this homogenous level or 'inner circle' and explore other perspectives on the MOU, moving from pronouncement to practice, from conceptualization to operationalization, by obtaining discourse as text and interviews from 'outliers' (Miles & Huberman, 1994, p.28.

These persons 'at the periphery' (Miles & Huberman, 1994, p. 34) were those, who in practical terms, translated the Agreement and gave the 'bones' of the Agreement 'flesh', in the context of implementation. They also had to communicate and translate the MOU into their everyday operations, converting and transforming policy discourse and text, into social action, structural and operational reality, communicating to public sector workers. By the inclusion of these other, multiple voices, new perspectives emerged, valued as a manifestation of diversity (Stockdill & Morehouse, 1992), a 'maximizing of the variation' (Maykut & Morehouse, 1994) and a broadening of the discussions within discourses.

The inclusion of each additional participant was due to their being able to expand the variability of the sample (Maykut & Morehouse, 1994). The researcher, according to Patton (1990), in engaging with the people, situations and phenomenon under study, can provide important insights and personal experience, as well as a critical understanding of the phenomenon. The research was contextualized (Bergman & Coxson, 2005) but with the researcher also as a voice in the study, altogether contributing to differential interpretation.

DATA COLLECTION

Interviews do not remain fixed but are constructed interactionally on each occasion" (O'Rourke & Pitt, 2007) and the standpoint, from which the information is offered is continually developed in relation to the ongoing interview interaction and constituted in relation to the developing context of the interview (Holstein & Gubrium, 1995, p. 15). The interviews conducted served as a tool for data gathering and a means of capturing perspectives, rich, in depth experiential accounts and constructs of knowledge on the phenomenon, to inform the process of analysis at the various levels for CDA. These oral accounts provided access to beliefs, understandings, interpretations, relationships and modalities of meaning held by the informants, enabling through observation and interactive dialogue, 'moments of text production' in the interface.

Scheduled, semi structured interviews where several thematic questions pertaining to the major components and themes within the text of the MOU Agreement were developed, along with an Interview Protocol. The key data collection methods included using semi structured face-to-face interviews and observations, which helped to provide a 'participant perspective', and obtain an appreciation of how they considered aspects of their interface with respect to the MOU process, its implementation and the nature of the partnership. Furthermore, the interviews were animated and sometimes emotional as the phenomenon of the MOU and its implementation affected the lives and roles of individuals differently according to their position or role in the MOU network and the implementation of the process.

Cognizant of ethical considerations commitments and assurances given to maintain their confidentiality, in terms of their data and anonymity were agreed accordingly. Several of the participants made themselves available and all welcomed the opportunity to be able to speak and 'tell their stories from their perspective, giving their account and interpretation of the MOU and elements and their own experiences with the MOU process.

Data was obtained from notes taken at meetings, by photocopying and scanning documents and media reports, preserving them in electronic form. Information was also extracted from websites, emails, electronic databases and book search sites, all of which helped to build an electronic database for easy access during the research and support an audit trail of data collection. The audio interviews from participants were transcribed with the assistance of a dictation computer software programme called Dragon Naturally Speaking 9, which assisted the accuracy of the verbatim transcription of interviews, using Microsoft Word. Listening repetitively to the recordings, and reflecting on information from interviews, memos, observations and notes made throughout the course of the research, served to make analysis a continuous inductive process over the period. These approaches assisted in maintaining a distance from the interview findings and to limit personal influence upon those being researched so that the data being received was not pre-interpreted in the process.

Secondary data, documents and economic reports assisted by contributing to a database of hard copy information, to support the electronic database of information which all together formed the 'corpus' of 'text' from which the research proceeded.

DATA ANALYSIS

Dimensions of Discourse Analysis

In Titscher et al, (2000), Fairclough (1993) portrays the "dimensions of discourse analysis' using the analogy of 'three boxes' concentrically aligned, representing the bringing together of three analytical traditions and levels of analysis beginning with text. The text is described by looking at language, vocabularies, linguistic, semantic categories, with the view to identify representations. This includes how the participant categorizes himself and the constructions of his relations and identity of subject, object and social position, noting the instances of the use of power through language. 'At this level, the analyses of the genres of the different discourses are made along with the 'underlying assumptions and presuppositions of the generic and discursive configurations of the text.' (Waller, 2006). In addition, how

Figure 1. Dimensions of discourse analysis: "the three boxes"
Source: Titscher, S., Meyer, M., Wodak, R., & Vetter, E. (2000). Methods of text and discourse analysis: In search of meaning. London: Sage. (p. 152)

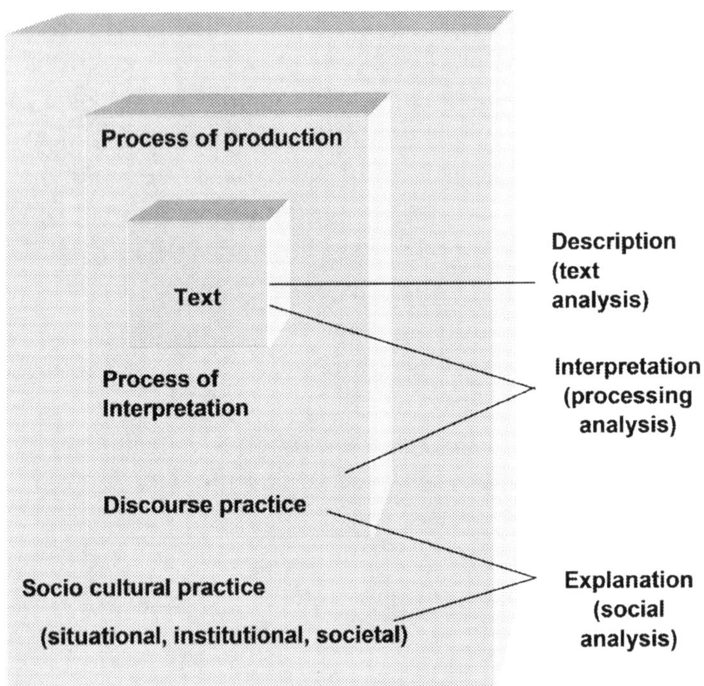

the text and the genres cohere, how the social events and their elements are represented, generalizations made and the ordering of events, in terms of what is fore grounded and what is back grounded.

The CDA analysis of the dimensions, as in the "Three Boxes" (Figure 1. (Box 1, Box 2 and Box 3), was applied to the text, which provided for a multilevel analytical approach and comparisons. Firstly, the text was described focusing on the language, vocabularies, linguistic, semantic categories, relations of identities, the discursive content, the productive and interpretive processes and how these texts link to other discourses, genres and styles, and what was represented within the text, - intertextuality'. Box 2 type analyses sought to establish the genre(s), how the text was created and represented by particular genres in 'ways of acting and being' how the social events, conjunctures and their elements were represented, and generalizations made and what was the angle or focus taken at different points in the text. Social factors with respect to the text being produced, distributed and consumed, the discursive practices, interdiscursivity and orders of discourse were also highlighted.

The "Three Boxes" analyses, was also applied with respect to the transcripts and the other texts, which aided an analysis of the 'dialectic' to show how systems of discourses were used in shaping institutions, social practices and structures and in activities of social action and agency. Being shaped, being transformative while being transformed. In conducting these CDA analyses, there was no standard method in approaching the texts, just broad theoretical guidelines. However, Fairclough (2003) has proposed several questions along with MacGregor (2003) which served to give guidance to the thought process involved in analysing the corpus of the text, from a CDA approach, which are indicated in Figure 1 so as to focus on reading 'against the text' (MacGregor, 2003) and to identify patterns of consistency and variation (Potter & Wetherall, 1987).

Data triangulation which provides multiple measures of the same phenomenon (Yin, 2003) can reduce the risk that the study will reflect methodological biases or limitations of one particular method (Maxwell, 1996). Furthermore, by making the descriptions context–rich and meaningful (Denzin & Lincoln, 2005), exploring converging explanations as well as examining 'rival' positions, competing positions and discrepant data and testing these conclusively, the study will truly reflect and represent the range of constructs accorded the phenomenon by the participants. There was an emphasis made to capture an inside view, detailed accounts and narrative of how the participants understood their MOU experience and by supporting empirical claims by utilizing numerous pieces of diverse empirical data, which cumulatively would create the evidence.

Critique of Methodology

The CDA process is not without its critics, such as Widdowson (1998) who asserts that CDA needs to be more empirically based, stronger in its ethnographic investigations and is too interpretative and biased due to the focus on the political. Laclau & Mouffe (2001) hold the view that everything is contingent in CDA and there is the overestimation of the possibilities of change as not all groups have the equal possibility for rearticulating elements in new ways to engender change. The discourse of persons are subject to constraints that do not emanate from the discursive level but from structural relations of dependency, such as, class, gender and ethnicity.

However, as indicated earlier, CDA has several strengths, one of which is that it can be used in conjunction with other methodologies and techniques. The weaknesses were mitigated using other methods in the study, such as elements of Constant Comparative Analysis of Grounded Theory (Strauss & Corbin, 1990) and Case Study Method (Yin, 1994). The use of Case Ordered Effects Matrices and Theme Ordered Effects Matrices (Miles & Huberman, 1994) assisted to display some of the salient findings allowing them to be mapped and compared to derive patterns and 'construct meaning' across and within groups while staying true to the perspectives of participants. Case Order Effects Matrices constructed according to the effects emerging on the part of the discourses, representations and social constructs of the phenomenon as communicated by participants helped, in the derivation of patterns. This was particularly useful when there is a wide variety of possible effects, and there is a need to reduce the data, while keep the data disaggregated, distinct and to reveal any deviant cases (Miles & Huberman, 1994) and to establish patterns or links between groups and within the data.

Using discourse and text as data and units of analysis, the nature of the power relations within the connectivity is explored through the discourse moment and deconstructed using CDA methodology of Norman Fairclough (1992; 2001) that concomitantly provides for the deconstruction of the power relations within the 'black box' of the MOU actor network.

CDA recognizes local norms and values and the relations among and between them while unearthing the inner workings of network interactions as conceptualized within ANT. However, CDA has the added facility of a critical approach in challenging established hegemonic networks, which contributes a strong emancipatory flavour. Norman Fairclough's approach to CDA was deemed the more appropriate methodology, on account of using discourse as the unit of analysis to deconstruct the discourses surrounding the MOU as a network and through which the research question could be answered. Its usefulness partly rests in being able to facilitate 'multiple points of analytic entry' (Janks, 1997) as well being a vehicle to investigate, describe, interpret and explain in depth the patterns within the moments of interactions within the study.

CDA, as a methodological tool, becomes a lens to "penetrate' and facilitate an exploration of power dimensions within the "black box' of network interaction reflected in the nature of the linkages and network relations created within the MOU actor network. These texts and revealed discourses, analysed using CDA, exposes the interpretations of experiences, social processes, events and moments during the formative period of the MOU network, its translation through the institutional constructs and discourses of the other actors in the network, adding "flesh' to the 'bones' of the Agreement.

The methodology also brought to the fore discourses hidden within and below discourses and explained the contests and the changing power relations evidenced in social practices and the material. Hegemonic relations of power born out of tradition and precedence within the public sector and union movement were contested and resisted the tenets of the MOU Agreement and discourse and the empowerment sought by those previously excluded.

By drawing upon discourses, texts, other 'voices', texts, social practices and genres in terms of social practices, orders of discourse and related interdiscursivity, whereby elements and or social practices in one discourse carries the social and or institutional meaning from other discourses.

Diverse implications emerged from the process of inscribing and aligning the traditional networks and discourses with that of the MOU Agreement as well as the inculcation of MOU discourse, revealing the inner ebbs and flows between partners and discoursal contests and the practice of discoursal power in the partnership.

- In exploring the possible implications of the MOU for governance of the public sector, trade unions and industrial relations practice, they could be perceived as having outcomes for the respective discourses and practices, for growth and development, their public image, representation, culture and raison d'être. Additionally, there would be implications for the governance of public administration, human resources, political and technical dimensions, structures, operations and procedures within institutions and in network relations.

Other discourses, of the key actors, gave form and meaning to the discourse of the MOU Agreement as through interdiscursivity reflected in the implementation outcomes and the modalities of the social practices affected.

The MOU had discoursal implications for governance and the actors in the accord, the public sector, and industrial relations practice within it. The book explores the ways in which the traditional discourses and social practices within the public sector and union movement were contested with that of the new discourse' of the MOU, as revealed in discourse and text considering the possible implications.

The approaches used in analysing text and discourses surrounding the Agreement are novel in terms of the leveraging of Actor Network Theory (ANT) and Critical Discourse Analysis (CDA) methodology, in their application to a labour agreement or social partnership, even more so within a Caribbean context.

The book advocates the utility of ANT and CDA in analyzing network relations which underlie the social processes and structures of governance and in this context the MOU network and related social processes. In addition, the case is made for the inclusion of discourse as a moment in actor network configurations. (Nelson, 2016).

What is also brought to the fore is the nature of the interactions within actor network relations and the need to analyse their mechanics, the dynamics of their cycle of formation - cohesion, divergence, convergence and reformulation. Both enable an understanding of the hidden mechanics and intricacies of power relations as revealed through actor network linkages and the deconstruction of text and discourse. Together, they enable an appreciation for the complexity of network interaction, hidden in the pages of agreements and texts, which arise as an outcome of implementation and decision making linked to processes of governance. To arise to the challenges of behavioural change conditioned by agreements and texts, that heterogeneous actors must negotiate and embrace together, metering their individualities and raison d'etre in contributing to balance needed and obligations to a framework of text, of governance and overall good governance.

In like manner, insight is provided into the operations of partnerships by Actor Network Theory (ANT), the sociology of translation, whereby there is the translation or negotiation of interests around, in this case, the Public Sector Memorandum of Understanding (MOU) Agreement, forged between the Government of Jamaica and the Public Sector Trade Unions, to create actor network relations.

On reflection, the book contributes to the institutional memory of the MOU partnership by capturing its earliest years. Furthermore, that the MOU came to fruition, is significant when one considers the limited success of the social partnership experiences of Jamaica, due in part to the legacy of political divisiveness and bipartisanship which permeates the institutional fabric of society and around which societal discourse subtly pivots.

Applied, as a tool to analyse the nature of the linkages in the actor network and relations, which are discoursal, CDA captured the relational ebb and flow of the network interface with other actors. By drawing upon discourse texts, other 'voices', texts, social practices and genres, orders of discourse and related interdiscursivity, numerous implications emerged from the dynamic process of inscribing and aligning the traditional networks and respective discourses with that of the MOU network and corresponding discourse. The CDA methodology, its concepts, critical origins and techniques of analysis revealed its utility by being able to uncover the inner workings of the network, probing into the nature of the connectivity which, apart from inscribing the negotiated text and obligations of the Partner within the MOU actor-network, also represents 'MOU discourse' in terms of social practices, orders of discourse and interdiscursivity.

The approaches used in analyzing discourses surrounding the Agreement and actors are novel in terms of the leveraging of Actor Network Theory (ANT) and Critical Discourse Analysis (CDA) methodology, in their application to a labour agreement or social partnership. CDA methodology is deemed 'relevant to studying the exercise of power' (Hastings, 1999, p. 93) and in-depth insider perspectives from discourse as text, by facilitating the deconstruction of texts. Verbatim elite interviews were garnered from persons, who were instrumental in the negotiations to forging of the MOU Agreement, providing in-depth, qualitative, experiential accounts and information as conceptualizers, policy makers, technical advisers, negotiators and implementers.

Once analyzed using CDA, these revealed the interpretations of experiences, social processes, events and moments during the formative period of the MOU network, its translation through the institutional constructs and discourses of the other actors in the network, adding 'flesh' to the 'bones' of the Agreement.

REFERENCES

Bergman, M. M., & Coxon, A. P. (2005). The quality in qualitative methods. In Forum: qualitative social research= Forum qualitative Sozialforschung: FQS (Vol. 6; No. 2, pp. Art-34). Freie Univ. Berlin.

Bowker, G. C., & Star, S. L. (1996). How things (actor-net) work: Classification, magic and the ubiquity of standards. *Philosophia*, *25*(3-4), 195–220.

Callon, M. (1986). Some elements of a sociology of translation: domestication of the scallops and the fishermen of St Brieuc Bay. In Power, Action and Belief (pp. 196-223). London: Routledge.

Callon, M. (1991). Techno-economic networks and irreversibility. In A Sociology of Monsters: Essays on Power, Technology and Domination. London: Academic Press.

Chouliaraki, L., & Fairclough, N. (1999). *Discourse in late modernity-rethinking CDA*. Edinburgh, UK: Edinburgh University Press.

Couldry, N. (2008). Actor network theory and media: do they connect and on what terms? In A. Hepp, F. Krotz, S. Moores, & C. Winter (Eds.), *Connectivity, Networks and Flows: Conceptualizing Contemporary Communications* (pp. 93–110). Cresskill, NJ: Hampton Press, Inc.

Denzin, N. K., & Lincoln, Y. S. (Eds.). (2011). *The Sage handbook of qualitative research*. Sage.

Dumas, J. R. P. (1995). *In the Service of the Public: Articles and Speeches 1963-1993, with Commentaries*. Canoe Press.

Fairclough, N. (1989). *Language and power*. London: Longman.

Fairclough, N. (1992). *Discourse and Social Change*. Cambridge, UK: Polity Press.

Fairclough, N. (1993). Critical discourse analysis and the marketization of public discourse: The universities. *Discourse & Society*, *4*(2), 133–168. doi:10.1177/0957926593004002002

Fairclough, N. (2001). The dialectics of discourse. *Textus*, *14*(2), 231-242. Retrieved from http://www.ling.lancs.ac.uk/staff/norman/2001a.doc

Frow, J. (1985). Discourse and power. *Economy and Society*, *14*(2), 193–214. doi:10.1080/03085148500000010

Gee, J. P. (1996). *Social linguistics and literacies: Ideology in discourses*. Taylor & Francis.

Habermas, J. (1984). *The theory of communicative action* (Vol. 2). Beacon press.

Harvey, D., & Braun, B. (1996). *Justice, nature and the geography of difference* (Vol. 468). Oxford, UK: Blackwell.

Holstein, J. A., & Gubrium, J. F. (1995). *The active interview* (Vol. 37). Sage. doi:10.4135/9781412986120

Janks, H. (1997). Critical discourse analysis as a research tool. *Discourse (Abingdon)*, *18*(3), 329–342. doi:10.1080/0159630970180302

Janks, H. (1999). Critical discourse analysis as a research tool. In J. Marshall & M. Peters (Eds.), *Education Policy* (pp. 49–62). Cheltenham, UK: Edward Elgar.

Jørgensen, M. W., & Phillips, L. J. (2002). Discourse analysis as theory and method. *Sage (Atlanta, Ga.)*.

Kooiman, J. (1993). Modern governance: New government-society interactions. *Sage (Atlanta, Ga.)*.

Kress, G. R., & Van Leeuwen, T. (1996). *Reading images: The grammar of visual design*. Psychology Press.

Kvale, S. (1996). The 1,000-page question. *Qualitative Inquiry*, *2*(3), 275–284. doi:10.1177/107780049600200302

Laclau, E., & Mouffe, C. (2001). *Hegemony and radical democracy in hegemony and socialist strategy*. Academic Press.

Latour, B. (1986). The Powers of Association. In J. Law (Ed.), Power, Action and Belief. A New Sociology of Knowledge? (pp. 264-280). London: Routledge.

Latour, B. (1991). *Technology is society made durable. Sociology of Monsters: Essay on Power. Technology. and Domination*. London: Routledge.

Latour, B. (1996). *Aramis, or, The love of technology*. Cambridge, MA: Harvard University Press.

Law, J. (2007). *Actor Network Theory and Material Semiotics.* Centre for Science Studies and Department of Sociology. Retrieved from www.heterogeneities.net/publications/Law-ANTandMaterialSemiotics.pdf

Law, J., & Hassard, J. (1999). *Actor network theory and after*. Oxford, UK: Blackwell.

Lincoln, Y. S., & Guba, E. G. (1985). *Naturalistic inquiry* (Vol. 75). Sage.

Lowe, A. (2001). After ANT: An illustrative discussion of the implications for qualitative accounting case research. *Accounting, Auditing & Accountability Journal*, *14*(3), 327–351. doi:10.1108/EUM0000000005519

Macgregor, J., Peterson, S., & Schuftan, C. (1998). Downsizing the civil service in developing countries: The golden handshake option revisited. *Public Administration and Development: The International Journal of Management Research and Practice*, *18*(1), 61–76. doi:10.1002/(SICI)1099-162X(199802)18:1<61::AID-PAD988>3.0.CO;2-N

Maxwell, J. A. (2012). *Qualitative research design: An interactive approach* (Vol. 41). Sage publications.

Maykut, P., & Morehouse, R. (1994). *Beginning qualitative research: a philosophic and practical approach*. Bristol, PA: Falmer.

Merriam, S. B. (1998). Qualitative Research and Case Study Applications in Education. Jossey-Bass Publishers.

Michael, M. (1996). *Constructing Identities: The Social, the Nonhuman and Change*. London: Sage. doi:10.4135/9781446279182

Miles, M. B., & Huberman, M. (1994). *Qualitative data analysis: An expanded sourcebook*. Sage.

Munroe, T. (2000). *Voice participation and governance in a changing environment: the case of Jamaica. Caribbean Group for Cooperation in Economic Development (CGCED)*. Washington, DC: World Bank.

Nelson, C. (2016). Beyond Actor Network Theory to the Marriage of Moments. *International Journal of Actor-Network Theory and Technological Innovation, 8*(3).

Neumann, L. W. (2006). *Social research methods*. Boston: Pearson Education.

O'Rourke, B., & Pitt, M. (2007). *Using the technology of the confessional as an analytical resource: Four analytical stances towards research interviews in discourse analysis*. Academic Press.

Patton, M. Q. (1990). *Qualitative evaluation and research methods*. SAGE Publications, Inc.

Pennycook, A. (2001). *Critical applied linguistics: A critical introduction*. Routledge.

Potter, J., & Wetherell, M. (1987). Discourse and social psychology: Beyond attitudes and behaviour. *Sage (Atlanta, Ga.)*.

Richardson, T., & Jensen, O. B. (2003). Linking discourse and space: Towards a cultural sociology of space in analysing spatial policy discourses. *Urban Studies (Edinburgh, Scotland), 40*(1), 7–22. doi:10.1080/0042098022008013 1

Stockdill, S. H., & Morehouse, D. L. (1992). Critical factors in the successful adoption of technology: A checklist based on TDC findings. *Educational Technology, 32*(1), 57–58.

Strauss, A., & Corbin, J. (1998). *Basics of qualitative research: Procedures and techniques for developing grounded theory*. Academic Press.

Teddlie, C., & Yu, F. (2007). Mixed methods sampling: A typology with examples. *Journal of Mixed Methods Research*, *1*(1), 77–100.

Titscher, S., Meyer, M., Wodak, R., & Vetter, E. (2000). Methods of text and discourse analysis: In search of meaning. *Sage (Atlanta, Ga.)*.

Van Dijk, T. A. (1993). Principles of critical discourse analysis. *Discourse & Society*, *4*(2), 249–283. doi:10.1177/0957926593004002006

Waller, L. G. (2006). Introducing Fairclough's critical discourse analysis methodology for analyzing Caribbean social problems: Going beyond systems, resources, social action, social practices and forces of structure or lack thereof as units of analysis. *The Journal of Diplomatic Language*, *3*(1), 5.

Waller, L. G. (2009). *The role of discourse in ICT for development: Lessons from Jamaica*. VDM Publishing.

Widdowson, H. G. (1998). Context, community, and authentic language. *TESOL Quarterly*, *32*(4), 705–716. doi:10.2307/3588001

Widdowson, H. G. (2008). *Text, context, pretext: Critical issues in discourse analysis* (Vol. 12). John Wiley & Sons.

Williams-Jones, B., & Graham, J. E. (2003). Actor-network theory: A tool to support ethical analysis of commercial genetic testing. *New Genetics & Society*, *22*(3), 271–296. doi:10.1080/1463677032000147225 PMID:15115034

Wodak, R. (Ed.). (1989). *Language, power and ideology: Studies in political discourse* (Vol. 7). John Benjamins Publishing Company. doi:10.1075/ct.7.11wod

Wodak, R., & Meyer, M. (Eds.). (2009). *Methods for critical discourse analysis*. Sage.

Yin, R. K. (1994). Case study research: Design and methods. Thousand Oaks, CA: Academic Press.

Chapter 1
Context:
Globalization, Crisis, and the Public Sector Memorandum of Understanding (MOU)

ABSTRACT

Globalization has played a transformative role with respect to social processes filtering from the global into the realm of the local. Governance and its modalities within globalization are highlighted and crisis elements are deconstructed leading to a discussion on key crisis "moments" within Jamaica's history, which together create the context from which the Public Sector Memorandum of Understanding Agreement or "MOU" social partnership emerged. The fragility of the Jamaican macroeconomy and key catalysts that precipitated the negotiations are examined as well as insight into issues of governance driving the decision making of the partners. A synopsis of the Public Sector Memorandum of Understanding or "MOU," namely, the principles, provisions, and areas of restraint, as well as specific measures in the areas of health, education, and fire services managed by local government, is highlighted. Social partnership emerges as a governance response to crisis.

DOI: 10.4018/978-1-5225-8961-7.ch001

INTRODUCTION

One recalls the view held by Neumann (2006, p.158) that 'the meaning of a social action depends on the context in which it appears'. Jamaica as a small island developing state has faced numerous challenges interfacing with and integrating within, the global economy (Hughes, 2006). Key historical snapshots of Jamaica, placed in the foreground against the interaction with the globalized environment, consist of the overexpansion of the bauxite industry in the 1970s and economic instability in the aftermath of the reduction in global demand. Other moments concern the crisis of debt and borrowing from the International Monetary Fund (IMF) from the 1980s, (Bernal, 1984), the financial crisis of the mid 1990s and the concomitant effect on the structure of the labour market within the Jamaican state. The resultant combination of globalization and a decline in state capabilities and resources has resulted in changing conditions for domestic policy choice and the need to create a counterweight in leveraging new modalities of governance and enhance government's leveraging of its political capacity.

Jamaica's historical and socio-economic context has contributed to shaping the national and specific legacies and characteristics of social dialogue (Martinez-Lucio & Stuart, 2002) especially with regards to dimensions of the state, (and the economy), the labour movement and the public sector, which, came together as stakeholders or actors to the bipartite arrangement.

GLOBALIZATION

Globalization as an evolutionary phenomenon has historically transformed and taken many shapes with a variety of unfolding and resultant impacts upon national and global life. As a process there is transformation in the spatial organization of social relations with associated transaction costs, involving new forms of space and time compression. There has been a diminishing of territoriality and supra territoriality rises as geographic distinctions become blurred.

The systemic institutional and organizational outcomes from the outworking of globalization processes have generated additional policy processes and priorities in addition to those concerns arising from within the domestic policy environment of the state. The changing arena of global public policy making and policies emanating from supra-national governance institutions and other global actors create challenges for the state in terms of its context, its role and functioning within the global market economy. There has been a transformation of the global political economy which has disrupted the traditional constructs of the state ordered within a Westphalian model of global political economy within in which they operate. There are consequent implications for sovereignty, autonomy and positioning within the power constructs of global political economy relations, which presents challenges for the state as how to relate within a domestic policy context and with the globalized environment and actors. It is at the nexus of policy making processes and decision making at the national level that globalization and global policy is integrated and becomes a reality defined by the capacity of the state to implement from within while still contesting with globalization effects from without.

Globalization (Held et al. 2001; Scholte, 1993; Pierre & Peters, 2000) and the 'hollowing out' of the state' (Jessop, 2002a) has created degrees of interdependence. The resultant reciprocal asymmetric relationships (Scholte, 1993), entails costs that impinge upon the welfare of states in mutual dependence (Keohane & Nye, 1989). Stiglitz (2002) argues that trade liberalization, as a mechanism of globalization, has led to inefficient industries in largely developing countries to succumb under the pressure of competition from other more mature international businesses. One could posit that globalization helped to precipitate the conditions for the creation of social partnership arrangements.

GOVERNANCE

Governance and its characteristics have been shaped by globalization's discourse, while the development literature, explores arguments about governance without government in both the national and international arenas. There are several authors that describe the governance phenomenon and the exercise of authority within the construct. Rosenau et al. (1992) understands governance to mean the capacity to get things done without the legal competence to command that they be done and distribute effectively in a way which is not authoritative but equally effective. These authors see the essence of governance being a focus on governing mechanisms which do not rest on the recourse to authority and sanctions of government. Kooiman (1993) also attests that governance is the creation of structure or order not externally imposed but results in the interaction of a multiplicity of the governing actors. Also seeing governance as interactive, Nettleford (2002) defines it as signifying the dynamics of interaction and interrelationships between the governed and the governor, between the people and the persons they elect/choose to administer their affairs as fiduciaries and the institutional and operational framework that guarantee the perpetual presence of the people who are the proffered beneficiaries of government organized and run in their interest.

O'Brien et al (2000) and Cheema and Maguire (2001) similarly indicate that the phenomenon of governance, is broadly, the sum of ways and interactions by which individuals and institutions manage their collective affairs, between and amongst government, groups and corporations.

Nettleford (2002) suggests six (6) features and new paradigms from the literature on governance which also has synergies with those espoused by Rhodes (1997) and Pierre and Peters (2000) as seen in Table 1 namely:

- Changes in the role of the state from a welfare or provider to a minimal state
- New role for government emphasizing corporate governance
- The application of private sector techniques and the introduction of 'New Public Management' (NPM) the thrust towards 'good governance', which refers to the systematic conception of broader government to include the distribution of internal and external political power. The introduction of Rhodes (1997) 'self-organizing networks'
- The new and enlarged role of civil society and the private sector

Table 1. Governance: different perspectives

ARRANGEMENTS/ USES	THEORIES
Corporate Governance	Traditional Hierarchical
New Public Management	Cybernetic Steering
Good Governance	Autopoesis/ Network Steering
Socio-cybernetic System	Policy Instruments
Self-Organizing Network	Rational Choice
Process	Institutional Analysis
Minimal State	Networks & Policy Communities
Global governance	Neo Marxist Critical Theory

Source: Derived from Rhodes, R. A. (1997). *Understanding governance: Policy networks, governance, reflexivity and accountability*. Open University Press and Pierre, J. & Peters, G. (2000). *Governance politics and the state*. London: MacMillan

Governance, through the dynamics of globalization and the interdependence of decision making embraced by the state, has resulted in 'the national interest', now being interpreted, prioritized and accepted beyond the state's hegemonic and unilateral determination of such, to one which absorbs, facilitates or becomes consonant, complementary or compatible with the goals of domestic sub actors and collective group interests, who are now included in the policy process and decisions making.

Jamaica as a small state has faced numerous challenges interfacing with and integrating within, the global economy (Hughes, 2006). Some challenges persist due to the structural attributes and vulnerabilities of the small island economy (Bernal, 1998) but also from its historical legacy as a former British colony, (Hart, 1999;) being one of dependency (Mandle, 1984) and being on the 'periphery' (Farkas, 2002) within the global productive order.

Key historical snapshots placed in the foreground in the interaction with the globalized environment, consist of the overexpansion of the bauxite industry in the 1970s and macroeconomic instability and crisis in the aftermath of the reduction in global demand. Other moments concern the crisis of debt and IMF borrowings from the 1980s, (Bernal 1984), the financial crisis of the mid 1990s and the concomitant effect on the structure of the labour market within the Jamaican state. Globalization (Held et al. 2000; Scholte, 1993; Pierre & Peters, 2000) and the 'hollowing out' of the state' (Jessop, 2002a) had created degrees of interdependence. Despite governance structures processes and issues being more complex, multi layered and interactive, which is being exacerbated by globalization, it describes and prescribes power arrangements in society. Governance embraces and also transcends government (Munroe 2005), which in turn interfaces with other centres of authority and contenders, either as adversaries or partners in the distribution and exercise of power.

The state regardless, still maintains a core role as the embodiment of the political gains and benefits of society, enshrining laws, fulfilling the outcomes of the political process, even as the representative of the polity. Furthermore, capital is reliant upon the state, through government, to maintain the rule of law, implement domestic policy and property rights that underpin commerce while the state must use its power through international, economic and social policy to monitor 'market forces', being democratically accountable to and protecting the interests of its citizens

The ideological shift towards the individualistic political culture of the market has uprooted the normative collective action image of the state as the epitome of collective interests. Hence the adoption of the role of 'steering' by the state to redeem itself as a political institution prioritizing on behalf of the polity, and in sync with harmonious public private action.

The resultant reciprocal asymmetric relationships (Scholte, 1993), entails costs that impinge upon the welfare of states in mutual dependence (Keohane & Nye, 1989). Stiglitz (2002) argues that trade liberalization, as a mechanism of globalization, has led to inefficient industries in largely developing countries to succumb under the pressure of competition from other more mature international businesses. With respect to Jamaica, one could argue that globalization helped to precipitate the conditions for the creation of social partnership arrangements.

The Triad of Social Dialogue

The question arises as to the circumstances or conditions that drive the emergence of social dialogue and the different processes and arrangements resulting in social partnership? It is apparent that in numerous instances across regions that globalization, through its various institutions and their ensuing effect upon the state, has contributed to or created turbulence within it leading to crises of various forms.

Baccaro and Lim (2006), from their studies on the social pacts of Ireland, Korea and Italy, are among several researchers that hold that a social pact begins when a governments are vulnerable and unable to manage crisis or when a state receives a shock to its system which threatens its stability and its international standing, it is forced into forms of governance which entails power sharing, and

what seems unthinkable under conditions of normal politics suddenly becomes possible when a country is struck by a shock to the system that threatens the national interest and international prestige. Actors that used to fight each other ferociously find themselves rallying around a shared cause (Baccaro & Lim, 2006, p.5)

From several cases of social dialogue, the experiences highlighted, and the diversity in the form of the arrangements that can result, one can argue that the three interacting elements or forerunners, contributing to the formation of social partnerships through social dialogue are globalization, a weakened state and crisis – The *Triad of Social Partnership*. These associations are modelled in Diagram 2 and several scenarios can be used in explaining them depending at which element you start at, A, B or C.

Figure 1. The triad of social dialogue: interdependent relations-globalization, the state and crisis

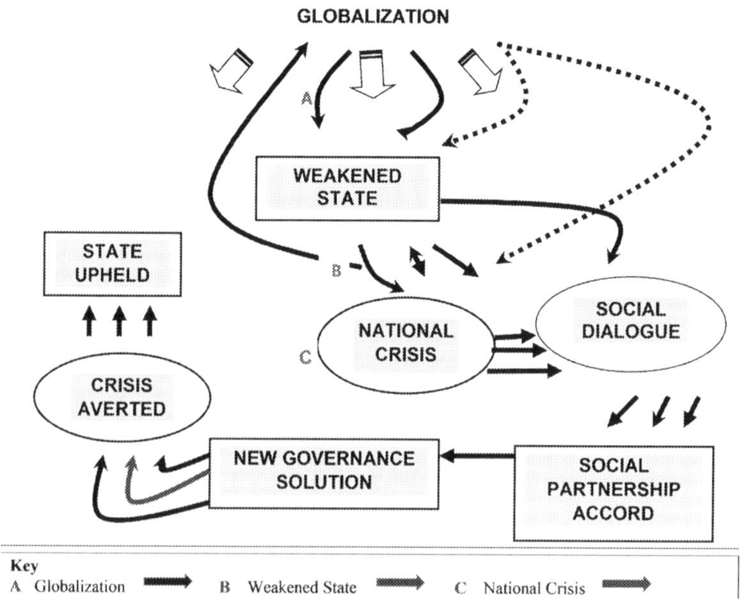

If the cycle begins with globalization (A) and its processes, one could argue that the effects upon the state contributed to it being weakened which in turn creates the propensity for crises to emerge. Similarly, beginning at the point of the weakened state, (B) the position can be taken that the state, inherently weak in terms of its internal structure and associated vulnerabilities, made it prone to crisis, and both are aggravated by globalization effects. Other societal stakeholders are eventually engaged in dialogue at the policy level and resultant arrangements to determine a solution through the vehicle of an accord. Vulnerability is measured by the costs imposed on an entity by external events that it must absorb for lack of being able to pursue alternatives that could minimize them (Keohane, Nye 1989), this also includes costs incurred even after policy adjustment.

Sensitivity, as an expression of the presence of power and liability, is evidenced where actions in the strategic interest of some, negatively affect others resulting in counteractive policy responses. States as a consequence become permeable to decisions taken elsewhere with interactions of power and resultant vulnerabilities unevenly balanced hence with the emergence of crisis, there is contagion.

National crisis, (C) could arise contextually from the nature of decisions taken at the political and national policy level which provides the environment for the crisis to be exacerbated by globalization processes, resulting in a 'weaker' state. The ability of the state to control the reins of power within its traditional jurisdiction – economy and society, diminishes simultaneously with its operations being severely altered. In response, the state seeks consensual participatory relationships with other actors in society (nationally and globally) as it seeks to implement policies or measures to ensure its continued control and address the crisis.

Complex interdependence is revealed in the multiple channels that connect societies diverse set of issues and policy agendas with priorities that fluctuate inconsistently, even those external to it. Strategic responses to vulnerability and sensitivity include more cooperation, tighter coordination and incremental policies that in adjusting create 'turbulence' especially within political structures.

HISTORICAL MUSINGS ON THE JAMAICAN MACRO ECONOMY: CRISIS

Jamaica as a small state has weathered the vagaries of economic crises and challenges from the effects of the overexpansion of the bauxite industry in the 1970s, debt and IMF borrowing in the 1980s, a depreciated dollar and the financial crisis of the mid1990s. Jamaica's fiscal returns from the imposition of a levy upon bauxite companies, declined between 1973-1980, (Bernal, 1984) when global market prices fell by 15%, causing a severe decline in GDP from capital flight and the depletion of foreign exchange reserves. Reduced domestic revenue and levels of public expenditure added to large external and fiscal imbalances in the economy, prompting social disintegration and the need to seek overseas assistance (DFID, 2001). Hughes (2006) stated that:

The period of the 1980s and 1990s, saw Jamaica relying heavily on a reform agenda approved by the International Financial Institutions, under the rubric of the Washington Consensus, was a period of growth stagnation. While the weak performance can also be related to internal policy failures and the impact of globalization, the weakening of the capacity of the state to play its critical developmental role was a major factor. (Hughes, 2006)

As a condition of structural adjustment loan agreements with the Bretton Woods Institutions, an initial phase of liberalization took place from 1986-1988, combined with thrusts to reform interest rate policies and develop money and capital markets (Peart, 1995). Governments' rapidly deregulated their economies and dismantled regulatory regimes in competition with one another to attract foreign direct investment (Woods 2000). Dean (1998) argued that Jamaica's liberalization of internal and external markets was premature, as the preconditions for undertaking the process, such as well-capitalized and supervised financial institutions, macroeconomic stability and an exchange rate close to equilibrium, were absent; hence, there was the propensity for problems to arise.

The Financial Crisis

Following liberalization, the vulnerability of the financial sectors had increased as well as their fragility, which engendered greater financial risk by banks and moral hazard, attenuated by weaknesses in the regulatory and supervisory systems (McBain, 1997). Rapid expansion of Jamaica's financial sector occurred between 1991-1997, with the sector widening and deepening qualitatively and quantitatively. Stennet et al., (1998), notes that the number of banks had grown, from 154 in 1985 to 201 in 1993. Peart (1995), records that assets totalled J$142.4 billion at the end of 1997 representing 50 per cent of the total assets of the financial sector.

There was a commensurate increase in size and vulnerability of the financial sector, which according to McBain (1997), engendered greater financial risk by banks and moral hazard, attenuated by weaknesses in the regulatory and supervisory systems. Support to institutions, such as Blaise Financial Entities (BFE) and Century Financial Entities (CFE), to protect the depositors with the eventual collapse of the sector in 1994 and 1995, cost the public sector J$10 billion and J$ 972 million respectively. In 1996, the Government had to intervene again to address illiquidity, insolvency, weak management, the structure of ownership and control as well as the regulatory framework (Davies 1998a).

Created by Government in 1997, the Financial Sector Adjustment Company Limited (FINSAC) (Kirkpatrick and Tennant 2002) served to intervene, rehabilitate and restructure financial institutions and divest the remaining assets. In 1999, it was noted by the Chairman of FINSAC, Dr. Hon. Kenneth Rattray, OJ, QC, that the assets that were protected involved

1.5 million accounts valued at J$68.7 million dollars and 569,000 insurance policies with a sum insured of J$174.4 million dollars. Fifty-five thousand pensioners with a fund value of J$19,023 million dollars (FINSAC Annual Report 1999), were also protected, altogether resulting in the assimilated costs of the public debt and fiscal deficit increasing debt servicing obligations to 60% of revenues in 1999/2000 (DFID, 2001).

Overall, there was a sharp decline in the profitability of the financial sector as the return on assets of the commercial banks were reduced, fuelled by the collapse of the real estate and equity markets, which generated liquidity problems from a shortage of capital. Financial sector liberalization underpinned by weak regulatory frameworks further contributed to the crisis. As these problems were revealed, concerns grew within the financial sector prompting Government to respond in a manner to preserve relative calm and bolster confidence (Kirkpatrick & Tennant, 2002). For example, efforts to protect the depositors of Blaise Financial Entities (BFE) and Century Financial Entities (CFE) in 1994 and 1995 led to a cost to the public sector of J$972 million and J$10 billion respectively. In 1996, the mismatch of assets and liabilities of insurance companies, arose again, which led to Government of Jamaica intervening to address issues in the sector concerning illiquidity, insolvency, weak management, the structure of ownership and control as well as the regulatory framework (Davies, 1998a).

The assimilation of the costs of absorbing the bad loans increased the public debt and fiscal deficit with debt servicing obligations already being 60 per cent of revenues in 1999/2000 (DFID, 2001). Government's macroeconomic policy had to be adjusted due to the growing fiscal deficit as one of the outcomes of the crisis. Consequently, the surplus gains of J$3,806.3 million in 1995/1996 turned into a deficit of J$14,966.1 million in 1996/1997 and a further J$19,961.6 million in 1997/1998 and J$18,693.1 million in 1998/1999 (Stennett, et.al., 1998).

The financial crisis caused distortion and instability, with respect to the labour market. apart from the structural effects on the economy of the process of liberalization and market competition, which cumulatively has been a contributory factor to the emergence of the informal economy. Ritchie (2000) highlights that of the total employed Jamaican workforce of 940,000 in 2001, that 496,330 were employed informally of which 60 per cent in the wholesale/retail trade or agriculture and further, that 70 per cent of them had no formal contract. In April 2001, Central Government assumed the remaining J$79,297.3 million of debt in the budget. With the cost of the financial sector intervention fully absorbed, the stock of domestic debt was high, having increased from 63.9% of GDP at end of March 2001 to 87.5% of GDP at April 1, 2002 (Davies 2003). Negative fiscal conditions worsened when the Jamaican Dollar depreciated, despite interventions by the Bank of Jamaica, which pushed up inflation rates. Higher oil prices internationally, had a concomitant effect on transportation, fuel costs and the price of commodities (Thorburn & Morris, 2007) which aggravated the fiscal situation.

The genesis of the dialogue leading to the social partnership arrangement of the Public Sector Memorandum of Understanding or (MOU) emerged from two main catalysts, namely the macroeconomic weaknesses and fragility prevailing which prompted several policy measures and actions by the Government as an actor, to address them.

Catalyst 1: 'The Bubble Burst'

The persistence of economic vulnerability and weakening resilience had its toll on the fabric of the state and economy in several dimensions persisting into 2000, where it precipitated the MOU process and the type of agreement derived.

Government's national economic challenges were revealed in the macroeconomic indices and trends in economic growth, debt, inflation and the fiscal balance. A high Debt to Gross Domestic Product (GDP) Ratio prevailed as in April 2001, Central Government assumed the remaining J$79,297.3 million of debt in the budget. Consequently, with the cost of the financial sector intervention fully absorbed, the stock of domestic debt increased from 63.9 per cent of GDP at end of March 2001 to 87.5 per cent of GDP at April 1, 2002 (Davies, 2003). The Central Government assumed the remaining debt, from its intervention in the financial crisis amidst efforts to avert the total collapse of the financial sector. These liabilities were converted into Local Registered Stock and cash payments to bond holders.

The debt imposed severe fiscal and budgetary constraints because of the debt from the financial crisis resulted in a significant addition to interest payments on both domestic and foreign debt, alongside servicing the stock of loans to multilateral creditors. As a percentage of GDP, foreign currency Government guaranteed debt trended upwards from 79.1 per cent in 1996-1997, levelled at 132.1 per cent from 2000-2002, then trended upwards again to 146.4 per cent in 2002/2003.

With respect to inflation, from the peaks of the early 1990s to 1996, the rate of inflation declined to single digit inflation in 1997. For calendar year

2002, however, inflation stood at 7.3 per cent comparing favourably with an 8.7 per cent inflation rate in 2001

In March 2003, the Jamaican Dollar experienced its most severe depreciation in value of 15.3 per cent from J$47.61:US$1.00 in March 2002 to J$56.24: US$1.00 one (1) year later. The stock of NIR also declined to US$1,339.7mn in March 2003 from US$1,941.7 million a year earlier, in March 2002, despite the interventions of the Central Bank in the economy. In December 2003, further pressure was brought to bear upon the foreign exchange market when Standard & Poor's, one of the major US credit rating agencies revised the outlook for Jamaica from stable to negative, on its local and foreign currency debt.

Catalyst 2: Circular 21- The Proverbial 'Straw That Broke the Camel's Back"

Government as an actor, against this background of crisis, macroeconomic vulnerability and the threat of destabilization, initiated through the Ministry of Finance and Planning (MOFP) a response to the fiscal challenges, geared specifically to address the public sector wage bill. The Ministry of Finance and Planning issued on 22, September 2003, an advisory entitled; '*Circular 21: Operation of Posts*', throughout the public service. This triggered an immediate and direct response by the Jamaica Confederation of Trade Unions (JCTU). Given the enormity of the implications for public sector management and employment for public sector workers, the Jamaica Confederation of Trade Unions, (JCTU) was compelled to respond with alacrity. 'Circular 21', as it was referred to, essentially capped the creation of new posts, the filling of vacant posts and the reclassification or upgrading of existing posts within the public sector. It was now conditional, that in order to fill vacancies the approval from the Ministry of Finance & Planning had to be sought, as well as the detailing of the rationale and justification why the request should be given. The Jamaica Confederation of Trade Unions (JCTU), took umbrage to this unilateral decision by Government, which prompted a series of meetings and negotiations.

'Circular 21', which was not anticipated or expected by the JCTU, but it represented an effort by the Government to address its expenditures, in effect, by imposing limits upon employment within the public sector and appointments which had implications for being able to curtail the size of the recurrent wage bill. The unilateral decision to promulgate Circular 21, inferred the Government lacked the ability to pay and fulfill its obligations. Concerns undergirded by the possibility that the Government also was unable to borrow, further compounded the political implications that loomed, to include a possible fallout if a rigorous tax package had to be entertained. 'Circular 21' issued by the Government sought to limit and reduce any additional costs of public sector salary related expenditures to the budget and to relieve the salary related fiscal pressure, driven by a growing public sector wage bill.

The Government, represented by the Ministry of Finance & Planning (MoFP), presented the three (3) choices that it had to deliberate upon in its dialogue with the JCTU. These were for (a) the Government to borrow money; (b) raise taxes: or (c) chop the public service, of which the first two options were dismissed by the Government as not being feasible.

Regarding the option of cutting jobs, the JCTU dismissed this option, moreover from the perspective of their experience. The JCTU recalled from its past relationships with successive Governments, the experience of mass redundancies in the public sector, which they viewed to be indiscriminately pursued, and being "stop gap' method of reducing recurrent costs to remedy fiscal challenges. Furthermore, given the recent occurrences at the time, of private sector redundancies the option was deemed even more untenable. The JCTU considered Governments' *ad hoc* approaches in the past in their handling of redundancies and the unlikelihood of those made redundant finding alternative employment. This would have proven extremely difficult because of the prevalence of a large percentage of unskilled labour in the workforce and limited opportunities prevailing in the job market. The Government considered reducing the wage bill by cutting 15,000 jobs which was resisted by the JCTU, especially in the context of the methodology and how redundancies were usually conducted in the past. A series of consultations ensued between the Government and the JCTU which led to negotiations and the brokering of an agreement to respond to the pending deepening of crisis conditions.

THE PUBLIC SECTOR MEMORANDUM OF UNDERSTANDING OR MEMORANDUM OF UNDERSTANDING (MOU)

The Public Sector Memorandum of Understanding (MOU) or Memorandum of Understanding (MOU) was signed between the Government of Jamaica and the Jamaica Confederation of Trade Unions (JCTU) 16, February 2004. This social partnership agreement between the Government of Jamaica and the JCTU in 2004-06, called the 'Public Sector Memorandum of Understanding', was coined the 'MOU' or 'MOU Agreement.

The major quid pro quo between the Government and the JCTU was the maintenance of the current size and cost of wage expenditure with a wage freeze, in exchange for not making 15,000 workers redundant. For the Government, the MOU contributed to fiscal savings by capping the wage bill and by providing a mutual 'breathing space' to address issues surrounding the macro economy, and overall, it supported the preservation of the existing political and economic governance framework and network of relations. For the unions, it was agreed that wage increases for public sector workers would be frozen or no more than 3 per cent where applicable and there would be no loss of employment, so workers were targeted to contribute to the growth of the economy by way of helping to reduce the debt burden (Witter, 2005). Additionally, there was a respite for the trade unions to become involved towards preparing the public sector for impending change and possible retrenchment, as a response to reduce salary related costs because of its size, (Macgregor et al. 1998), which was part of the underlying problem which led to the formation of the MOU.

For the public sector, however, the wage freeze as stipulated by the MOU, followed on the unresolved fulfillment of existing commitments under previous Heads of Agreement for Civil Servants, where salaries were to be increased to 80 per cent of market equivalent. The freezing of salaries was indicative of the beginning of negative responses to the MOU. This led to the surfacing of new, the resurfacing of old issues, (Downes, 2003; Bissessar, 2002; Mills & Robertson, 1990; Stone, 1989; Schoburg, 2006; Taylor, 2001) and those that had remained dormant, latent or hidden, or even glossed over. Consequently, the implementation of the MOU pushed these issues to the forefront.

In the MOU negotiations, three groups were targeted to receive benefits from specific training programmes according to the assessed need. Training programmes undertaken by the Ministry of Health (MOH), would address the severe shortage of nurses and ministry staff, in addition to developing training partnerships with various tertiary institutions. The Ministry of Education, Youth and Culture (MOEYC) was committed to carrying out a needs assessment to facilitate the training of Secondary School Principals in School administration. Similarly, the Ministry of Local Government and Community Development (MLGCD) had to implement training programmes to develop the current cadre of staff and fill the deficits in the staff complement of the Fire Services. The Cabinet Office had responsibility to examine the feasibility of an 'exchange programme' within government departments and 'cross training' between government departments and the private sector. A training plan produced within the first year of the MOU, would help prepare the public sector work force for the needs of a modern labour market.

THE TEXT OF THE PUBLIC SECTOR MEMORANDUM OF UNDERSTANDING (MOU) AGREEMENT

The Government of Jamaica and the JCTU, signed the Public Sector Memorandum of Understanding (MOU) on 16 February 2004. The Agreement captured the commitment of both Partners to the:

- sustained growth and development of the public sector;
- establishment of social dialogue mechanisms that would strengthen collaboration and consensus building in the public sector; and
- development of a framework for the conduct of good industrial relations in the public sector.

The scope of the Agreement was applicable to all employees in the entire public sector and all Government entities and statutory bodies. For ease of understanding the text of the MOU Agreement holistically, the major components are explained, and the key aspects summarized using three (3) sections headings which are termed the 'Three Ps' namely:

- **Section A- Principles**: Which are qualitative in character and speaks to the objectives, purpose and goals.
- **Section B- Provisions:** Identifiable, quantifiable and measurable in certain dimensions and the rationale for selection; and
- **Section C- Processes**: Looks at the mechanisms, institutions and structures established to carry out the work of the Agreement.

SECTION A: PRINCIPLES

Several principles laid the foundation for the Agreement and the identification of certain strategies that were to be pursued. These had the purpose of trying to be equitable in the treatment afforded to the groups involved, reaffirm the adherence to core International Labour Organization (ILO) Conventions or labour standards as well as good industrial relations practices. These Conventions were supported and had reflected in domestic labour policy through the legislation of Acts by Parliament, such as the Labour Relations and Industrial Disputes (Amendment) Act (2002) (LRIDA) signed into law on March 28, 2002, which was chiefly designed to manage industrial disputes.

SECTION B: PROVISIONS

The Partners to the MOU supported three overarching provisions reflecting strategic actions to be taken, in the areas of:

- Restraint - covering three sub components, namely, wages, employment and expenditure;
- Macroeconomic Management.
- Public Sector Development

RESTRAINT

Wage Restraint

This sub component, sought to achieve a reduction in the wage bill in nominal terms, being applicable to all remuneration under contracts of employment, full or part time in the public sector. Employees received exceptional or differential treatment, through promotion or increment, in respect of existing contracts, according to the status of contractual negotiations already in force, or for the purposes of pension calculations and those who would have proceeded on retirement during the period of restraint. No reclassifications were permitted during the period of restraint and the Government committed itself to reviewing the tax threshold.

Employment Restraint

The Employment Restraint sub component specified the preservation of jobs and no separation of employment, except by 'justifiable dismissals' and through the agreed restructuring and mergers of entities. The Office of the Services Commission (OSC) had to task to ensure that, as far as is possible;

no officer should be acting or employed in a clear vacancy for more than six months, without being evaluated for confirmation or otherwise, according to their performance, providing valid reasons.

Expenditure Restraint

The Expenditure Restraint component identified common areas of excessive expenditure but did not limit the restraint to these areas only. Entities were required to monitor systematically expenditure patterns and the use of assets, so that there would be a reduction in the abuse of Government resources and overall expenditure. Each agency was also required to establish a Cost Saving Committee (CSC) and submit quarterly reports detailing the savings achieved from their efforts. The CSC had a broad application to achieve energy savings as well as financial management and policy related efficiencies. Also considered was the examination of the operational activities and internal workflow processes, to garner efficiencies through quantitative structural changes as well as qualitative. Entities would receive as an incentive 40% of the savings achieved, allocated for staff welfare activities of their choice.

MACROECONOMIC MANAGEMENT

This provision captured the Government's agreed macroeconomic targets consistent with the medium-term economic policy. Government would manage economic policy to ensure that the inflation rate remained within the targeted band of 8% to 9% in 2004/2005 and 6% to 7% in 2005/ 2006. Fiscal policy measures sought to generate a deficit in the range of 3% - 4% in 2004/2005, a balanced budget in 2005/2006 and to deliver outcomes consistent with the medium-term profile.

Public Sector Development

This Provision specified training initiatives for public sector groups such as nurses, firemen, and secondary school principals. Other initiatives were wider in scope and included staff exchanges between public and private sector and cross training within the public service. The commitment to the development of the public sector, included efforts to make it modern, efficient, to be properly equipped and suitably rewarded, commensurate with determining an optimum size for the sector.

The text of the MOU Agreement itself and extracts derived from research undertaken, served to identify the tangible outcomes from the implementation of the MOU Agreement. There was a consensus, that the MOU provided a potential benefit to accrue overall to society, through the exercise of voluntarism and other sectors restraining prices. Several Government Circulars were promulgated, applicable to the entire public sector, to provide advice and policy support in addition to demonstrating control of the crisis situation. These circulars also functioned to communicate the requirements and activities stipulated under the MOU and further, to strengthen the discourse and practice of the MOU's mandate around which the Partners had to converge and conform.

SECTION C: PROCESSES

Public Sector Monitoring and Evaluation Committee/ (Monitoring Committee) (MC)

The Public Sector Monitoring and Evaluation Committee or 'Monitoring Committee', (MC) was created by Cabinet and vested with the responsibility to oversee and monitor the processes of operationalizing and implementing the Agreement. The MC became a tool for contributing and supporting good industrial relations conduct and practice, a forum for reconciliation and arbitration, and for collaboration and consensus building on the national landscape beyond (on occasion) the scope of the public sector. Three smaller committees, the Macroeconomic Sub Committee, the Special Sub Committee and the MOU Review Sub Committee, assisted the MC, as well as a Liaison Officer, selected from within the MOFP to assist in the administration of the MOU process.

The Memorandum of Understanding (MOU) and the International Labour Organisation (ILO)

According to Iankova and Turner (2004), the strategy of promoting social dialogue by the ILO became in effect a mechanism or mode of governance (ILO, 2007) to manage the effect of rapid globalization (Bangs, 2006; Mulvey, et. al., 2003). The emergence of the Public Sector MOU can be viewed as a mechanism or typology of social dialogue or a type of partnership which has promised mutual benefits to the parties as well as contributing to the amelioration of national economic challenges. The MOU as an output of the institutionalization of social dialogue or social partnership has led to the development of additional mechanisms and structures within the public sector on its execution, that had implications for the governance of the sector and its interface with the labour movement.

The text of the MOU Agreement 2004-2006 was formulated utilizing the typology and conceptual language of the ILO, contributing to the underlying principles, rhetoric and discourse. For example, Provisions 4 (i) and (ii) (See Appendix A) of the text, utilizes ILO discourse in the phrase "achieving harmonious labour management relations," which under certain conditions can contribute to growth and development in the national economy and the public sector.

Other phrases include in 4 (i) "conformity to good industrial practices" and in 4 (ii) by the "acceptance of bipartisan agreements as an effective strategy to achieve the same end." Provision 4 (ii) also mentions the "acceptance of bipartisan agreement as an effective strategy through which growth and development" may be realized. The aspect of peace and harmony in relations through bipartism, one of the ILO models of social partnership is also noted, especially against the background of Provision 3. Page 1 Item 4 (iii) of the MOU text makes specific reference to the principles laid down in the International Labour Organization's Conventions Nos. 87, 89 and that relating to Social Dialogue, being consistent with those underlying the MOU. At the discursive level, Provision 4 (iii) of the MOU text exhibits intertexuality by drawing upon ILO Conventions which subsume certain orders of discourse. There are associated discourses and socially ordered networks of social practices in the field of labour relations with its own genres, language and terminologies associated with industrial relations globally. These associations can be viewed as being hegemonic as there is "organizational control of linguistic variation and their elements." (Fairclough, 2003, p.24).

The manifest intertexuality in the text and the expected social practices associated with commitments to the Conventions by states e.g., freedom to associate, right to organize, etc., carry their own protocols and standards of best practices to which the discourse become aligned. Similarly, states who are signatories will have concomitant social practices and regulations to effect.

The latter line of provision 4 (iii) speaks to the Convention relating to Social Dialogue and the Labour Codes of Jamaica, which reflect how the Jamaican state has assimilated ILO discourse, language, terminologies, meanings and ideology. Jamaica has entrenched ILO Conventions within local labour relations practices, standards, conduct and the modus operandi of employers, displayed in the types of legislation put into effect. The affirmation in the text that sound industrial relations may be maintained by the commitment to the MOU principles and ILO Conventions to which Jamaica is already signatory, suggests an ideological commitment in principle. In the framing of the text of the Agreement elements of the Social Partnership of Barbados as well as that of the Bauxite MOU are drawn upon and articulated together as other voices (Fairclough, 2003) in the text. At the interdiscursive level, there is a possibility that the successful social partnership experiences of other countries, such as Ireland and Barbados (not bipartite agreements) are alluded to and a recognition of their value in the context.

Contending with globalization and its effects, the fragile Jamaican macroeconomy and demands from the programmes of assistance pursued, (Peart, 1995) coupled with a financial crisis (Kirkpatrick & Tennant, 2002; Davies, 1998), elicited varying domestic policy responses (Dean, 1998). The immediate macroeconomic environment, leading to the creation of the MOU was the key focus in the dialogue surrounding the negotiations, and directly influenced the type of inclusions in the text of the Agreement. Jamaica's historical and socioeconomic legacies, within the context of globalization, has contributed much to the shaping the of national and specific modalities of social dialogue (Martinez-Lucio & Stuart, 2002) exercised, especially regarding dimensions of the state, (and the economy), the labour movement and the public sector. These come together as stakeholders or actors to the social partnership arrangements, possessing their own agendas and characteristic.

Social Partnership Governance

The Public Sector Memorandum of Understanding or (MOU) created in 2004-06, could be considered as a governance response to crisis conditions and issues forefront in the Jamaican economy, given its scope, reach, application and coverage of a largest percentage of the employed workforce that reside in the public sector. The 'MOU' has enjoyed a degree of success and longevity, proving the possibility, even within the highly politicized Jamaican context, that such an Agreement could be forged. The MOU stimulated the eventual divestment of government centered authority, promoting and fostering government by networking and relationships which were further decentralizing in their effect. It has been expressed that social partnerships emerge as forms of governance which reflect a broadened governance capacity by incorporating relatively autonomous institutions, networks and actors (Jessop, 1998; Kooiman, 2000; Rhodes, 1997) which are then integrated into the political system to enhance the governability of the political system as a whole.

REFERENCES

Baccaro, L., & Lim, S. H. (2006). Social Pacts as Coalitions of" weak" and" moderate": Ireland, Italy and South Korea in Comparative Perspective. International Labour Organization (International Institute for Labour Studies).

Bernal, R. (1984). The IMF and class struggle in Jamaica, 1977-1980. *Latin American Perspectives, 11*(3), 53-82.

Bernal, R. L. (1998). *The Integration of Small Economies in the Free Trade Area of the Americas*. Center for Strategic and International Studies.

Bissessar, A. (2002). The introduction of new public management in small states. In Governance in the Caribbean. University of the West Indies.

Cheema, G. S., & Maguire, L. (2001). Governance for human development: The role of external partners. *Public Administration and Development, 21*(3), 201–209. doi:10.1002/pad.178

Davies, O. (1998a). *Public sector response to the problems of the financial sector. Ministry Paper, no. 13/98*. Kingston: Government of Jamaica.

Davies, O. (2003). *Fiscal Accounts: Performance & Implications*. Paper presented to the Jamaica Confederation of Trade Unions, Ministry of Finance and Planning, Kingston, Jamaica.

Dean, J. W. (1998). Can financial liberalization come too soon? Jamaica in the 1990s. *Social and Economic Studies*, 47–59.

Department for International Development (DFID). (2001). *Jamaica: Country Strategy Paper*. Author.

Downes, A. S. (2003). *Productivity and competitiveness in the Jamaican economy*. Economic and Sector Studies Series. Washington, DC: Inter-American Development Bank. (RE3/OD6)

Fairclough, N. (2003). *Analysing discourse: Textual analysis for social research*. Psychology Press. doi:10.4324/9780203697078

Farkas, P. (2002). *Development theory on relations between the state and the market and on their effects on the peripheries of the world economy (No. 127)*. Institute for World Economics-Centre for Economic and Regional Studies-Hungarian Academy of Sciences.

Financial Sector Adjustment Company. (1999). *Annual Report*. Kingston, Jamaica: Author.

Hart, R. (1999). *Towards Decolonization: Political, Labour and Economic Developments in Jamaica 1938-1945* (Vol. 3). Canoe Press.

Held, D., McGrew, A., Goldblatt, D., & Perraton, J. (2000). Global transformations: Politics, economics and culture. In *Politics at the Edge* (pp. 14–28). London: Palgrave Macmillan.

Hughes, W. (2006). *Strategic structural transformation*. Paper presented at the Conference on Globalization and the Problems of Development, La Asociacion Nacional de Economistas y Contadores (ANEC), Havana, Cuba.

Iankova, E., & Turner, L. (2004). Building the new Europe: Western and eastern roads in social partnership. *Industrial Relations Journal*, *35*(1), 76–92. doi:10.1111/j.1468-2338.2004.00301.x

International Labour Organisation (ILO). (2007). *Report of the Meeting on the Project "History of ILO Ideas and Their Impact"*. Geneva: International Labour Organisation.

Jessop, J. (1998). The rise of governance and the risks of failure: The case of economic development. *International Social Science Journal*, *50*(155), 29–45. doi:10.1111/1468-2451.00107

Jessop, D. (2002a). *The future of the capitalist state*. Wiley Blackwell.

Keohane, R. O., & Nye, J. S. (1989). *Power and interdependence* (2nd ed.). New York: Harper Collins.

Kirkpatrick, C., & Tennant, D. (2002). Responding to financial crisis: The case of Jamaica. *World Development*, *30*(11), 1933–1950. doi:10.1016/S0305-750X(02)00116-X

Kooiman, J. (1993). Modern governance: New government-society interactions. *Sage (Atlanta, Ga.)*.

Kooiman, J. (2000). Societal Governance: Levels, models, and Orders of Social-political interaction. In J. Pierre (Ed.), *Debating governance: authority, steering, and democracy* (pp. 133–164). Oxford, UK: Oxford University Press.

Macgregor, J., Peterson, S., & Schuftan, C. (1998). Downsizing the civil service in developing countries: The golden handshake option revisited. *Public Administration and Development: The International Journal of Management Research and Practice*, *18*(1), 61–76. doi:10.1002/(SICI)1099-162X(199802)18:1<61::AID-PAD988>3.0.CO;2-N

Mandle, J. R. (1984). Caribbean dependency and its alternatives. *Latin American Perspectives*, *11*(3), 111–124. doi:10.1177/0094582X8401100306

Martinez-Lucio, M., & Stuart, M. (2002). Assessing the principles of partnership, workplace trade union representatives' attitudes and experiences. *Employee Relations*, *24*(3), 305–320. doi:10.1108/01425450210428462

McBain, H. (1997). Factors influencing the growth of financial services in Jamaica. *Social and Economic Studies*, 131–167.

Mills, G. E. (1990). *A Reader in Public Policy and Administration*. Institute of Social and Economic Research, University of the West Indies.

Mills, G. E., & Robertson, P. (1990). The attitudes and behavior of senior civil servants in Jamaica. In *A Reader in Public Policy and Administration*. Sir Arthur Lewis Institute of Social and Economic Studies, University of the West Indies.

Munroe, T. (2005). On Strengthening Foundations for Regional Governance. *Caribbean Imperatives: Regional Governance and Integrated Development*.

Nettleford, R. (2002). Governance in the contemporary Caribbean: towards a political culture of partnership: In Governance in the Caribbean. St Augustine, Trinidad: Social and Economic Studies, University of the West Indies

Neumann, L. W. (2006). *Social research methods*. Boston: Pearson Education.

O'Brien, R., Goetz, A. M., Scholte, J. A., & Williams, M. (2000). *Contesting global governance: Multilateral economic institutions and global social movements* (Vol. 71). Cambridge University Press.

Peart, K. (1995). Financial Reform and Financial Sector Development in Jamaica, Sir Arthur Lewis Institute. *Social and Economic Studies*, *46*(2&3), 131–167.

Pierre, J., & Peters, G. (2000). *Governance politics and the state*. London: MacMillan.

Rhodes, R. A. (1997). *Understanding governance: Policy networks, governance, reflexivity and accountability*. Open University Press.

Ritchie, A. S. (2000). The informal sector in Jamaica. Inter-American Development Bank Economic and Social Studies Series, RE3 -06-010. Washington, DC: Inter-American Development Bank.

Rosenau, J. N., Czempiel, E. O., & Smith, S. (Eds.). (1992). *Governance without government: order and change in world politics* (Vol. 20). Cambridge University Press. doi:10.1017/CBO9780511521775

Schoburgh, E. (2006). *Taking Responsibility; The Jamaican Economy Since Independence Institutional and Administrative Capacity*. Presentation.

Scholte, J. A. (1993). *International Relations of Social Change*. Buckingham, UK: Open University Press.

Secretariat, C. (2002). *Progress in the Implementation of the Recommendations of the Commonwealth*. Academic Press.

Stennett, R. R., Batchelor, P. M., & Foga, C. S. (1998). *Stabilization and the Jamaican Financial sector 1991-1997*. Bank of Jamaica.

Stiglitz, J. E. (2002). *Globalization and its Discontents* (Vol. 500). New York: Norton.

Stone, C. (1989). Power, policy and politics in independent Jamaica. *Jamaica in Independence: Essays on the Early Years*, 19-53.

Taylor, O. W. (2001). The Employment Relationship (Scope) National Study 2001 (Jamaica). Academic Press.

Thorburn, D., & Morris, D. M. (2007). *Jamaica's Foreign Policy: Making the Economic Development Link*. Caribbean Policy Research Institute.

Witter, M. (2005). *Macroeconomic Developments in Jamaica, 2004-2005: A component of the review of the MOU*. Unpublished report prepared for the MOU Monitoring Committee, October 17, 2005, Department of Economics, University of the West Indies, Mona.

Woods, N. (2000). *The Political Economy of Globalization*. Basingstoke, UK: Macmillan. doi:10.1007/978-0-333-98562-5

Chapter 2
Social Partnership

ABSTRACT

This chapter explores themes surrounding social partnership, the epistemological and etymological relations of social dialogue, models, and associated themes. Theories, concepts, and dimensions of social partnership, its characteristics, emergence, and etymology are deconstructed. Various perspectives on the meaning and interpretation of associated interpretive themes such as partnership, trust, mutual benefit, and social capital are explored, including typologies of partnership. This conceptual review covering social partnership examines the discourses and knowledge associated with social partnerships and the philosophy of social partnership. The language of partnerships and social dialogue are embedded within the context of the International Labour Organization's (ILO) epistemological discourse and practice. This chapter provides a comprehensive framework for the purposes of understanding and identifying the philosophies within the current global discourses of social partnership and an appreciation of how our experiences have been influenced and interpreted through the lens of the parameters of the global discourses.

INTRODUCTION

In this chapter, the phenomenon of social partnerships is discussed, examining the origins and ancillary concepts associated with it. There is an exploration of the different types of social partnerships, models used and the institutional discourses surrounding how they are represented and the benefits. Building

DOI: 10.4018/978-1-5225-8961-7.ch002

on this, there is a discussion on the types and models of social partnership and those exhibited in the Jamaican context. I also reflect on the different ways that social partnerships have been analyzed and linked to the global discourse on social partnerships. Finally, I explore some of the limitations of these approaches and present a basis to build a case for the utility of a network approach as an alternate yet supporting role to analyze social partnership.

What Is Social Partnership?

The Copenhagen Centre for Partnership Studies (Boyd, 2002, p.1) defines social partnership as:

a tri or multi partite arrangement involving employers, trade unions, public authorities, ... and or others (voluntary sector). ... usually concerned with areas of economic and social policy and might be based upon a binding agreement of declaration of intent. Social Partners is the term used to designate the representative organisations of trade unions and employers.

Similarly, Iankova and Turner (2004) place social partnership within the context of an arrangement of regularized bargaining between business and labour, with the view to establish wages, work and employment standards, as well as to influence broader economic and social policy.

Regarding the etymology of social partnership, Wahl (2004) there are multiple names describing the phenomenon, such as "social contract", or "consensus policy" which suggests that there is the establishment of relatively stable power relations and peaceful cohabitation between labour and capital. This perspective is further supported by others (Boyd, 2002; Djuric 2002; Martinez-Lucio & Stuart, 2002) who suggest that the term also characterises collective actors in labour and industrial relations but embraces a wider concept to include any process directed towards the accommodation of conflicting interests.

CONCEPTS OF SOCIAL PARTNERSHIP

Critical concepts of partnership and dialogue emerge from deconstructing the phenomenon of social partnership which are implicit in these arrangements. Boyd (2002), from his studies on European partnership models, has determined key concepts about social partnerships, namely that:

- it means different things in different countries as it is nation specific, models cannot be transposed successfully from one country to another,
- it is more appropriate in small countries as they are more able to bring together principle economic actors,
- partnerships convey economic benefits.
- institutions are not critical to successful partnerships and
- agreement on the economic benefits to be derived by parties is a critical factor to success.
- powerful representative bodies are important and
- the most successful partnerships originate as responses to serious national problems such as war, inflation etc.

Other related aspects are issues of trust, mutual benefit and social capital. Social capital is a multidimensional and complex theory around which there appears to be very little consensus, with different researchers using different approaches in conceptualizing and operationalizing it as the definition varies from context to context. There is controversy as to whether 'social capital' is really 'capital' and even more obscure is where the theory originally came from. Easterley et al., (2006) indicates that much of the interest in social capital among economists, however, has been fuelled by a definition that includes not only the structure of networks and social relations, but behavioural dispositions (such as trust, reciprocity, honesty) and institutional quality measures ('rule of law,' 'contract enforceability,' 'civil liberties,' etc.)

Robert Putnam (2001) in his approach to social capital referred to features of 'social' organization, such as trust, norms, and networks, that can improve the efficiency of society by facilitating coordination and cooperation for mutual benefit. He elaborated on the importance of trust in people and institutions, norms of reciprocity, networks, and membership in voluntary associations and offered a four-part definition of trust, whereby:

- Placement of trust allows actions that otherwise are not possible.
- If the person in whom trust is placed (trustee) is trustworthy, then the trustor will be better off than if he or she had not trusted. Conversely, if the trustee is not trustworthy, then the trustor will be worse off than if he or she had not trusted.
- Trust is an action that involves the voluntary placement of resources (physical, financial, intellectual, or temporal) at the disposal of the trustee with no real commitment from the trustee.

- A time lag exists between the extension of trust and the result of the trusting behaviour.

Some attitudinal criteria, identified by the Trade Union Council UK (1999) as being key for successful social partnerships include mutual openness, a willingness to dialogue, a shared understanding and a commitment to agreed goals. Other authors (Boyd 2002; Ghellab & Vylitova, 2003; Martinez-Lucio & Stuart, 2004) also emphasize agreement and the mutual sharing of economic benefits. Trust in partnerships can be enhanced based upon the sharing of information and disclosure, that aligns the objectives of partners (Kelly, 2004) and also fosters a more equitable joint decision making process and possible change in the 'feelings' between parties (Coupar & Stevens, 1998). The analysis of trust by Kelly (2004), is instructive, as he is of the view that a higher trust is likely to be created when each perceives the other to be acting cooperatively out of choice and with reciprocity in bargaining. The principle of 'mutual benefit' suggests that it is unfair for one party to incur significant costs and risks if other parties are not prepared to accept similar sacrifices. In terms of efficacy, it is unfair for one party to incur risks and costs if it would only benefit those unwilling to behave in a similar manner (Martinez-Lucio & Stuart, 2004).

The willingness to dialogue and co-operate to find common responses under crisis as well as prosperity have also been highlighted by Boyd (2002) and Ghellab and Vylitova (2003) who specify the importance of institutions, noting that parties should be willing to cooperate and reach a consensus, having implications for governance. There is the recognition of a necessary spontaneity and intent to reach mutual understanding by listening and learning, amidst diverse perspectives, leading to the reconciliation of differences through interactive learning. Governments however, may be compelled to cooperate with the social partners — unless they are able to reform the governance structure to regain sufficient control. According to Ballantyne (2004) it is possible to achieve a level of understanding without agreement and create a consensus and mutual understanding through interactive learning, which engenders common agreement and the reconciliation of differences.

Origins of Social Partnerships

In reflecting upon the ontology why social partnerships exist, some root conditions obtain, that precipitate the formation of social partnership agreements contributing to what is exhibited globally and locally for the state to entertain and sustain such relationships which results in degrees of power sharing. Boyd (2002) from his studies has also noted that the most successful partnerships originate as responses to serious national problems or crises, (Baccaro & Lim, 2006; Mellahi & Wood, 2004; O' Donnell & O' Reardon, 1996), such as war and inflation.

From their studies on the social pacts of Ireland, Korea and Italy, Baccaro and Lim (2006) hold that a social pact begins when a weak government unable to manage a crisis unilaterally (Gourevitch, 1986; Kelly, 2004: Mellahi & Wood, 2004) and in pursuit of adjustment policies, is forced to build broad alliances around them. Each crisis involves a sequence of events which can be summarized quickly... preceding the crisis, a policy approach and support coalition developed. Then came crisis, challenging both policy and coalition. (Gourevitch, 1986, p. 21-22)

This text infers, that social dialogue and partnerships originate from within the context of globalization (Frenkel & Peetz, 1998; Strauss, 1998) as unitary bipartite or tripartite structures mediated by historical cultural and political environments. They blossom out of conflict or the need to solve problems that threaten and seek to destabilize or unseat existing hierarchical power structures and the social multilevel networks that cohere and bind them together.

On the other hand, Fashoyin (2004) contends that it would be misleading to suggest that mechanisms of consultation are only useful in times of crisis or are born out of them, as there are antecedent consultative initiatives without crisis. He argues that tripartite labour advisory boards existed in several countries prior and a crisis does not determine the policy response but is a contributor which conveys limitations upon the range of options available to policy-makers. Other authors (Baccaro & Lim, 2006; Bangs, 2006) posit that social partnerships have helped to order and manage the effects of globalization as labour and capital relations are reconstructed (Goolsarran, Mulvey & Gomes, 1997) and industrial relations, are modernized, replacing hostility with consensus (Martinez-Lucio & Stuart, 2002) in relation to a new organization of work.

The position that social partnership arrangements involve labour and actors in industrial relations, are consonant with Kelly (2004, p. 217) in that they are positioned as a special kind of labour co-operative agreement. However, Kelly (2004) adds another dimension by suggesting that these arrangements vary in the balance of power relations along a continuum. He is of the view that these types of agreements exist along a continuum between being an 'employer dominant' agreement where the agenda primarily reflects employers' interests and the compliance of labour predominates. Boyd (2002) argues that the term 'social partnership' was not a commonly used and understood term in Europe, except in Austria, Denmark, Germany and Ireland. The term "social partner" was used in France and The Netherlands, with 'concertation' used in Austria, France, Italy and Spain.

This compares to 'labour parity' agreements at the other end of the continuum where the balance of power is more even, to reflect interests of both parties. Boyd (2002), notes that the term has its origin in the German language characterising collective actors in industrial relations but applied subsequently to a wider concept. He argues that it was not a commonly used and understood term in Europe, except in Austria, Denmark, Germany and Ireland. However, the term 'social partner' was used in France and The Netherlands, with 'concertation' used in Austria, France, Italy and Spain. Other authors (Baccaro & Lim, 2006; Bangs, 2006) posit that social partnerships have helped to order and manage the effect of rapid globalization as labour and capital relations are reconstructed (Mulvey et.al., 2003) and industrial relations, are modernized, replacing hostility with consensus (Martinez-Lucio & Stuart, 2002) in relation to a new organization of work.

Under the effects of globalization, the terms and conditions underlying existing accords are revisited and Kelly (1996), suggests that during economic downturns, pressure is exerted on actors, resulting in recurring patterns of power shifting to the hands of employers. This infers that social partnerships, through coordination and orchestration, is a means to broaden governance capacity, to integrate and include relatively autonomous institutions, networks and actors (Jessop, 1998; Kooiman, 2000; Rhodes, 1997) to enhance the governability of the political system on a whole and to preserve its integrity (Sorensen, 2006). From this we can infer nevertheless, three interrelated and interacting elements, of globalization and its processes, a weakened state and pending national crisis or the threat of crisis as being prerequisites of the pathway towards social partnership.

UNION CONTROVERSIES

From the perspective of the trade union movement participating in such arrangements, social partnerships may unwittingly create controversies as partnerships are brokered towards a consensus and problem solving. There is a downside of partnership, noted by Martinez-Lucio and Stuart (2004) relating to the changing perception of the unions participating in such relationships. By pursuing participation and alternate occupational interests or compensation, such as training under these arrangements, there is a relinquishing of the adversarial industrial relations practice in embracing an agenda of consensus, so that the conciliatory process within labour becomes legitimate. A more managerial union (Mellahi & Wood, 2004) representative emerges with positions seemingly at odds with labour members concerns, which can accelerate the decline of internal democracy or governance within unions. Consequently, the practice of partnership can create problems of legitimacy and vitality in the workplace (Taylor & Ramsay, 1998). The unions' collusion with its traditional adversary, according to Iankova and Turner (2004), compromises the capacity of the unions with respect to the degree of representativeness and its mandate of agitating for worker interests. As the language of partnership is used to make legitimate a more conciliatory process within organized labour, it is alleged by Martinez-Lucio and Stuart (2004) that it becomes a rhetorical device for external and internal political agendas.

A similar outcome obtains when unions also become political actors (Frege & Kelly, 2004) and signs of political unionism (Ebbinghaus, 2004, p. 578) emerge. These tensions arise between the interests of union leaders and their members in the pursuit of creating orderly and stable industrial relations via partnership, a tension Hyman refers to as the relationship 'between power for and power over' (Hyman, 1975, p. 90).

There is an inherent dichotomy which relates to shifts between conflict and cooperation in unions' strategic choices described by the metaphor 'boxing and dancing,' which was coined by Huzzard et al. (2004). The dichotomy resides in the fluctuations between adversarial negotiations as against amicable discussions in the development of consensual, employee related programmes. Partnership or dancing therefore becomes a trade union strategy when choosing to, for example, extend union activities from distributional to developmental issues which may necessitate a co-operative industrial relations stance or "taking the dance floor" (Huzzard et al., 2004). In contrast, Kelly (1998) holds the opinion that unions gain more through militant mobilization which is where their strength lies, rather than cooperation, concluding that unions enter partnership arrangements as a measure of self-preservation (McCartan, 2003).

Despite social partnership having its discontents, it has served as an avenue for union renewal (Ackers & Payne, 1998; Martinez-Lucio & Stuart, 2002a ; van Klaveren & Sprenger, 2005) and their emergence as a political force (Cowell 2006 ; Frege & Kelly, 2004; Friedman & Hochstetler 2002 ; Ramalho, 1996 ; Stone, 1989). Social partnership has afforded gains through joint problem solving (van Klaveren & Sprenger, 2005) and advances in the status of unions with improvements in working conditions.

Partnership has enabled unions to 'come in from the cold' (Ackers & Payne 1998, p. 527) with a new identity (Guest & Peccei, 2001) and in support of industrial peace (O'Donnell & O' Reardon, 1997) which has furthered the formal acceptance of the legitimacy of trade unions (Martinez-Lucio & Stuart 2004, p.416 ; Iankova & Turner, 2004). Overall, as unions pursue partnerships in industrial relations (Ackers & Payne 1998; Coupar & Stevens, 1998; Guest & Peccei, 2001) they adopt a less militant stance which contributes to a greater likelihood for cooperative displays with employers and the building of trust.

TYPES OF PARTNERSHIPS

The New Zealand Department of Labour describes partnership as being a mechanism that can accommodate diversity and a tool to manage conflict and is:

A collaborative approach to bargaining; wide union and employee consultation practices; a focus on extracting mutual gains from negotiations; a preference for consensus over conflict; and mutual investment in protecting relationships. ... Partnership nonetheless, respects the existence of a diversity of interests, ... recognizes the potential for legitimate conflict ... but promotes restraint and protection of the relationship in the management of conflict.

Partnership involves the sharing of power, work, support and/or information with others for the achievement of joint goals and/or mutual benefits (Kernaghan, 1993) according to Hodgett & Johnson (2001). They also identify four different types of partnership (Kernaghan, 1993) dependent on the nature of the power sharing relationship as shown in Table 1, useful for classification purposes.

These broad categories also assist the understanding of a particular partnership arrangement, by assessing the power base, the purpose, the key actors involved, the life stage that the partnership is in, and the implementation mechanisms (Nilson, 2004). However, as a concept, Guest and Peccei (2001) state that there is no agreed definition (Armistead & Pettigrew, 2004; Haynes & Allen, 2000) of partnership in academic and policy literature, as different definitions have different emphases, different elements and dimensions, according to the researcher and the research objective.

Table 1. Types of partnerships

Description	Characteristics
Collaborative	Ideal type characterized by mutuality of interest, pooling of resources and labour to meet compatible objectives. Each forgoes autonomy
Operational	Less equality of power and shared decision making. Sharing of work than executive decision making. Collaborate for administrative tasks, usually public sector entity dominant actor.
Contributory	One actor provides resources, finances, personnel towards a shared objective but exercise little or no operational involvement. Granting strategic and operational power to other actors – "silent business partner".
Consultative	Public organizations solicit advise from entities outside of government and are able to influence policy
.	

Source: Data from Hodgett, S., and D. Johnson. 2001.

Different definitions have different emphases which focus on different elements and dimensions according to the researcher and the research objective. An example of this diversity is the concept of enhanced partnership (De Waal, 2002; Luiz, 2006) from the context of African economies, which lies at the core of the New Partnership for Africa"s Development (NEPAD) which transformed the aid relationship between African countries and donors. This "enhanced partnership" reflected a common commitment by the partners in the NEPAD initiative to a set of development outcomes (defined by African countries), whereby donors pool funds, guarantee them for an extended period and channel them through budgetary processes, which are then jointly monitored on the basis of outcomes.

Isaacs (2004), notes that partnership has become the 'preferred approach to government administration and is a powerful approach for a shared national agenda', recognizing that it is not a panacea with challenges and opportunities. She explains that they pose challenge to existing power relations, the values of the partners and affords the consolidation of resources, insight and expertise which increase the chances of success

SOCIAL DIALOGUE

In examining another core concept, namely "dialogue", it has the etymological roots, "dia" meaning "through" and "logos" meaning "word" and involves the use of words to achieve a deeper understanding between parties. There is the recognition of a necessary spontaneity and intent to reach mutual understanding by listening and learning, bringing to the surface diverse perspectives where the reconciliation of differences can be enhanced (Ballantyne, 2004). These elements are intertwined in the definition of social dialogue on the website of the International Labour Organization"s (ILO) which:

includes all types of negotiation, consultation or simply exchange of information between, or among, representatives of governments, employers and workers, on issues of common interest relating to economic and social policy.

Founded after World War 1, the ILO was created to give expression to the growing concern for global social reform, diminishing labour rights and the decline in global living standards in the aftermath of World War global political crises and social decay (ILO, 2007).This global institution, devoted to advancing opportunities for women and men to obtain decent and productive work in conditions of freedom, equity, security and human dignity (Kuruvilla, 2003), has an epistemology which places social dialogue as its core constitutional obligation (Minet, 2008) demonstrated in its mandate (ILO, 2001 ; Kuruvilla, 2006; Minet, 2008) and discourse . The Resolution adopted by the International Labour Conference at its 90th Session held in Geneva, November 2002 – concerning tripartism and social dialogue, became effective.

Minet (2008), states that the ILO's work is based on the core concept of social dialogue, (Somavia & General, 1999) which is its 'constitutional obligation' and that it seeks to ensure that tripartite dialogue occurs widely in policy making, labour law reform and implementation to help build the capacities of workers and employers to influence socio economic policies (Somavia & General, 1999). Kuruvilla (2006), also supports this view in that the decline in living standards of the world's populations and union density internationally has pushed the ILO's discourse on 'Decent Work' which has social dialogue as one of its core principles, being a strategic objective of ILO's programming.

The ILO has enshrined tripartism as a form of social dialogue in a number of ILO Conventions and Recommendations. The Tripartite Consultation International Labour Standards) Convention, 1976 (No. 144)1 specifically requires effective consultation between government, employers and worker representative. Social dialogue (Kuruvilla, 2003) is also incorporated inclusive of four principal goals (ILO, 2001) to further information sharing, consultation, mechanisms of collective bargaining and joint decision making. See Table 2.

Table 2. Goals of social dialogue

Goals	Description
Information-sharing	Implies no real discussion or action on the issues although an essential part of the process, valued by influencing the quality of decision making, promoting mutual understanding, building trust and reducing conflict
Consultation	Involves an exchange of views which can lead to more in-depth dialogue and discussion on issues of mutual benefit. It is a vehicle enabling greater understanding of the concerns of stakeholders, as well as enhancing sustainability and ownership.
Collective bargaining or negotiation mechanism	At the enterprise, sectoral, regional, national and multinational level and is an indicator of the capacity within a country to engage in national level tripartism. It involves debates and the exchanges of position in order to arrive at a consensus which could be captured within an agreement, based purely upon the honour of the parties to fulfill the terms without enforcement or it can be binding
Joint decision making	A highly structured negotiation where the conclusion or decisions, of which may be final, or may be subject to ratification by the appropriate governmental authority e.g. Cabinet. Such decisions are enforced and monitored for implementation (Fashoyin 2004).

Source: ILO. 2001. http://www.ilocarib.org.tt/Promalco_tool/productivity-tools/introilopro.htm.

MODELS OF SOCIAL PARTNERSHIP

The ILO recognizes different forms and modalities of social dialogue based upon partnership composition, consonant with Kernaghan's (1993) identification of a collaborative partnership typology mentioned earlier. These are 'tripartite', 'bipartite' and 'concertation' type relationships. Concertation', is a planned process of consultation and negotiation on issues, involving government authorities and the civic community. It facilitates coherence amongst diverse perspectives, mutual respect, consensus, a shared responsibility and a sense of civic duty which encourages the sustainability of the process. Over time it can precipitate behavioural change due to associated social practices and procedures, within a framework of total transparency, focus and respect of participants willing to explore alternative perspectives and arrangements. This process also requires a methodology to be determined as well as the tools whereby an ethical relationship between parties is established. 'Concertation' has a cost in terms of time and energy, information generation, surveys and the expertise needed to support the process.

Through the agency of the ILO, there has been the establishment of standards, criteria for assessments, educational and social practices reinforcing the ILO discourse, which holds that the inclusion of social partners in the process of social dialogue at the level of the enterprise and also within the national context is 'indispensable for increasing competitiveness and accomplishing social objectives' (ILO, 2001). Two arrangements occurring at the national, regional or at enterprise level pertinent to this book involves the 'tripartite' relationship - with representatives of government, employers and workers; or a 'bipartite' relationship - between labour and management (or trade unions and employers' organizations only, with or without indirect government involvement. A comparison of key features of tripartism and bipartism are reflected in Table 3.

It is to be noted that employers' organizations can be involved in some cases in issues such as disputes and strikes, wages and terms and conditions of employment. However, it may be argued that when an employers' organization enters such negotiations, the matter is taken out of the enterprise level.

Bipartism may also operate in the form of workplace information-sharing through group activities without the union, and at the corporate level through joint consultation committees consisting of management and union representation.

Tripartism is enshrined in a number of ILO Conventions and Recommendations, such as the Tripartite Consultation (International Labour Standards) Convention of 1976 No. 144), which presume consultation between government, workers' and employers' organizations leading to the formulation of socio-economic policies at the national and industry levels, as well as on the legal framework of labour relations and related policies.

Katz, et al., (2004) go further to describe variations in tripartism indicating that contemporary tripartism has placed emphasis on workplace change and

Table 3. Comparative table examining bipartism and tripartism

Bipartism	Tripartism
Operates at all levels	Operates at the national, industry or provincial levels not the enterprise level
Policy-oriented at the national and industry level. Practical, specific operational concerns at the enterprise level	Policy-oriented issues
Representatives of employers and employees, at the national, industry or provincial level. At the enterprise level, there is less scope for the involvement of employers' organizations. Bipartism can take place at the enterprise level even if there is no union at different levels. **	Representatives of employers and employees, at the national, industry or provincial level
Bipartism is not a process intended only to give effect to tripartite decisions but can have an impact upon the effectiveness of tripartism.	Tripartism can become an important means to settle issues when bipartism does not result in a consensus
There is interplay and interaction between tripartism and bipartism. Since macro level decisions (taken through tripartite consultation) have little value if they are not translated into practice at the enterprise level, bipartism can be a process for giving effect at the enterprise level to tripartite decisions.	

Source: Derived from De Silva, S. (1997). Tripartism, employers and their organizations, Geneva:ILO

time flexibility, as compared to a macro level focus on inflation and incomes policy as in the past. Tripartism, prevalent in most European countries involves the government's direct presence in communications between union and employers. Also identified is a "tripartite –plus" relationship, where the tripartite partners may choose to open the dialogue to other relevant actors in society in an effort to gain a wider perspective, to incorporate the diverse views of other social actors and to build a wider consensus; and an informal or institutionalized "concertation," which can be can be inter- professional, sectoral or a combination of them occurring at the national, regional or at enterprise level.

Bipartism on the other hand, specifically relates to the relationship between the organizations of employers and employees at the enterprise, industry and national levels, as in Britain and the United States, where it is common. Comparatively, bipartism differs in approaches made to maintain the cooperation of labour and capital according to Hethy (2001), as there is no sharp divide between tripartism and bipartism and they only differ in approaches to maintain the cooperation of labour and capital, in that the former (prevalent in most European countries) involves the government's direct presence in communications between union and employers while the latter, common in Britain and the US, is limited to relations between trade unions and employee associations and can be complementary. Unitary bipartite tripartite structures mediated by historical cultural and political environments.

Bipartism operates at all levels and consists of representatives from both employers and employees from the national, industry or provincial arenas. Tripartism on the other hand, consists of representatives that operate at the national, industry or provincial levels but not the enterprise level as compared to bipartism, and is concerned with policy-oriented issues. There is interplay and interaction between tripartism and bipartism. Bipartism can be a process for giving effect at the enterprise level to tripartite decisions, since macro level decisions (taken through tripartite consultation) have little value if they are not translated into practice at the enterprise level. Tripartism can also become an important means to settle issues when bipartism does not result in a consensus. (De Silva, 1997). However, it may be argued that when an employers' organization enters such negotiations, the matter is taken out of the enterprise level. Bipartism may also operate in the form of workplace information-sharing through group activities without the union, and at the corporate level through joint consultation committees consisting of management and union representation. The Tripartite Consultation

(International Labour Standards) Convention, 1976 (No. 144)1 specifically requires effective consultation between government, employers' and workers' representatives.

A number of other Conventions presume consultation between government, workers' and employers' organizations leading to the formulation of socio-economic policies at the national and industry levels as well as on the legal framework of labour relations and related policies. The ILO holds tripartism as one of the founding principles of the ILO which facilitates governments and social partner organizations of member states to enjoy equal status and opportunities to make decisions on issues of consequence to labour and employment. Promotion of social dialogue has been integral to ILO's core mandate ever since the Organization was born and Yi and Yi (2004), go further to describe variations in tripartism, identifying four levels such as being '*insignificant*' as in the USA, '*on the decline or in decline*' as in Japan Australia and Italy, '*sporadic*' and limited in application, as in the case of Korea and '*flourishing*' as in Ireland, the Netherlands and Germany.

Contemporary tripartism has placed emphasis on workplace change and time flexibility, as compared to a macro level focus on inflation and incomes policy as in the past. Tripartism, prevalent in most European countries involves the government's direct presence in communications between union and employers.

Kuruvilla (2006), notes that tripartism is used as primary avenue for social dialogue and has been operationalized by collective bargaining between employers and workers and social concertation between labour employers and government. Tripartism assumes that the views of the social partners are adequately represented with contributions being made to social economic development broader in scope than that of the direct employment relationship concerning members (De Silva, 1997).

From the ILO's perspective the tripartite arrangements can be both formal and informal and should give effect to the basic objectives of tripartism. The ability of the tripartite consultative mechanisms to influence the formulation of broader national and social policy on issues, that will be consistent so as to achieve broader development goals, is not guaranteed, but tripartite social dialogue is flexible and a learning process, which does not require a full-tfledged institutional framework or a clear and precise agenda to commence (Ghellab & Vylitova, 2003). Five conditions are specified that need to be met for effective tripartite social dialogue, such as:

- Independent, strong and representative social partners, able to represent the interests of their constituencies. (Boyd, 2002)
- The parties should be willing to cooperate, reaching a consensus about the challenges and problems faced and to find common responses, both in times of crisis and of economic prosperity.
- The existence of well-functioning institutions of social dialogue, including at lower levels (sectoral, enterprise, workplace) of decision making.
- An agenda and agreed procedures.
- Practice in the conduct of tripartite social dialogue.

Tripartism – plus includes the broadening of dialogue to include non-traditional stakeholders which is a reflection of how the labour market has been influenced. Non-governmental organizations and civil society are now seen as integral as the structure and composition of the labour market institutions consist of aspects that apply to persons outside the traditional forms of employment with concerns for example, such as social security

However, Djuric (2003) acknowledges the importance of bipartite mechanisms as being critical for the creation of durable tripartite relations without which, industrial relations are much more dependent on current political processes of the state. Where bipartite mechanisms are developed, institutionalized and politically established, inclusive of proper negotiating structures, these augers well for the creation of durable tripartite relations. In the absence of these, then industrial relations become much more dependent upon the current political processes in the state and although tripartism has been institutionalized relatively fast, transition countries structures such as in the EU, were based upon a weak and problematic bipartism. Nevertheless, Kuruvilla (2006), opins that the ILO has demonstrated that it is possible to channel the interests of non-governmental parties into representative and accountable structures of decision-making and implementation, even at the global level. Additionally, entertaining the idea that issues should be resolved with the active involvement of employers and workers as well as governments.

SOCIAL PARTNERSHIP GLOBAL DISCOURSE

The ILO has been instrumental in driving the discourse concerning social dialogue with it being one of the core pillars of its institutional mandate. It has categorized forms of dialogue and discusses how these forms are born out in the social processes of states globally from their experiences.

The historical origins of the discourse of the ILO emerged from the context of responding to political crises and turbulence, driven by the impetus to rebuild the social decay and revitalize and standardize labour relations in the world of work to improve the basic needs of the worker. Its thrust was that of social policy and its relevance strengthened with the effects of globalization on transition economies and diminishing labour rights, by redirecting employment and development within the global economy (ILO, 2007; Maata, 1993).

Possessing the dominant worldview on social dialogue, the International Labour Organization as an institution, has captured the discourse of and made popular the pursuit of governance structures centered upon social dialogue and partnership, and its hegemony in establishing standards of operationalizing social partnership and co-opting support from other global governance institutions. The ILO has built up a level of authority, exercised globally in consolidating, disseminating the discourse and practice of social dialogue inclusive of conventions that are adopted by states. Elements of the evidence presented in the social world and experiences of several states and regions worldwide are weighed in terms of new forms of social partnership developed -tripartite and bipartite arrangements, through explorations that reveal the benefits and value of them and the rationale and insight as to why the course of social dialogue is pursued.

One could argue that tripartite collaborative efforts aimed at the improvement of the conditions of workers, has also directly enhanced their rights, which is evidenced by an indicative shift from worker focused pursuits towards a more rights-based governance approach by the ILO. Consistent with their epistemological approach and consonant with other global social concerns such as human rights, equal justice and rights-based development, the ILO has become a conduit in helping these other social dimensions to become institutionalized in the framework of states through its global influence and activity (ILO, 2007). The mandate of the ILO, as noted by the Governing Body, is to engage in various activities and methods that inter alia:

- Enhance the role of tripartism and social dialogue in the Organization;

- Promote the ratification and application of ILO standards specifically addressing social dialogue;
- Promote the involvement of the social partners in a meaningful consultative process in labour reforms;
- Carry out in-depth studies of social dialogue with a view to enhancing the capacity of labour administrations and workers' and employers' organizations to participate in social dialogue;
- Reinforce the role and all the functions of the Social Dialogue Sector within the Office
- Further develop technical cooperation programmes with the social partners and governments to help strengthen their capacities, services and representation (ILO, 2002)

The ILO therefore, reinforces and supports social dialogue processes wherever they exist, enhancing the capacity of Governments and the social partners to participate in social dialogue which is advocated as compared to adversarial approaches. By encouraging Governments and social partners to start or intensify social dialogue, they provide information on best practices, monitor and analyzes the outcomes of these approaches. The ILO promotes at the enterprise level, a greater readiness on the part of management and labour to adopt social dialogue practices (ILO, 2001).

The form of social dialogue or partnership arrangement differs greatly from country to country. This results in diverse institutional arrangements, legal frameworks, traditions and practices (ILO 1999a) as derived from the experience of labour movements from countries, such as Latin America (Cook, 2000 ; Ramalho, 1996), Africa (Alby et al., 2005 ; Bassett, 2004 ; Buhlungu, 2005 ; Etukudo, 1995) Asia, (Fashoyin, 2004 ; ILO, 2000 ; Katz, et al., 2004) and Europe (Boyd, 2002 ; Iankova, 2008).

As an institution of global governance, the ILO has also furthered industrial democracy (Farnham et al., 2003) within global space by involving multiple stakeholders to yield mutual benefits as outcomes of the consensus reached. Trade unions were the prime agents of industrial democracy, since they had enforced their Regulations by three distinct instruments or levers - the Method of Mutual Insurance, the Method of Collective Bargaining and the Method of Legal Enactment. Of these three methods, collective bargaining and legal enactment were to become the prime instruments for advancing industrial democracy within global space by involving multiple stakeholders to yield mutual benefits as outcomes of the consensus reached.

ILO AND BRETTON WOODS: INSTITUTIONAL CONVERGENCE

On reflection, other global and financial institutions apart from the ILO, have integrated social dialogue forms and institutions as part of their policy framework and discourse (Friedman & Hochstetle, 2002; Oelbaum, 2002) as a conditionality to access benefits. In furthering a social dialogue discourse the ILO has become a conduit to forming institutional networks in support of institutionalizing social dialogue at the global and local levels (ILO, 2007). The ILO Strategy No. 4, on Strengthening Social Dialogue, emphasizes the critical need to extend social dialogue, bipartite and tripartite networks, improve its links to international financial institutions, i.e., the World Bank and to the United Nations (UN) specialized agencies, e.g., the World Health Organization, to deepen the use of such mechanisms within their membership.

Iankova and Turner (2004) contend that ILO's discourse of social dialogue is supported and reinforced by other global policy institutions in finance and development assistance in that;

The World Trade Organization (WTO), World Bank, International Monetary Fund (IMF) and the European Union (EU) have also contributed to the development of tripartism. The ILO has packaged its philosophy of tripartism with practical expert assistance. While international lending institutions favoured neoliberal policies (fiscal and monetary austerity, anti-inflation policies, and shock therapy) for states extricating themselves from state socialism, they have also supported the establishment of social dialogue among governments, unions, and employers. Negotiations have been broadened to include labour and employer federations, and IMF and World Bank missions have required the conclusion of national social peace agreements as a condition for granting loans. (Iankova & Turner, 2004, p. 78)

Other global governance institutions have been enlisted in parallel efforts noted by Singh and Zammit (2000, p. 1) stating that there have been;

intense policy debate in various international fora in response to policy proposals by a few advanced countries to establish multilateral rules permitting punitive trade measures to be taken against countries deemed to be failing to uphold core labour standards. ... parallel efforts have been made to have a social clause introduced into WTO trade rules. This would allow trade sanctions against countries deemed to be failing to uphold core labour standards.

Model standards or norms (Beschoner & Muller, 2007) are established by the ILO in the form of conventions to be ratified and incorporated within the legislation and policy discourse of member states, (ILO, 2007, p. 3) influencing their development. Maatta (2008) highlights that, at the national level, the countries adjusted their policy discourse according to the international rights discourse. It can be said that the ILO's policy approaches and Convention No. 100 did begin to direct the policies of the countries. The institutionalization process of the principles of the Convention varied from country to country, especially between the developed and developing countries, even though similar patterns and processes can be found. The national level policy discourse underwent changes that resulted in the reframing of policy approaches also in legislation. (Maatta, 2008)

According to Iankova and Turner (2004), the strategy of promoting social dialogue by the ILO became in effect a mechanism or mode of governance (ILO, 2007) to manage the effect of rapid globalization (Bangs, 2006; Mulvey, et.al., 1997). Labour and capital relations were reconstructed around partnership, a global pluralist dialogue and modernized, industrial relations, replacing hostility with consensus (Martinez-Lucio & Stuart, 2002).

Typologies of social partnerships have been discussed, highlighting dominant as well as institutional discourses, as demonstrated through the institutions of global governance and governance arrangements in states, including some benefits from pursuing various modalities of social dialogue. Contrasting views are explored, examining contending arguments to the dominant discourses and their relevance within the context of developing states and their experiences. Emerging from this, the hegemony exercised in the relationship between pursuits of the ideal versus the relevance to realities, precipitates the need to chart a new course or discourse.

Focusing on these dimensions cumulatively, provides a comprehensive framework for the purposes of understanding and a means to identify the philosophies within the current global discourses of social partnership, which exert an influence on the subject and contribute indirectly to how one can interpret and contextualize the phenomenon. The manner in which tripartism and social dialogue has been a pathway chosen in response to globalization's effect and pending crisis or instability in varied forms, is highlighted in that, the status quo and established order and authorities within states becomes threatened or unstable, economically and or politically.

CONCLUSION

The phenomenon of social partnerships were explored with a view to deconstruct its essence by reflecting upon the inherent concepts of social dialogue, partnership, mutual benefit and trust and the associated controversies. Possessing the dominant worldview on social dialogue. Explorations were made concerning the emergence of the dominant world view of social dialogue, embedded within social partnerships, through the discourse and practice of the International Labour Organization (Somavia & General, 1999). Models – bipartite and tripartite social partnerships their modalities and importance, linked to social dialogue and governance were discussed. Institutional convergence and the forming of institutional networks by the ILO in support of institutionalizing social dialogue at the global and local levels, with other global policy institutions in finance and development and the distillation and inclusion of norms in global policy discourses are discussed.

In deepening this exploration, there is reflection concerning the question of what are the root conditions that precipitate social partnership agreements generally and what obtains globally and locally for the state to entertain and sustain such relationships which results in degrees of power sharing?

The exercise of deconstructing the conceptual themes in social partnerships, the hegemonic global discourses, regional and national experiences with the phenomenon, considered in tandem, serves to locate the MOU Agreement within the current discourses concerning social partnerships. Discussions about origins and the role of hegemonic global governance regimes have captured social partnership discourse, as social governance, showing their influence on the trajectory of its development.

Given its root, representation and expression within global space, social partnerships have been used as devices in relation to changing governance. In supporting the neoliberal philosophies that undergird the process of globalization, social partnerships have been a vehicle with respect to the labour movement, in support of a shift towards social governance models and industrial relations practices that are participative and democratic.

REFERENCES

Ackers, P., & Payne, J. (1998). British trade unions and social partnership: Rhetoric, reality and strategy. *International Journal of Human Resource Management*, *9*(3), 529–550. doi:10.1080/095851998341062

Alby, P., Azam, J. P., & Rospabé, S. (2005). *Labour Institutions*. Labour Management Relations.

Armistead, C., & Pettigrew, P. (2004). Effective partnerships: Building a sub-regional network of reflective practitioners. *International Journal of Public Sector Management*, *17*(7), 571–585.

Baccaro, L., & Lim, S. H. (2006). Social Pacts as Coalitions of" weak" and" moderate": Ireland, Italy and South Korea in Comparative Perspective. International Labour Organization (International Institute for Labour Studies).

Ballantyne, D. (2004). Dialogue and its role in the development of relationship specific knowledge. *Journal of Business and Industrial Marketing*, *19*(2), 114–123. doi:10.1108/08858620410523990

Bangs, J. (2006). Social Partnership: The Wider Context. In *FORUM: for promoting 3-19 comprehensive education* (Vol. 48; No. 2, pp. 201-208). Symposium Journals.

Beschorner, T., & Müller, M. (2007). Social standards: Toward an active ethical involvement of businesses in developing countries. *Journal of Business Ethics*, *73*(1), 11–20. doi:10.100710551-006-9193-3

Boyd, S. (2002). *Partnership Working: European Social Partnership Models. Scottish Trade Union Congress (STUC)*. Social and Economic Partnership Project.

Cook, M. L. (1998). Toward Flexible Industrial Relations? Neo-Liberalism, Democracy, and Labour Reform in Latin America. *Industrial Relations*, *37*(3), 311–336. doi:10.1111/0019-8676.00090

Coupar, W., & Stevens, B. (1998). Towards a new model of industrial partnership: beyond the "HRM versus industrial relations" argument. In Human Resource Management: The New Agenda. London: Financial Group of Public Administration Conference.

De Silva, S. (1997). *Tripartism, employers and their organizations*. Geneva: ILO.

De Waal, A. (2002). What's new in the 'New Partnership for Africa's Development?' *International Affairs*, *78*(3), 463–476. doi:10.1111/1468-2346.00261

Frege, C., Kelly, J., & Kelly, J. E. (Eds.). (2004). *Varieties of unionism: Strategies for union revitalization in a globalizing economy*. Oxford University Press. doi:10.1093/acprof:oso/9780199270149.001.0001

Frenkel, S. J., & Peetz, D. (1998). Globalization and industrial relations in East Asia: A three-country comparison. *Industrial Relations*, *37*(3), 282–310. doi:10.1111/0019-8676.00089

Friedman, E. J., & Hochstetler, K. (2002). Assessing the third transition in Latin American democratization: Representational regimes and civil society in Argentina and Brazil. *Comparative Politics*, *35*(1), 21–42. doi:10.2307/4146926

Ghellab, Y., & Vylitova, M. (2005). *Tripartite social dialogue on employment in the countries of South Eastern Europe*. International Labour Organization.

Goolsarran, S. J. (2002). *Caribbean Labour Relations Systems: An Overview*. International Labour Office-Caribbean.

Goolsarran, S. J. (Ed.). (2006). *Industrial relations in the Caribbean: issues and perspectives*. International Labour Office-Caribbean.

Gourevitch, P. A. (1986). *Politics in hard times: comparative responses to international economic crises* (1st ed.). Cornell University Press.

Guest, D. E., & Peccei, R. (2001). Partnership at work: Mutuality and the balance of advantage. *British Journal of Industrial Relations*, *39*(2), 207–236. doi:10.1111/1467-8543.00197

Haynes, P., & Allen, M. (2001). Partnership as union strategy: A preliminary evaluation. *Employee Relations*, *23*(2), 164–193. doi:10.1108/01425450110384697

Héthy, L. (2001). Social Dialogue and Expanding World. *New Internationalist*.

Hodgett, S., & Johnson, D. (2001). Troubles, Partnerships and Possibilities: A study of the making Belfast work development initiative in Northern Ireland. *Public Administration and Development: The International Journal of Management Research and Practice*, *21*(4), 321–332. doi:10.1002/pad.181

Huzzard, T., Gregory, D., & Scott, R. (Eds.). (2004). *Strategic unionism and partnership: boxing or dancing?* (1st ed.). Palgrave MacMillan.

Hyman, R. (1975). What is Industrial Relations? In *Industrial Relations* (pp. 9–31). London: Palgrave Macmillan. doi:10.1007/978-1-349-15623-8_2

Iankova, E., & Turner, L. (2004). Building the New Europe: Western and eastern roads to social partnership. *Industrial Relations Journal*, *35*(1), 76–92. doi:10.1111/j.1468-2338.2004.00301.x

Iankova, E. A. (2007). Europeanization of social partnership in EU-acceding Countries. *Journal for East European Management Studies*, *12*(4), 297–317. doi:10.5771/0949-6181-2007-4-297

International Labour Organization, (1999). Employment policy in a small island economy: Barbados. In *Country employment policy review*. Trinidad: ILO Sub regional Caribbean Office.

International Labour Organization. (2001). *The ILO in the Caribbean: its objectives and activities: Strengthening tripartism and social dialogue*. Retrieved from http://www.ilocarib.org.tt/Promalco_tool/productivity-tools/introilopro.htm

International Labour Organization. (2002). *Governing Body Resolution GB.285/7/1, in Record of Decisions, adopted at the 90th Session, Geneva, November 2002*. Retrieved from https://www.ilo.org/public/english/standards/relm/gb/refs/pdf/rod285.pdf

International Labour Organization. (2007). *Report of the Meeting on the Project "History of ILO Ideas and their Impact."* Geneva: ILO. Retrieved from http://www.ilo.org/wcmsp5/groups/public/dgreports/nst/documents/genericdocument/wcms_192674.pdf

Isaacs, H. (2004). *Short Form for the Institutional Assessment of Civil Service Systems: Case of Barbados*. Inter-American Development Bank.

Jessop, B. (1990). *State theory: Putting the capitalist state in its place*. Penn State Press.

Jessop, B. (1998). The rise of governance and the risks of failure: The case of economic development. *International Social Science Journal*, *50*(155), 29–45. doi:10.1111/1468-2451.00107

Katz, H., Wonduck, L., & Joohee, L. (2004). *The new structure of labor relations: tripartism and decentralization.* Ithaca, NY: Cornell University Press.

Kelly, J. (1996). Union militancy and social partnership. *The New Workplace and Trade Unionism, 3*, 77-109.

Kelly, J. (2004). Social partnership agreements in Britain: Labour cooperation and compliance. *Industrial Relations*, *43*(1), 267–292. doi:10.1111/j.0019-8676.2004.00326.x

Kelly, J. (2012). *Rethinking industrial relations: Mobilisation, collectivism and long waves*. Routledge. doi:10.4324/9780203213940

Kernaghan, K. (1993). Partnership and public administration: Conceptual and practical considerations. *Canadian Public Administration*, *36*(1), 57–76. doi:10.1111/j.1754-7121.1993.tb02166.x

Kernaghan, K. (2005). Moving towards the virtual state: Integrating services and service channels for citizen-centred delivery. *International Review of Administrative Sciences*, *71*(1), 119–131. doi:10.1177/0020852305051688

Kooiman, J. (1993). Modern governance: New government-society interactions. *Sage (Atlanta, Ga.)*.

Kooiman, J. (2000). Societal Governance: Levels, models, and Orders of Social-political interaction. In J. Pierre (Ed.), *Debating governance: authority, steering, and democracy* (pp. 133–164). Oxford, UK: Oxford University Press.

Kuruvilla, S. (2006). *Social dialogue for decent work. In Decent work: Objectives and Strategies*. Geneva: International Institute of Labour Studies, International Labour Organization.

Luiz, J. M. (2006). The wealth of some and the poverty of Sub Saharan Africa. *International Journal of Social Economics*, *33*(9), 625–648. doi:10.1108/03068290610683422

Maatta, P. (2008). *Equal pay: just a principle of the ILO?* BoD–Books on Demand.

Martinez Lucio, M., & Stuart, M. (2002). Assessing the principles of partnership: Workplace trade union representatives' attitudes and experiences. *Employee Relations*, *24*(3), 305–320. doi:10.1108/01425450210428462

Martinez-Lucio, M., & Stuart, M. (2004). Swimming against the tide: Social partnership, mutual gains and the revival of "tired' HRM. *International Journal of Human Resource Management*, *15*(2), 410–424. doi:10.1080/0958519032000158581

McCartan, P. (2002). Towards social partnership– or cooperative industrial relations? *Irish Journal of Management*, *23*(1), 53–70.

Mellahi, K., & Wood, G. T. (2004). Variances in social partnership: Towards a sustainable model? *International Journal of Social Economics*, *31*(7), 667–683. doi:10.1108/03068290410540873

Minet, G. (2008, July). Some aspects of social dialogue from an ILO standpoint. In Expert Group Meeting on Economic and Social Councils (pp. 24-25). Academic Press.

Mulvey, M., Goolsarran, S. J., & Gomes, P. I. (2003). *Strategic Visions for Labour Administration in the Caribbean*. International Labour Organisation: ILO Sub-regional Office for the Caribbean.

New Zealand Department of Labour's Partnership Resource Centre. (2006). *Partnership and productivity in the public sector: A Review of the Literature*. New Zealand: Department of Labour, TeTari Mahi. Retrieved from http://www.publicworld.org/files/pandp.pdf

Nilson, C. (2004). *Partnerships in urban aboriginal housing projects: a theoretical perspective: A Report for the Bridges and Foundations Project (CURA)*. University of Saskatchewan. Retrieved from http://bridgesandfoundations.usask.ca/reports/Nilson.pdf

Nolan, P. (1999). John Kelly, Rethinking Industrial Relations: Mobilization, Collectivism and Long Waves, London: Routledge, 1998, paper 177 pp. *Work, Employment and Society*, *13*(3), 563–577. doi:10.1017/S0950017099280397

O'Donnell, R., & O' Reardon, C. (1997). Ireland's Experiment in Social partnership 1987-96. *Social pacts in Europe*, 79-95.

Oelbaum, J. (2002). Populist Reform Coalitions in Sub-Saharan Africa: Ghana's Triple Alliance. *Canadian Journal of African Studies/La Revue canadienne des études africaines*, *36*(2), 281-328.

Putnam, R. (2001). Social capital: Measurement and consequences. *Canadian Journal of Policy Research, 2*(1), 41-51.

Ramalho, J. R. (1996). Labour, Restructuring of Production, and Development. A Point of View from Latin America. *The Ecumenical Review, 48*(3), 369–378. doi:10.1111/j.1758-6623.1996.tb03486.x

Rhodes, R. A. (1997). *Understanding governance: Policy networks, governance, reflexivity and accountability*. Open University Press.

Singh, A., & Zammit, A. (2000). The global labour standards controversy: Critical issues for developing countries. South Centre No. *South Perspectives*, 1-101.

Somavia, J., & General, I. D. (1999, June). Decent work. In *Report of the Director-General to the 87th Session of the International Labour Conference*. Geneva: ILO.

Sørensen, E. (2006). Metagovernance: The changing role of politicians in processes of democratic governance. *American Review of Public Administration, 36*(1), 98–114. doi:10.1177/0275074005282584

Stone, C. (1989). Power, Policy and Politics. In R. Nettleford (Ed.), *Jamaica in Independence: Essays on the Early Years*. Kingston: Heinemann Caribbean.

Taylor, P., & Ramsay, H. (1998). Unions, partnership and HRM: Sleeping with the enemy? *International Journal of Employment Studies, 6*(2), 115–143.

van Klaveren, M., & Sprenger, W. (2005). *Boxing and dancing: Dutch trade union and works council experiences revisited*. Amsterdam Institute for Advanced Labour Studies.

Waal, A. D. (2002). What's new in the 'New Partnership for Africa's Development?'. *International Affairs, 78*(3), 463–476. doi:10.1111/1468-2346.00261

Wahl, A. (2004). European labour: The ideological legacy of the social pact. *Monthly Review- New York, 55*(8), 37-49.

Yi, W. D., & Yi, C. H. (2004). *The New Structure of Labour Relations: Tripartism and Decentralization*. Cornell University Press.

Zhu, Y. (1995). Major changes under way in China's industrial relations. *Int'l Lab. Rev., 134*, 37.

Chapter 3
Social Partnership:
Global Expressions

ABSTRACT

Social partnership is a dynamic construction tailored to the context of globalization, the state, time, society, and culture. Snapshots of the experiences of regions and countries globally with modalities of social partnership arrangements are discussed. Further, global reflections on the contexts from which social partnerships were forged—economic chaos and recovery, weak political governance capacities, fractured political regimes, financial instability and governance responses, such as the institutionalization of social dialogue and social partnerships as prerequisites for European accession—are highlighted. Social partnership becomes the outcome of adjustments made by governments, sometimes reluctantly, in power-sharing arrangements, incorporating multiple actors and stakeholders in the way societies are reorganized, to respond and treat with destabilizing forces in the struggle for self-preservation. The chapter concludes around the value and benefits of social partnership as well as some recommendations for effective social dialogue arrangements.

INTRODUCTION

The social dialogue experiences of several states and regions worldwide are highlighted, giving rise to various types of tripartite and bipartite arrangements in reality which reveals the weaknesses in the ILO hegemonic discourse.

DOI: 10.4018/978-1-5225-8961-7.ch003

Attempts are made to establish any patterns or trends evident from examining the conditions that initiate social dialogue arrangements.

Dominant as well as institutional discourses are explored and how they are represented by the states and the benefits of pursuing social dialogue as a form of governance. The review also provides a balance by examining the contending arguments to the dominant discourse and relevance within the context of developing states and the hegemony exercised in the relationship between the pursuit of the ideal versus the relevance to realities and the need to chart a new course or discourse. Elements of the evidence presented in the social world and experiences of several states and regions worldwide, in terms of types of tripartite and bipartite arrangements which reveal the benefits and value held and the rationale and insight as to why the course of social dialogue is pursued.

Benefits and Ways of Analyzing Successful Partnerships

The literature is replete with the beneficial outcomes from social partnerships (Bangs, 2007; Haynes & Allen, 2000; Goolsarran, 2006). Social partnerships have been transformative (Katz et al., 2004) and viewed as the backbone of economic policy (Baccaro & Simoni, 2004) as it promotes economic recovery (McCartan, 2003; O' Donnell & O' Reardon, 1996) and the shaping of social policy (Buhlungu, 2005; Iankova, 2008). Becoming a framework for consensus (Cook, 1998; Fashoyin, 2004) social partnership has reduced the potential for industrial relations conflict (Hethy, 2001) emerging as an instrument for building better understanding between social partners (Etukudo,1995; Tokman, 2007; Weeks, 1999).

Three interacting elements have been presented as part of a triad of conditions precipitating the formation of social partnerships through social dialogue, namely globalization's effects, a weakened state and crisis conditions. The view of crisis being a prerequisite for social partnerships is evidenced also by the decline in such arrangements in states that are more developed and who do not exist within a cycle of crises as compared to many developing countries. One could argue that once the crisis has receded within the context of particular economies, that the need for such arrangements wane or decline, as exhibited in Italy and Japan. Furthermore, the motivation for pursuing social dialogue and subsequent arrangements could be temporary once the imposed dialogue process has satisfied a specific goal, e.g., EU membership on the part of Italy and Eastern European states under transition.

In the case of Belgium, the Central Council of the Economy produced a report in July 1993, that argued that Belgium was losing market share in international trade more rapidly and its wage costs were also increasing faster than its competitors. This led to the social partners beginning discussions on a social pact, but while agreeing on the diagnosis, they failed to reach an agreement. This was due to the government intervening in an area traditionally reserved for collective autonomy which led to one of the union confederations, leaving the bargaining table, while also taking issue with employers for tolerating the intervening action.

Despite the other union confederation to the dialogue, being willing to continue negotiations, the government ignored this offer and acted unilaterally by releasing its own *Global Plan*, with the employers, who also expressed their preference for unilateral state intervention to a negotiated approach. The unions responded by organizing the first 24- hour general strike since 1936. The 1993 episode was not unique as again in 1994, history repeated itself, so when the social partners failed to reach agreement on the Global Plan, once again, the government proceeded unilaterally.

In 1996, new peak level negotiations for a social pact on employment and wage moderation failed again because one union group refused to approve the tentative deal. Government then used legislative means to introduce a new wage system breaking collective bargaining autonomy and hence constrained wage growth to mimic wage increases in Belgium's three main partners, France, Germany and the Netherlands. (Baccaro & Lim, 2006)

How Have Social Partnerships Been Used?

Social partnership can be construed as a natural outcome, a strategic response and as a development strategy in reconstituting relationships under crisis or times of intense challenge, i.e., to undo the legacy of apartheid (Bassett, 2004, p.546) or those between state, market and civil society (Jones & Schoberg, 2004) where governance is viewed as self-organizing and inter organizational networks (Rhodes, 1997, p. 53) consisting of state and non-state actors resting upon relations of exchange and trust rather than on informal institutional roles and boundaries. Social partnerships have been analyzed in terms of the circumstances from which they emerged and the models employed, from the perspective of ILO global discourses, classification and modalities of social dialogue, e.g., whether the arrangements are bipartite or tripartite (Hála et al., 2002; Iankova, 2008; Taylor & Mathers, 2002).

PARTNERSHIP AND SOCIAL DIALOGUE

In every EU member state, except the U.K. and France, during the 1990s, there was a surge of social partnership development modeled after tripartite and bipartite relationships, even in states where there was no predisposition to this tradition, such as in Ireland, Portugal and Spain (Boyd, 2002).

Other approaches and perspectives on social partnerships consider how the state and governance modalities are affected positively to achieve economic and societal benefits. The process over time is considered in analyzing how negative socio economic and political processes have been turned around and broader benefits derived. During the transition to a market economy in Central and Eastern Europe states as aforementioned, the labour market was characterized by jobless growth and unemployment, which increased poverty, the informal economy and movement towards agricultural subsistence and migration. The informal economy includes activities that are not covered by law, or to which the law is not applied, or again where the law is discouraging compliance because it is inappropriate, burdensome or imposes excessive costs (Trebilcock, 1996).

Labour force participation rates were much lower than in the EU in general (UNESCAP 2006). Within the global climate of economic crisis and instability (Collins 2003), social partnership became a condition for membership in the EU (Grabbe 1999, 13; Iankova 2008).

The process of European integration also resulted in the development of new forms of partnership at the enterprise level. Labour and capital relations were reconstructed around partnership, a global pluralist dialogue and modernized, industrial relations, replacing hostility with consensus (Martinez-Lucio & Stuart, 2002). The institutionalization of social dialogue in Europe, became a prerequisite for acceding (Grabbe, 1999) to membership within the EU and the associated benefits. Many Central and Eastern European (CEE) countries managed their transition from socialist to market economies through tripartite social partnership mechanisms. They established national (Taylor & Mathers, 2002) bodies, so that tripartism (Kuruvilla & Erikson, 2002; International Labour Organization (ILO), 2002; Katz et al., 2004) and social dialogue (Hethy, 2001) would become the militating pathway. The ten CEE applicants for membership were Bulgaria, the Czech Republic, Estonia, Hungary, Latvia, Lithuania, Poland, Romania, Slovakia and Slovenia. An eleventh applicant, Cyprus, began negotiations in 1998 at the same time as five of the CEE countries (the Czech Republic, Estonia, Hungary, Poland and Slovenia).

The term *'Accession Partnership'* is used in this case, intended to make conditionality stricter on financial assistance and ultimately on accession itself, by uniting all EU demands and assistance for meeting them in a single framework. Albania, Bulgaria, Czech Republic, Estonia, Hungary, Latvia, Lithuania, Moldova, Poland, among others, all established tripartite national bodies from the beginning of their transition periods, which yielded some successes.

Through EU regulation (Grabbe, 1999) highly productive employment relations were supported and encouraged initiating labour market renewal (Taylor & Mathers, 2002) and the participation of multiple stakeholders in support of labour and social policy (Hethy 2001). Social partnership philosophies have been incorporated into law, e.g., in Spain (Boyd, 2002) and have been used to maintain statutory forms of employee participation, reflected in the EU Directives (Gollan & Patmore, 2005). These Directives from the European Council in 1994 and 1997 related to employee participation, namely the European Works Council Directives (EWCD) and the National Directive Establishing a General Framework for Informing and Consulting Employees Within Member States. EWCD is an employee committee consulted by management and play a role in workplace decision making. The autonomous actions of the social partners have been institutionalized and legalized, gradually translated into the economic, social and political life of transition countries (Djuric, 2002).

Owing to their active participation in social partnership (Hála et al., 2002; Iankova, 2008) the countries acceding to the EU have embraced a broader philosophy in that governments and stakeholders of Central and Eastern Europe, held the belief that tripartism could peacefully solve conflict and mitigate social tension. With respect to the experience of the states, Djuric (2002), argues that well developed bipartism is a precondition for the development of tripartism. Where bipartism is well developed, institutionalized and politically established, with proper negotiating structures, tripartite relations are more durable. Without this framework, there is a greater dependence of industrial relations on national political processes. He explains that autonomous action of social partners have been gradually translated into the economic, social and political life of transition countries and have also become institutionalised and legalised owing to their active participation.

With regards to Africa, trade unions in the pursuit of social partnership have played a political role (Van der Walt 1998, p. 3) in ending one party regimes in Mali, Zambia and Malawi and have contributed to the restoration of democratic rights in collaboration with civil society (Gallin, 2000; Percival 1996).

Deepening crisis during the 1990s, the pursuit of structural adjustment programmes and the effects of globalization, prompted dialogue between labour and the state with a view to adopt macroeconomic and structural measures and address the resulting distortions in the labour market. Based on the conditionality of dialogue and 'good governance' as a prerequisite to access international development assistance, African political leaders sought to include social partners in modalities of governance to help foster ownership of programmes and as they restructured labour legislation and industry as a means to catalyze economic growth.

A report from the International Confederation of Free Trade Unions (ICFTU-AFRO) notes that politicians are again tempted to employ repression in stabilising society so that the requirements of conditionality are accepted unopposed'. The offer of a 'docile workforce' facilitates external investment. 'Dialogue has become a condition for intervention by international financial institutions and an indicator of 'good governance'. On the other hand, an increase in violations of labour and trade union freedoms by governments has been seen (Percival, 1996).

There are examples where under dictatorship, trade unions have faced state repression or are forced underground, and Webster (2005), lists Indonesia the Philippines under Marcos, Poland from 1976 to 1981 with the Workers. Defense Committee (Komitet Obrony Robotników (KOR), the Republic of Korea in the late 1980s, and South Africa in the early 1970s.

Webster (2006), explains that under Nigeria's military dictatorship, the International Federation of Chemical, Energy, Mine and General Workers. Unions (ICEM) worked with human rights NGOs to campaign for the release of imprisoned trade unionists. However, challenges emerge with respect to issue of power as Landell-Mills (1992), mentions the weaknesses of union leaders who are drawn in by elites in several African countries. Additionally, Etukudo (1995), criticizes the notion of development held which involves the co-opting of certain interest groups into socio economic decision making, whereby they forego their legitimate right to protect their sectional interests and in return government grants them privileges.

Several African states had begun to create presidential task forces to advise heads of state which have served to promote multipartite consultations

(Etukudo, 1995) and should be encouraged to support not derail tripartite efforts at the lower level. The tendency to rely upon structures and institutions to order functions are a feature of the culture of authoritarianism in many African states and a rules-based approach to governance which contrasts with political democratization and pluralist approaches with tripartism. In Kenya for example, the business community has led in the tripartite discussions there, with the informal process becoming institutionalized in 1997 and being included in the dialogue and governance consultations with the Bretton Woods Institutions. Ghana has enjoyed a rich history of social dialogue institutions with an initial attempt in 1972, with the formation of the National Tripartite Committee (NTC) by the National Redemption Council (NRC). It was charged with responsibility for fixing the national minimum wage, but tripartite consultations became more effective during the Third Republic in 1979 where the Committee was made up of five representatives of labour, employers and Government.

The post- repression period in South Africa, saw unions leading the movement towards democracy which has contributed to development based on social partnership which has been institutionalized in the structures of governance at various levels of organization. Within the tripartite alliance, the African National Congress (ANC) refers to itself, and is variously referred to by others, as 'the leader of the alliance' or 'the leader of the forces of change'. The close relationship between union and political party was strengthened by social regulation which fostered a consensus, multivariate alliances and social partnerships. The social safety nets created provided labour with opportunities to influence policy as they 'ameliorated the ravages of capitalism' (Buhlungu, 2005).

Recognizing the political dimension of power and the positioning of trade unions as actors in industrial relations shaping Africa's political economy (Kraus 1976; Van der Walt 1998, Andrew Kailembo, Secretary General of the Africa regional section of the International Confederation of Free Trade Unions (ICFTU-AFRO) noted that:

In this democratization process, some governments fear the role of the trade union movement. This is particularly so when they see that it is independent and working with a free press, conversing with society. (Percival, 1996, p.1). This has resulted in governments being antagonistic towards trade unions, reflected in their exclusion from consultations in the design of Bretton Woods programmes (Etukudo, 1995; Percival, 1996) and retarding progress on labour rights and greater participation (Percival, 1996).

Economic crisies in Latin America in the 1980s, compounded by debt, an ideological shift and the forced restructuring of production has had serious implications for labour in this region (Weeks, 1999; Tokman, 2007, Trebilcock, 1996) Concerns circled the guaranteeing of social and labour rights, the maintenance of levels of employment, the rate of poverty and rising social exclusion. The crises of the 1980's saw a decline in real wages in countries implementing structural adjustment programmes which aggravated the standard of living and poverty (Trebilcock, 1996) for which Latin America was not exempt. Political change in transitioning from dictatorial military regimes towards more democratic forms in the 1990s, also served to shape the form of social dialogue emerging in this region, with the state being the major architect (Cook, 1998). The modalities of liberalization in the context of globalisation in the Latin American region severely curtailed national decision-making capacity which gave rise to low growth and productivity, weak labour demand and high levels of unemployment and inequality evidenced by deteriorating labour market indicators. The increased inequities within the context of enormous market deregulation and speculative financial flows, contributed to the removal of social programmes and to increased exclusion.

Since distortions in the distributional aspects of an economy reflect political coalitions in which some groups benefit to the detriment of others, measures to strengthen the position of the most marginalized within a society was required that would ultimately lead to their receiving a more equitable share benefit from economic growth (Trebilcock, 1996). The international financial institutions demonstrated their support for dialogue (Oelbaum, 2002; Friedman & Hochstetler, 2002) and the term '*concertation sociale*' or '*concertation*' emerged from this region referring to bargaining relations with formerly antagonistic sectors. Trade unionism was thereby perceived as moving from '*a discourse of protest to one of proposals*' (Ramalho, 1996, p. 6).

The ILO posits that 'concertation' can be informal or institutionalised, and often it is a combination of the two, occurring at various levels whether national, regional or at the enterprise level, and it can be inter-professional, sectoral or a combination of all of these. '*Concertacion*' has led to various reforms in Brazil, Chile, El Salvador, Mexico, Honduras, Peru and Venezuela and although there have been improvements within the labour markets since 2003, there are still huge employment problems which will lead to the continuation of social dialogue processes and the emergence of varied forms

In Latin America, the powerful unified and centralized unions used their political (Madrid, 2003; Ramalho, 1996 ; Van der Walt 1998, 3) economic clout and relationships with the state and political parties, (Cook, 1998 ;

Levitsky & Way, 2000 ; Madrid, 2003) to make the latter responsive to their wishes. It is noted that the Argentine labour movement has not hesitated to use its power to block policies that it has opposed. Madrid (2003) explained that the strength of the unions (Cook, 1998) and their ability to influence policy rested on their density which relates to their financial resources and capacity to disrupt the economy. Unified and centralized unions are able to act as a single voice, mobilize more workers and make commitments. Secondly, the relationships of the trade unions with political parties are such that the latter can be responsive to union wishes and so use their political or economic clout in their favour. Insomuch that, 'the success of an adjustment policy often depends on a government's capacity to negotiate wage restraint or public sector retrenchments with influential trade unions (Trebilcock, 1996, p. 8). The trade unions played a political role, forging a legitimacy, in the midst of the changes in regime. They participated in nationwide strikes, in the bargaining for industrial and social development activities and the processes of the transformation of industry and business, in search of a common ground which would safeguard jobs, wages and preserve society overall.

Recollecting the financial crisis of 1997, this was the catalyst for change and industrial relations restructuring (Kuruvilla & Erikson, 2002; Sig Choi, et al., 2008) in several of the affected economies of the Association of Southeast Asian Nations' (ASEAN), resulting in the loss of the traditions of lifetime employment (Frenkel & Peetz, 1998). The crisis led to social dialogue over the issue of job losses, the planned or policy-driven measures towards privatization, a focus by trade unions on negotiation and the reorganization of work with improved labour-management cooperation. For example, a survey of 425 Malaysian companies undertaken in early 1998 revealed that, in a majority of cases, a wide range of alternatives to layoffs had been deployed and that, at that date, retrenchments had been relatively few (ILO, 2000).

In Indonesia, the crisis and collapse led to a contraction in employment at a time when social dialogue was in its infancy and the mechanisms for resolution were inadequate. Labour repression and the absence of a tradition of labour management cooperation and tripartism prevented the coming to fruition of meaningful agreements from the attempts at social dialogue, after the rise and fall of four successive governments from 1998 – 2001. In 1999 however, the institution of a tripartite task force and the sensitization to dialogue of the partners provided a framework of consensus alongside informal consultations (Fashoyin, 2004). Post-crisis scenarios led to the decline of authoritarian governance modes (Erickson & Kuruvilla, 2002) within Asia and movement towards increased social dialogue and political democratization, evidenced by the forging of consensus at various levels. Efforts were initiated through social dialogue to address issues of job losses, (Cook, 1998; Friedman & Hochstetler, 2002) planned or policy-driven measures towards privatization, trade unions activism and the reorganization of work with improved labour-management cooperation (Zhu, 1995).

The enterprise provided the focus for bargaining and the union organization in Japan, but in recent years traditional enterprise industrial relations has been demoted by management's replacement of full-time workers with 'non-regular workers.' It was suggested that a new form of union movement was emerging representing these 'non-regular workers' to circumvent existing enterprise unions. Constitutional rights were established and rights assured to collective bargaining in South Korea and Japan where consultation is regarded as a peaceful attempt to reach convergence, whereas collective bargaining is recognized as confrontational. (ILO, 2000; Fashoyin, 2004). Labour bargaining efforts were strengthened as well as the promotion of consensus politics at the national level (Katz, et al., 2004) and the emergence of creative alternatives to minimize layoffs (ILO, 1999c). In 2001, China created a tripartite consultation mechanism resulting in new laws for dispute settlement and contracts to foster harmonious labour relations and collective bargaining.

Crises and the fluctuation in primary commodity prices globally contributed to the accrual of debt by many Third World countries, between the 1970s and the 1990s. This situation exacerbated the existing colonial driven, economic dependency (Frank 1967) of Third World states that had remained oriented around a primary product creating the vulnerability of economic dependence upon the income of one export, subject to fluctuating commodity prices within global markets.

The nature or basis of competition appears to have changed, and "human resources" has emerged as the critical factor of production, as economic activity in the most internationally competitive industries is increasingly "knowledge-based". There is a constant drive to maintain a greater level of skills based and a more educated population in order just to keep up with certain standards of production. There is an enhanced importance placed upon the individual's human capital endowment as the theme of the organizational basis of competition, and the assumption that new varieties of interpersonal working relationships are as critical, if not more critical, to competitiveness than "technology'.

The "social basis" of competition suggests a new set of policy challenges not only for developed economies, but for developing countries as all are forced reformulate the very social models upon which economies are based (Campbell 1991). Examples are in seen in levels of employment displacement – which occurs more and more as a result of import market shares, rather than purely domestic competition. There is a rise in the protection of uncompetitive industry to stave off massive employment loss and in both developed and developing countries, wages can and have adjusted downward to meet international competition.

Caribbean countries however, also faced the challenge of weak infrastructure for enforcement. In fact, there is an increasing awareness that approaches are needed that will facilitate global competitiveness, attractiveness to investors and the creation of new employment opportunities, while at the same time meeting decent work standards. The requirement for a more consensual approach among government, management and labour to improve productivity and enterprise performance, and to promote human, social and economic development, offers new opportunities to achieve a reassessment on the part of enterprise management of the advantages of compliance with international labour standards

The most cited case of successful social partnership in the Caribbean is that of Barbados, where social dialogue, was born out of economic crisis and the need to avoid the IMF's prescription of devaluating the currency, which propelled a focus upon competitiveness and productivity. Difficult economic decisions had to be made and implemented with dialogue aimed to achieve stabilization and economic growth. At the beginning the objectives of the pact involved the retention of jobs as well as the acceptance of a wage freeze until productivity gains were achieved. The success of the first 'protocol' was followed by a second, covering 1995-97. There was an acknowledgement that the tripartite protocol agreements helped to resolve a major economic crisis which has led to continued social dialogue on major economic and social policy issues to promote stability and economic prosperity (Fashoyin, 2004), the details of which are discussed in Chapter 2.

In the case of Barbados in the Caribbean, their social partnership arrangement can be located within the framework of a collaborative partnership typology (Kernaghan, 1993; Hodgett & Johnson, 2001). A tripartite social partnership model emerged in response to pending economic crisis (O' Donnell & O' Reardon, 1996; McCartan, 2003) triggered by a downturn in the world economy, which, (through relations of economic interdependence (Keohane & Nye, 1989), led to the destabilization of the Barbadian economy.

Tables 1- 4 summarizes the main elements of these arrangements termed 'Protocols'.

Table 1. Summary of protocols on social partnership 1993-1995: Barbados

Protocol	Date	Rationale	Agreement	Objectives
Protocol for the Implementation of a Prices and Incomes Policy.	April 1, 1993 to March 31, 1995	Developed as part of the response to the grave economic crisis which faced Barbados in 1991 and 1992. Clear economic focus to strengthen the economy and a core strategy to avoid the prescriptions of the IMF which included the devaluation of the Barbados dollar. Stabilization through prices and incomes	Establish a Tripartite Consultative Mechanism (TCM) The Social Partners encompassing Prices and Incomes Policy for Barbados 1. Maintaining *the* existing parity of the rate of exchange. 2. Expansion of the economy. 3. Competitiveness through productivity 4. Industrial relations harmony Collective bargaining. Meetings held quarterly and chaired by the PM	1. Freeze on basic wages and salaries in the public and private sectors with increases permitted on the basis of productivity improvement. 2. Prices to be kept under review and increases based only in higher" input costs. 3. Establishment of a National Productivity Board to develop and improve productivity.

Successive protocols evolved in depth and helped to avert the crisis through continued social dialogue on major economic and social policy issues (Fashoyin, 2004) forming the foundation of the modality of governance reflected in the National Development Strategy 2005-2025 of Barbados (Farley, 2000).

Crisis conditions, leading to the need to avoid an intervention by the International Monetary Fund (IMF) as well as a currency devaluation, fuelled the mutuality of interest (Hodgett & Johnson, 2001; Martinez-Lucio & Stuart, 2004) and the realization that more could be gained through dialogue. Sectoral consultations began which resulted in the Tripartite Consultative Mechanism (TCM) being created, composing of representatives from government, private sector and labour unions.

The priority was to maintain the value of the Barbadian dollar to control inflation, preserve employment and create an environment of stability for business. The benefits gained from the first protocol or tripartite social partnership, involving the retention of jobs and a wage freeze was followed by a second protocol and the expansion of the stakeholder base for 1995-97.

Decline in Tripartism

Some authors, (Turner, 2004; Katz, et al., 2004) have argued that there has been a fluctuation in the active pursuit of social pacts in some countries that have traditionally held tripartite dialogue and established formal relations and structures. They indicate that contemporary tripartism has emphasized workplace change and time flexibility as against in the past a macro level focus on inflation and incomes policy.

Table 2. Summary of protocols on social partnership 1995-1997: Barbados

Protocol	Date	Rationale	Agreement	Objectives
Protocol II Restrain Wages and Prices	1995 -1997	Second protocol essentially reaffirmed commitment to the objectives and principles of the first protocol. Protocol Two was extended for one year whilst Protocol Three was being drafted.	Consolidation of the process of tripartite consultation. Restructuring of the economy. Sustainable expansion of the economy through competitiveness. National commitment to increased productivity. Reduction "of social disparities through increased employment. Maintenance of a stable industrial relations climate. Achievement of a balance between prices and incomes. Maintenance of the existing parity of the rate of exchange	Major changes were: Agreement to wage and price restraint The establishment of a TCM Sub-Committee of the Social Partners to meet at least once per month. The Social Compact to create a modern, efficient economy and sustainable economic growth and for achieving industrial harmony. Joint approaches to the formulation of policies, problem solving and to the management of social development Strategies to expand the private sector. Reduction in the benefits of labor in context of long-term improvement in numbers employed and or conditions of "labour

Table 3. Summary of protocols on social partnership 1998-2000 Barbados

Protocol	Date	Rationale	Agreement	Objectives
Protocol III Social Pact	1998-2000	Protocol Three further departed from the two previous Protocols by listing, in addition to the joint commitments, undertakings taken on board by each of the three partners. Government, Employers and Worker representatives	Growth, employment, equity, growth of an efficient modern economy, increased productivity.	Additionally, addressed national employment policy, labour market changes, and sub- standard wages, taxes, widening the partnership to include NGOs, church etc., and reduction of child labour, crime. 4th of February Accord - Protection of the rights to operate for unions and foster a stable industrial relations climate

Katz et al., (2004) notes that Italy, for example, experienced the resurgence in tripartite dialogue during the 1990s and several tripartite agreements were designed to achieve economic stability, reduce inflation and foster greater coordination between national and local levels of collective bargaining. A series of social pacts were established, primarily to meet the 'Maastricht parameters' for European Monetary Union entry. and since attaining entry tripartism has lost its momentum (Meardi, 2007); Katz et al., 2004) with movement towards a less regulated bargaining. evidenced also by the Berlusconi government of Italy moving further towards market-oriented economic policies and less regulated bargaining.

Reference is also made to Australia's industrial relations system, which has been one of the most centralized going through three stages, managed

Table 4. Summary of protocols on social partnership 2001-2004: Barbados

Protocol	Date	Rationale	Agreement	Objectives
Protocol IV	1st April, 2001 to 31st March, 2004	The repositioning of the Barbadian economy (by the year 2005) through the protection, consolidation and advancement of Barbados" best economic interests in the regional, hemispheric and global economic environment such that the country can succeed in building a fully developed society in which all are afforded the opportunity to secure the highest standard of living.	The reduction of social disparities through those protections which are inherent in an acknowledgement of the right to decent work freely chosen and the provision of opportunities for access to increased employment. (iii) The national commitment to increased competitiveness through improved productivity and efficiency in the workplace. (iv) The maintenance of an industrial relations environment conducive to a continuation of stable industrial relations. (v) The protection of the domestic economy specifically through the preservation of the existing parity of the exchange rate and the achievement of balance between prices and incomes. (vi) The consolidation of the process of tripartite consultation.	National employment policy. Industrial harmony. Labour market changes. Widening of the social partnership. Productive sectors of the economy. Training. Reduction of social disparities. Crime. Public Sector Reform Persons "with disabilities. Child Labour National Productivity Council Prices policy. Incomes policy. Sub-standard wages. Tax regime

decentralism from 1987 to 1990, (Gardner, 1996) coordinated flexibility from 1991 to 1996) and fragmented flexibility from 1997 to the present. With the recent re-election of a coalition government the increased majority and control of the Senate, no initiative has been taken by the union movement to re-establish an Accord-style arrangement which existed prior. It would appear that tripartism has been abandoned and the prospects for both tripartism and centralised bargaining seem to be very dim (Lansbury & Niland, 1995).

Japan similarly, had previously experienced a significant level of tripartism but is now in decline. From the mid-1950s, inter-union coordination; and from the 1970s, a significant degree of tripartite bargaining had taken place but both of these trends have waned in recent years. The corporation traditionally provided both the main focus for bargaining and for union organization, but traditional enterprise industrial relations have been eroded by management replacement of full-time workers with 'nonregular' workers. Enterprise based unions whose membership has been confined to full time workers are challenged as it is possible for new form of union movement representing these workers may emerge circumventing existing enterprise unions (Katz et al., 2004). From the perspective of Katz et al (2004), it would appear that states that have achieved a degree of global economic strength and resilience and who fall outside of any crisis scenario, show a diminishing interest or need for such social dialogue processes as they had in the past.

CHALLENGES

Social partnerships as operationalized globally, reflect ILO discourses and have used the ILO world view as benchmarks to grade success, being analyzed as a process partnership under tripartism et al. (ILO, 2002; Kuruvilla, 2003). However, the literature also suggests that the approaches and the standards established by the ILO are inadequate to analyze the special features and experiences of Third World society, as noted by Kuruvilla (2003) who observed that the ILO's concept of social dialogue and tripartism is restricted in its relevance. An underlying assumption of the ILO is that the traditional employment relationship – employers and unions is universal and organized urban industrial society governance structures and policies, become the assumed base upon which labour analyses are predicated, (Kuruvilla, 2003) influencing and defining subsequent models and criteria to benchmark worker protection.

In reality, a large majority of the world's population have no access to social dialogue mechanisms and many countries outside of Europe have decentralized bargaining processes hence they do not have tripartite structures. Further, that amidst a declining union membership worldwide, collective bargaining coverage rates are low even with respect to the results of bipartite negotiations and with declining densities, the proportion of the world's workers do not have the right to participate.

There are limitations to the use of tripartite models as artifacts as they are premised on certain assumptions which do not necessarily hold true in all circumstances. There is concomitantly an implicit assumption that an employment relationship between workers and employers is necessary for social dialogue to occur, which becomes negligible compared to the realities and characteristics of the labour market in the context of developing countries.

A characteristic of most developing countries, which is increasing, is the size of the informal sector that shows very little of the employment relationship, a key element in the analysis of social dialogue (de Silva, 1997). Comparatively this informal unorganized sector, which is significant and a true representation of labour conditions, has been insufficiently captured or represented within the framework of norms and standard setting nor are they adequately protected within the structure, as social partners lack the mandate to represent the interests of these groups (Alby et al., 2005; Etukudo, 1995). The process towards tripartism assumes that the views of the social partners are adequately represented (de Silva, 1997). In the developing world a large majority of the populace have no access to social dialogue mechanisms and many countries outside of Europe have decentralized bargaining processes hence they do not have tripartite structures.

In Central Europe, economic programmes proved to be successful only at the cost of the social, resulting in increased social tension and risk of a social explosion (Hethy, 2001). The hope of mitigating these effects by the resolution of conflict and the sharing of remedial measures with social partners was a motivation for the pursuit of tripartism. During the first decade of the transition process, Djuric (2002) noted that the social price paid for the reforms was higher, whereby countries gradually acknowledged the need to devote more attention to the social price of reforms as a whole, with the hope that tripartism would resolve conflict and engender the mutual sharing of remedial measures between partners. Further, that amidst a declining union membership worldwide, collective bargaining coverage rates are low even with respect to the results of bipartite negotiations, and with declining densities, the proportion of the world's workers do not have the right to participate. It is argued by Lado (2002) that the neoliberal discourse pursued by many developing and transition states, with or without overt political authoritarianism, prevents the institutionalization of labour in civil society and restricts the potential benefits to be derived as demonstrated in Africa and Latin America.

In the fast-growing economies of East and Southeast Asia, a culture of deference to hierarchy, avoidance of open conflict and a preference for affective-personal rather than rational-legal means to resolve problems, were recognized as being obstacles to trade union organization and impediments to engaging the full participation of the workforce (ILO 1998). Regarding gender issues, some countries on the South Asian continent do not acknowledge or afford the minimum recognition of being a worker to women in the labour force who are disenfranchised, being unable to associate and bargain collectively or enter into dialogue. The largest proportion of the unorganized or informal sector workers are women Webster (2005) who entered the sector during crises, for e.g., in Moscow, two thirds of the jobless are women (Auvergnon, 2006). The informal economy includes activities that are not covered by law, or to which the law is not applied, or again where the law is also discouraging compliance because it is inappropriate, burdensome or imposes excessive costs (Trebilcock, 1996).

FUTURE RESEARCH

In reflecting upon social partnership agreements and what conditions precipitate social partnership agreements generally, globalization has emerged as affecting the state globally and locally, to form relationships which results in having to entertain various degrees of power sharing.

As the source of the dominant discourse and literature on social dialogue, the ILO ideology of global social policymaking implicitly suggests a neoliberal 'one size fits all' philosophy supported and replicated in other 'global public policy' institutions such as the Bretton Woods Group. In relation to ongoing debates and how ILO approaches and the institutionalization of social partnership has been translated into the state domain in the developing world, there are challenges as born out in their experiences which have affected power relations, having a political dimension. There are also limitations to the degree that the process can be universally applied, especially in the application of labour conventions.

New methodologies are therefore required to fully explore the employment relationship and to treat with the unorganized sector. This phenomenon is not peculiar to any particular country or region and even represents 30-50 per cent of the labour market in the new European Union member states (Auvergnon 2006). Labour market changes during the transition period in Central and Eastern Europe were characterized by jobless growth and unemployment that was larger, long-term and structural. These conditions made the propensity to move towards poverty, an informal economy or towards agricultural subsistence and migration more apparent, with labour force participation rates much lower than in the European Union in general (UNESCAP, 2006)

There will continue to be debates as to what extent ILO norms can be universally applied and factored in with respect to different types of economies. Furthermore, as to how effective they can be in empathizing and understanding cultural diversity and localized societal norms of acceptance, that contravene Western conceptualizations of appropriate practice and acceptability, inclusive of balancing political perspectives on modes of governance.

Auvergnon (2006) suggests that norms, particularly related to the industrial and trade union practices of states, can be imposed for the long term if they reflect social, economic, and cultural realities. Consequently, calibrations of worker participation must be determined through alternative institutions or mechanisms that can, accommodate and represent the grey area that ILO philosophy has yet to appropriate in furthering the discourse of social dialogue and worker rights in developing countries in a meaningful way. These 'grey' areas have to be analysed and understood in trying to further the discourse of social dialogue and worker rights in developing meaningful and relevant indicators of social dialogue, under these circumstances. New approaches must be pursued to capture relevant indicators of social dialogue within these diverse scenarios.

There is also an underlying belief that development will be greater furthered with dialogue than without it and the more inclusive the process is, involving multiple stakeholders, consensus can be achieved and hence mutual benefits gained. Through social dialogue there has been the integration of the social dimension into economic policy-making and through participation, providing a means whereby the demands of social partners can influence the decision-making processes on economic and social policy reform (Fashoyin, 2004). International experience shows that effective social dialogue cannot operate in a vacuum and that it requires:

- A well organised institutional framework endowed with the necessary human and financial resources within which interactions facilitate the reaching of necessary compromises building consensus on social and economic policies.
- Political will on the part of the government to engage in meaningful social dialogue on economic and social policies is of paramount importance for the success of transition.
- The commitment to the social partnership not to be diminished with a change of political regime (Ghellab & Vylitova, 2003)

The literature positions social partnership as a governance response to crisis conditions, examining outcomes and effects in terms of institutions – labour and the state, political economic and socioeconomic contexts, the types and models of partnership relationship employed and from leadership perspectives and processes. In global discourses, it is positioned as a solution to the resolution of conflict, measured as deliverables from labour and social policy making within conciliatory governance regimes which promotes nation building.

There are additional dimensions that need consideration in the analyses of social partnerships, such as past legacies, leadership attitudes to dialogue, a lack of knowledge and information, that all contribute to weaknesses in the institutionalization of social partnerships, some of which have been highlighted by Djuric (2002). The institutionalization of social dialogue and new legislation alone are insufficient to offset the legacy of negative, often anti-unionist practice in the countries of this region. There are examples that tripartite institutions, although formally established, are actually hollow, ineffective, faced with the problems such as lack of willingness for dialogue, lack of knowledge for resolution of complex social, economic and general developmental problems.

Other authors, Ghellab and Vylitova (2003) have identified the need to consider the attitudes of parties who should demonstrate in word and deed, the willingness to cooperate and reach a consensus and find common responses, both in times of crisis and economic prosperity. Several general and idiosyncratic factors contribute to differentiated results in social partnerships, such as the nature of the politics, the political culture, the vibrancy of the trade union movement, the immediate circumstances of each country before the introduction of the policy style and state capacity for policy management, which have also been identified

In all the regions mentioned, social dialogue has had value in reducing industrial conflict, contributing to labour peace and social stability and economic and social development. In cases, negotiation, consultation, discussion and information sharing has been used to seek consensus on policy options and has defused opposition to proposals or break a deadlock.

Social dialogue has also contributed to good governance and democracy, by the way in which decisions are reached, facilitating the contribution concerns of stakeholders in the policy process. This chapter provided the global contextual frame and overview of the main discourses around social partnership within which Jamaica's experience with social partnership agreements can be located. These analyses further a better understanding of some of the social processes and theoretical considerations behind contemporary experiences with social partnership agreements.

The review has discussed the typologies of social partnerships, dominant as well as institutional discourses, as demonstrated through the institutions of global governance and governance arrangements in states as well as the benefits from pursuing various modalities of social dialogue. Contrasting views are explored, examining contending arguments to the dominant discourses and their relevance within the context of developing states and their experiences. Emerging from this, the hegemony exercised in the relationship between pursuits of the ideal versus the relevance to realities, precipitates the need to chart a new course or discourse. From the explorations undergone it is observed that:

- Social partnerships - forged from within contentious arenas of negotiation for the establishment of new and the changing of traditionally held power relations within the state and between its actors - are political.
- The rationale driving the process is one of actors minimizing losses in the face of changing relative power positions and maximizing the possibility of benefits and maintenance of position, through reciprocity and compromise in the new arrangements.

REFERENCES

Armistead, M., & Pettigrew, P. (2004). Effective partnerships: Building a sub-regional network of reflective practitioners. *International Journal of Public Sector Management*, *17*(7), 571–585. doi:10.1108/09513550410562257

Baccaro, L., & Lim, S. H. (2006). Social Pacts as Coalitions of" weak" and" moderate": Ireland, Italy and South Korea in Comparative Perspective. International Labour Organization (International Institute for Labour Studies).

Baccaro, L., & Simoni, M. (2004). *The Irish social partnership and the" celtic tiger" phenomenon*. Academic Press.

Ballantyne, D. (2004). Dialogue and its role in the development of relationship specific knowledge. *Journal of Business and Industrial Marketing*, *19*(2), 114–123. doi:10.1108/08858620410523990

Bangs, J. (2006). Social partnership: The wider context. *FORUM*, *2*(48), 201–208. doi:10.2304/forum.2006.48.2.201

Boyd, S. (2002). *Partnership Working: European Social Partnership Models)*. Scottish Trades Union Congress (STUC). Retrieved from http://www.scotland.gov.uk/Resource/Doc/25954/0028681.pdf

Buhlungu, S. (2005). Union-party alliances in the era of market regulation: The case of South Africa. *Journal of Southern African Studies*, *31*(4), 701–717. doi:10.1080/03057070500370464

Collins, H. (2003, April). *The evolving direction of European labour law: social inclusion, competitiveness and citizenship*. Paper presented at the Annual Labour Law Conference — Rethinking the Law of Work: Perspectives on the Future Shape of Employment Regulation, Sydney, Australia.

Cook, M. L. (1998). Toward Flexible Industrial Relations? Neo-Liberalism, Democracy, and Labor Reform in Latin America. *Industrial Relations*, *37*(3), 311–336. doi:10.1111/0019-8676.00090

De Silva, S. (1997). *Tripartism, employers and their organizations*. Bangkok: International Labour Organisation Act Emp Publications.

Djuric, D. (2002). Social dialogue, tripartism and social partnership in the South East European countries, including recommendations for Serbia and Montenegro. *Europe Revie for Labour and Social Affairs*, *3*, 87-100. Retrieved from www.ceeol.com

Etukudo, A. (1995). Reflections on the role of African employers' organizations in tripartism and social dialogue. *Int'l Lab. Rev.*, *134*, 51.

Fashoyin, T. (2001). *Fostering economic development through social dialogue*. Geneva: ILO.

Fashoyin, T. (2004). Tripartite Cooperation, Social Dialogue and National Development. *International Labour Review*, *143*(4), 341–372. doi:10.1111/j.1564-913X.2004.tb00553.x

Frenkel, S. J., & Peetz, D. (1998). Globalization and industrial relations in East Asia: A three-country comparison. *Industrial Relations*, *37*(3), 282–31. doi:10.1111/0019-8676.00089

Friedman, E. J., & Hochstetler, K. (2002). Assessing the third transition in Latin American democratization: Representational regimes and civil society in Argentina and Brazil. *Comparative Politics*, *35*(1), 21–42. doi:10.2307/4146926

Gallin, D. (2000). *Trade unions and NGOs: a necessary partnership for social development (No. 1)*. Geneva: United Nations Research Institute for Social Development.

Gardner, G. T., & Stern, P. C. (1996). *Environmental problems and human behavior*. Allyn & Bacon.

Ghellab, Y., & Vylitova, M. (2005). *Tripartite social dialogue on employment in the countries of South Eastern Europe*. International Labour Organization.

Gollan, P. J., & Patmore, G. (2006). Transporting the European social partnership model to Australia. *The Journal of Industrial Relations*, *48*(2), 217–256. doi:10.1177/0022185606062832

Goolsarran, S. J. (2006). *Industrial Relations in the Caribbean, Issues and Perspectives*. International Labour Organization.

Grabbe, H. (1999). *A partnership for accession: the implications of EU conditionality for the Central and East European applicants*. European University Institute, Robert Schuman Centre.

Hála, J., Kroupa, A., Mansfeldová, Z., Kux, J., Vašková, R., & Pleskot, I. (2002). *Development of social dialogue in the Czech Republic*. Prague: Research Institute of Labour and Social Affairs.

Haynes, P., & Allen, M. (2000). Partnership as union strategy a preliminary. *Employee Relations*, *23*(2), 164–193. doi:10.1108/01425450110384697

Héthy, L. (2001). Social Dialogue and Expanding World. *New Internationalist*.

Hill, M. (2014). *Policy process: A reader*. Routledge. doi:10.4324/9781315847290

Hodgett, S., & David, J. (2001). Troubles partnerships and possibilities - a study of the 'Making Belfast Work' initiative in Northern Ireland. *Public Administration and Development*, *21*(4), 321–332. doi:10.1002/pad.181

Iankova, E. (2008). *Europeanization of social partnership in EU-acceding countries*. Paper presented at the annual meeting of the International Studies Association (ISA's) 49th Annual convention, "Bridging Multiple Divides," San Francisco, CA.

Iankova, E., & Turner, L. (2004). Building the new Europe: Western and eastern roads in social partnership. *Industrial Relations Journal*, *35*(1), 76–92. doi:10.1111/j.1468-2338.2004.00301.x

International Labour Organisation. (2000). *Towards full employment: Technical report for discussion at the Asian Regional Consultation on Follow-up to the World Summit for Social Development, Bangkok, January 13-15, 1999*. Retrieved from http://www.ilo.org/public/english/region/asro/bangkok/feature/f-emp32.htm

International Labour Organisation. (2007). *Report of the Meeting on the Project "History of ILO Ideas and Their Impact"*. Geneva: International Labour Organisation.

Isaacs, H. (2004). The allure of partnerships: Beyond the rhetoric. *Social and Economic Studies*, *53*(4), 125–134.

Jessop, B. (1998). The rise of governance and the risks of failure: The case of economic development. *International Social Science Journal*, *50*(155), 29–45. doi:10.1111/1468-2451.00107

Jones, E., & Schoburgh, E. (2004). Deconstructing policy-making and implementation issues in a Caribbean context. *Social and Economic Studies*, *53*(4), 35–61.

Katz, H., Wonduck, L., & Joohee, L. (2004). *The new structure of labor relations: tripartism and decentralization*. Ithaca, NY: Cornell University Press.

Kernaghan, K. (1993). Partnership and public administration: Conceptual and practical considerations. *Canadian Public Administration*, *36*(1), 57–76. doi:10.1111/j.1754-7121.1993.tb02166.x

Kooiman, J. (2000). Societal Governance: Levels, models, and Orders of Social-political interaction. In J. Pierre (Ed.), *Debating governance: authority, steering, and democracy* (pp. 133–164). Oxford, UK: Oxford University Press.

Kraus, J. (1976). African trade unions: Progress or poverty? *African Studies Review*, *19*(3), 95–108. doi:10.2307/523877

Kuruvilla, S. (2003). *Social Dialogue for Decent Work, Education Outreach Programme, International Institute for Labour Studies*. Geneva: International Labour Organisation.

Kuruvilla, S., & Erickson, C. L. (2002). Change and transformation in Asian industrial relations. *Industrial Relations*, *41*(2), 171–227. doi:10.1111/1468-232X.00243

Kuruvilla, S., & Erickson, C. L. (2002). Change and transformation in Asian industrial relations. *Industrial Relations*, *41*(2), 171–227. doi:10.1111/1468-232X.00243

Landell-Mills, P. (1992). Governance, cultural change, and empowerment. *The Journal of Modern African Studies*, *30*(4), 543–567. doi:10.1017/S0022278X00011046

Lansbury, R., & Niland, J. (1995). Managed Decentralization? Recent Trends in Australian Industrial Relations and Human Resource Policies. *Employment Relations in a Changing World Economy*, 59-90.

Levitsky, S., & Way, L. A. (1998). Between a shock and a hard place: The dynamics of labour-backed adjustment in Poland and Argentina. *Comparative Politics*, *30*(2), 171–192. doi:10.2307/422286

Maatta, P. (2008). *Equal pay, just a principle of the ILO? Abstract*. Tampere University.

Madrid, R. L. (2003). Labouring against neoliberalism: Unions and patterns of reform in Latin America. *Journal of Latin American Studies*, *35*(1), 53–88. doi:10.1017/S0022216X0200665X

Martinez-Lucio, M., & Stuart, M. (2002). Social partnership and mutual gains organization and remaking involvement and trust at the British workplace. *Economic and Industrial Democracy*, *23*(2), 177–200. doi:10.1177/0143831X02232003

Martinez-Lucio, M., & Stuart, M. (2004). Swimming against the tide: Social partnership, mutual gains and the revival of "tired' HRM. *International Journal of Human Resource Management*, *15*(2), 410–424. doi:10.1080/0958519032000158581

McCartan, P. (2002). Towards social partnership-or co-operative industrial relations? *Irish Journal of Management*, *23*(1), 53.

Meardi, G. (2007). More voice after more exit? Unstable industrial relations in Central Eastern Europe. *Industrial Relations Journal*, *38*(6), 503–523. doi:10.1111/j.1468-2338.2007.00461.x

Messenger, J. C. (2009). TRAVAIL Policy Brief No. *Work Sharing: A Strategy to preserve Jobs During the Global Economic Crisis*.

Minet, G. (2008). *Some aspects of social dialogue from an ILO standpoint*. Paper prepared for the Expert Group Meeting on Economic and Social Councils, Vienna, Austria.

Momm, W. (2001). *Strategies and activities of the ILO Caribbean Office in relation to the labour agenda of the Americas*. ILO Caribbean Office.

Mulvey, M., Goolsarran, S. J., & Gomes, P. I. (2003). *Strategic Visions for Labour Administration in the Caribbean*. International Labour Organisation: ILO Sub-regional Office for the Caribbean.

Nilson, C. (2004). *Partnerships in urban aboriginal housing projects: a theoretical perspective: Report for the Bridges and Foundation Project (CURA).* Retrieved from: http://bridgesandfoundations.usask.ca/reports/BF_Final_Report.pdf

O'Donnell, R. (1996). *Ireland's experiment in social partnership, 1987–96. In Social Pacts in Europe* (pp. 79–95). Brussels: ETUI.

Oelbaum, J. (2002). Populist Reform Coalitions in Sub-Saharan Africa: Ghana's Triple Alliance. *Canadian Journal of African Studies/La Revue canadienne des études africaines, 36*(2), 281-328.

Percival, D., (1996, March–April). The changing face of trade unionism in Africa. *The Courier ACP-EU*, (156), 76–77.

Qiao, J., & Applebaum, L. D. (2011). *Tripartite Consultation in China* (Research & Policy Brief No. 9). UCLA Institute for Research, on Labor and Employment. Retrieved from https://pdfs.semanticscholar.org/f609/749d5150b3649228d3e760334b57bd16bd11.pdf

Ramalho, J. R. (1996). Labour, Restructuring of Production, and Development. A Point of View from Latin America. *The Ecumenical Review, 48*(3), 369–378. doi:10.1111/j.1758-6623.1996.tb03486.x

Rhodes, R. A. W. (1997). *Understanding governance: policy networks, governance, reflexivity and accountability*. Buckingham, UK: Open University Press.

Shen, J., & Benson, J. (2008). Tripartite consultation in China: A first step towards collective bargaining? *International Labour Review, 147*(2-3), 231–248. doi:10.1111/j.1564-913X.2008.00032.x

Sig Choi, D., Michell, P., & Palihawadana, D. (2008). Exploring the components of success for the Korean chaebols. *Journal of Business and Industrial Marketing, 23*(5), 311–322. doi:10.1108/08858620810881584

Somavia, J., & General, I. D. (1999, June). Decent work. In *Report of the Director-General to the 87th Session of the International Labour Conference.* Geneva: ILO.

Sørensen, E. (2006). Metagovernance: The changing role of politicians in processes of democratic governance. *American Review of Public Administration, 36*(1), 98–114. doi:10.1177/0275074005282584

Taylor, G., & Mathers, A. (2002). Social partner or social movement? European integration and trade union renewal in Europe. *Labor Studies Journal*, *27*(1), 93–108. doi:10.1177/0160449X0202700106

Tokman, V. E. (2007). The informal economy, insecurity and social cohesion in Latin America. *International Labour Review*, *146*(1-2), 81–107. doi:10.1111/j.1564-913X.2007.tb00045.x

Trebilcock, A. (1996). Structural adjustment and tripartite consultation. *International Journal of Public Sector Management*, *9*(1), 5–16. doi:10.1108/09513559610693233

UNESCAP. (2006). *The Millennium Development Goals: Progress in Asia and the Pacific*. Author.

Walt, L. V. D. (1998). Trade unions in Zimbabwe: For democracy, against neo-liberalism. *Capital and Class*, *22*(3), 85–117. doi:10.1177/030981689806600105

Weeks, J. (1999). Wages unemployment and workers' rights in Latin America 1970-98. *International Labour Review*, *138*(2), 151–169. doi:10.1111/j.1564-913X.1999.tb00064.x

Zhu, Y. (1995). Major changes under way in China's industrial relations. *Int'l Lab. Rev.*, *134*, 37.

Chapter 4
Social Partnerships:
Jamaican Expressions

ABSTRACT

The pattern from international experience suggests that social partnerships emerge as forms of governance reflecting to a broadened governance capacity, which enables better governance of the political system. Crisis has been a catalyst for the co-opting of multiple stakeholders into governance models globally, which resonates the global context with the local context of Jamaica. In the previous chapter, the global, regional, and national contextual frames within which the discourses around Jamaica's social experience could be located were established. In the context of Jamaica, reasons are posited to account for the low pursuance of tripartite social partnership and why deeper models appear elusive or limited in scope. This would suggest that other factors of context, culture, issues of power, capacity, structure, and institution have an influence in determining modalities and models.

INTRODUCTION

From country experiences of social partnership, there are undeniably benefits realized from creating these arrangements but vary in scope, depth of success and duration. There is even the view that crisis is critical for the development of social partnerships from the experience of Belgium that tried to create one without a crisis scenario. Regardless of the challenges in operationalizing social dialogue and the different forms taken as a result of country history

DOI: 10.4018/978-1-5225-8961-7.ch004

and context, the process has proven to be valuable and has yielded some positive outcomes.

Given its root, representation and expression within global space, social partnership has been used as a hegemonic device in relation to changing governance. Firstly, towards participative, democratic industrial relations practice with respect to the labour movement and in support of a shift towards social governance as a model supporting the neoliberal philosophies that undergird the process of globalization.

There have been benefits where tripartite arrangements have been instituted within Europe with varied results in developing countries with the degree of transformation dependent upon the state context and capacity as in post tripartite scenarios the labour movement has become fragmented and less resilient to the state in terms of its original mandate. The dominant and institutional discourses and their representation by institutions of global governance bring to the forefront the benefits of pursuing social dialogue, noting that social partnerships are contentious arenas of negotiation, dealing with threats to stability of the existing order and distributions of power within the network of the state towards a new equilibrium or consensus.

International Labour Organisation

In the case of Jamaica, the fundamental rights afforded the labour market reflect accords of the International Labour Organisation (ILO) of which Jamaica is a member and are predicated on the assumption of the traditional contract of employment, whereby a number of these are only available to unionized workers. With respect to the fundamental rights at work, Jamaica has adopted a number of ILO Conventions, as reflected in Table 1. which operate within the framework of the traditional contract of employment, applicable in scope and effect mainly to unionized workers. As aforementioned, for many developing countries, a large proportion of the workforce falls within the informal sector and the challenge is to also enable this larger group some modicum of benefit and protection. It is argued that Jamaica has extensive worker protection in the formal sector and these coupled with strong trade unions may limit labour market flexibility and the ability of employers to replace unproductive workers with productive ones.

The ILO has facilitated the development of trade unions as political institutions within their own individual country context, which fundamentally alters the distribution of power relations within them as they become agents

Table 1. International Labour Organization Conventions Ratified by Jamaica

Year Adopted	Convention #	Convention
1962	29	ILO Convention No. 29, the Forced Labour Convention
1962	87	Freedom of Association, and the Right to Organize
1962	98	Right to Organize and to Collective Bargaining
1962	105	Abolition of Forced Labour Convention
1975	111	Discrimination (Employment and Occupation)
1975	100	Equal Remuneration
2003	138	The Minimum Wage Convention
2003	182	The Worst Forms of Child Labour Convention and other Conventions on Social Dialogue alongside the Labour Relations Code of Jamaica, Industrial / Labour Relations

Source: ILO website

of change, whether positively or negatively. Concomitantly, the ILO has influenced traditional indigenous labour practices and forms of work, through its discourse of homogenizing or harmonizing policy direction towards social governance forms.

Globalization, Crises, and Social Partnership in the Jamaican State

The decline in the state capabilities, in many developing countries resulted in drafting in of private interests into public service delivery to maintain their service levels, blurring the public private divide. Fox and Taylor et al., (2005) explain that Jamaica, as a small developing state has not been excluded from the effects of globalization and notes the changing patterns of the labour force since 1990. Trade liberalization and technological development has facilitated efficiencies in foreign production causing the displacement of local domestic production reducing the need for unskilled labour. Unemployment rates were stable at about 15% between 1991-2002 with a dominance of low skilled employment as well as declining participation rates (Jones and Cruickshank, 2004) becoming 13.1% in 2003 and 11.4% 2004 and 10.9% in 2005 (STATIN). There has been a resultant change in the labour profile which reflects the structural changes in the economy caused by globalization, especially as Jamaica moves towards being more of a service economy. Crises in varying dimensions have levied a toll in terms of diminishing resources in the 1980s and 1990s and later macroeconomic crises due impacting increases in public expenditures, economic restructuring and flailing efforts to stem falling state revenues within the context of limited taxation and also fiscal expenditures. The labour unions that emerged during the 1930s in Jamaica, gave rise to an industrial relations culture that was combative with weak dialogue between the unions and management fostering a labour relations environment characterized by work stoppages and disruptions in productivity. The major unions were outgrowths of the two major political parties- the Jamaica Labour Party (JLP) and the Peoples' National Party (PNP), which prefaced and influenced their discourse, world view and negotiating stances within the bargaining process and in contexts of their interface..

This combination precipitated an environment of low trust between capital and labour aggravated by the difficulties of sustaining and broadening policy cooperation, coordination and coherence especially within and even external to episodes whereby the Government had been engaged in the implementation of structural adjustment programmes in intervals over the years. This apparent vacuum at the interface between capital, government and labour became accentuated with the continued effects of globalization which contributed to an already unstable labour market. There was an 'erosion of the capacity to cooperate for collective purposes, or manage risk, impairing the capacity to fabricate policy and institutional congruence' (Jones & Cruickshank, 2004).

With regards to Jamaica's social partnership experience, the role of leadership, personality and the ability to forge consensus between antagonists had implications for the survival of the bipartite Bauxite Memorandum of Understanding of 1998 (Bauxite MOU) or the 'Michael Manley Accord,' social partnership between the trade union movement and stakeholders of capital in the Bauxite sector.

The overexpansion of the bauxite industry in the 1970s and the resultant economic instability in the aftermath of the reduction in global demand, placed the Jamaican economy in a vulnerable position and looming crisis, due to the heavy reliance upon earnings from this sector which was now in jeopardy. Fiscal returns from the imposition of a levy upon bauxite companies declined between 1973-80 (Bernal, 1984) when global market prices fell by 15 per cent causing a severe decline in GDP from capital flight and the depletion of foreign exchange reserves. The reduction in domestic revenue and levels of public expenditure added to large external and fiscal imbalances in the economy prompting social disintegration and the need to seek overseas assistance (DFID, 2001).

An initial phase of liberalization took place from 1986-88 encouraged by the Bretton Woods Institutions combined with thrusts to reform interest rate policies and develop money and capital markets (Peart, 1995). Governments' rapidly deregulated their economies and dismantled regulatory regimes in competition with one another to attract foreign direct investment (Woods, 2000). Dean (1998,) argued that Jamaica's liberalization of internal and external markets was premature as the preconditions for undertaking the process, such as well-capitalized and supervised financial institutions, macroeconomic stability and an exchange rate close to equilibrium were absent; hence there was the propensity for problems to arise.

Trade Unions and Memoranda of Understanding

Despite the failures of creating a national social partnership, there exists a unanimous agreement in principle to the need for a national social partnership and of its value to furthering national development. The JCTU which as an institution, had already established a policy position to pursue sectoral partnerships, continued in this vein towards developing Memoranda of Understanding, as it had before with the Banana, Shipping and Bauxite industries, the Jamaica Public Service Company and the National Water Commission years before.

Memoranda of understanding' have some of their foundations in treaty law where treaties were designated as such, reflecting an agreement and in less formal cases a convergence of understanding between states. Generally, MOUs describe an intended path of action, between parties, being a formalized alternative to a gentlemen's agreement, which does not necessarily make it legally enforceable, but it can possess contractual obligations and be binding depending on the composition of legal elements in the text. However, being used in the context of the labour relations, it represents one form of an agreed social partnership relationship between parties, allowing the text and framework to vary and accommodate multiple concerns.

These sectoral MOUs have had implications for framing the conduct of relations between worker and management and the culture of the operations. They have engendered consensus building and the buffering, dispersing and conditioning of the expectations of parties amidst the negative effects of globalization on the livelihood dimensions of the worker and on the profitability and productivity of the firm.

Sectoral MOUs, such as that of the National Water Commission was not far reaching in scope national coverage but served to address the internal culture and relationships between management and labour in the workplace, establishing greater collaboration, performance incentives and assessments and strengthening of industrial relations practices and dispute resolution to enable operational efficiency and productivity. Goolsaran (2006) describes it as serving to achieve 'fundamental transformation in employment relations'.

With respect to the partnership experience of Jamaica however there are a variety of approaches taken in the literature with respect to the sectoral Bauxite Memorandum of Understanding, which aided the recovery of the industry by increasing its global competitiveness and encouraging greater corporate social responsibility. Furthermore, the involvement of Prime Minister Michael Manley after which the MOU was named "The Michael Manley Accord', is noted, due to his success in getting warring union factions to agree as well as negotiating a consensus with the foreign investor companies, established its significance in terms of the role of leadership.

The Bauxite Memorandum of Understanding: The "Michael Manley Accord'

Leading up to the Bauxite MOU partnership, United States and Canadian companies were dominant investors in the mining of bauxite and alumina industries, so that Jamaica became a world leader in exports in the 1970s.

The ownership structure in 1990 was the Kaiser Jamaica Bauxite Company, Alcoa Minerals of Jamaica and Revere Jamaica Alumina. The major unions involved were the University and Allied Workers Union (UAWU), the Union of Technical and Supervisory Personnel (UTASP) and the National Workers Union. (NWU). One union delegate interviewed, recollected that the NWU was initially the only union in the sector at the time, then UTASP entered, representing supervisors and the white-collar groupings. There were challenges in the sector, such as the UAWU taking over worker representation in ALCOA and Kaiser, from the NWU precipitating and continuing antagonistic relationships between groups.

In terms of political processes, Jamaica was prominent in its support of and positioning as being a socialist state with respect to the Non-Aligned Movement (NAM) and pursued appropriate policy approaches similar to that of nations from the Black Liberation Movement of Africa in the 1950s. These states implemented programmes to redistribute wealth such as nationalizing banks, reclaiming property and undertaking institutions of agrarian reform. Under the rubric of democratic socialism, Jamaica sought to follow suit, seeking to improve equity through the redistribution of wealth, the nationalization of foreign-owned companies, acquiring foreign owned companies e.g., Barclay's Bank and overall reducing the dependency on foreign investment (Bernal, 1994). Michael Manley wrote in his book that;

The coincidental nature of the presence of the bauxite deposits in Jamaica and the relationship between these and the North American economy came across forcefully as did the moral implications that this industry owed a decent standard of living to its Jamaican workers. (p. 108)

In terms of economic policy in concert with the political agenda, Jamaica abrogated its 1967 agreement with the bauxite companies by imposing a levy of 7.5% on bauxite production in 1974 and 1978, providing fiscal earnings of J$200 million from January 1974 to March 1975 in the first year of the tax. The other motivation, noted by Stone (1985, 8) was the desire of the Prime Minister, Michael Manley; to establish himself as a Third World leader.

This leadership promotion required close collaboration with the existing radical leftist leadership in the non-aligned Third World movement all of whom were ostensibly committed to socialism as a development approach and embraced varying versions of so-called non-capitalist development strategies. These leaders included Fidel Castro of Cuba, Julius Nyerere of Tanzania, Colonel Maummar Gaddafi of Libya and Colonel Boumedienne of Algeria.

The crisis situation developed after Jamaica abrogated its agreement with the bauxite companies (Bernal 1994) which effect was compounded by the exodus of these foreign companies, reducing the investment capital to the sector. There was also a fall in global demand with competition from Australia, Guinea and new competitors, i.e., Brazil and Indonesia, which began to export bauxite at a lower price than the cartel of which Jamaica was a member. This was in the context of Jamaica pursuing Structural Adjustment Programmes (SAPS) with the International Monetary Fund (IMF). Hughes (2007) also noted that in the 1970s, there was a major policy shift towards an activism which emphasized social policy and equity, but with the caveat that the state did not hold the reins to drive private sector investment processes.

The industry was further threatened by adversarialism (Cowell 2006; Goolsarran 2003, 2006) that blossomed between union and management and between other unions (Johnson 1980). These were prompted by the fear of job losses due to layoffs, vying for worker representation (Alexander and Parker 2004) and combative power struggles, (Munroe 2000) based on political alignment and rivalry (Johnson 1986; Stephens and Stephens 1986). The charismatic leadership style of Michael Manley played a significant role in negotiating consensus between warring groups of unions who were allied to different companies and national political parties and in brokering the bipartite social partnership between the foreign companies and unions.

The rivalry between the union groups, (Acosta and Alleyne 2006; Johnson 1980; Stephens and Stephens 1986) which threatened negotiations were so intense, that they were specifically referred to in the Bauxite Agreement itself under the list of union undertakings, to refrain from engaging in rivalry which is detrimental to the stability of the industry. The bipartite partnership created through consensus improved productivity and the industrial relations climate of the industry so that one newspaper reported that the Bauxite MOU 1998 was dubbed the "Michael Manley Accord" in honour of his orchestration of the Agreement. The social partnership in the bauxite industry (the Manley Accord) has given that industry the long-term confidence to make the largest bauxite investments in Jamaica"s bauxite history. (Buddan, 2006)

There is evidence that suggests initiatives were taken to nationalize social partnership in Jamaica, as Goolsarran (2006), indicates that a Social Partnership Secretariat was created under the Peoples' National Party (PNP) administration in the late 1990s, which produced a document entitled 'Draft Agreement for the Implementation of a National Economic and Social Understanding: Social Partnership 1996-1997, which was coined a 'social contract', premised on the need to adopt the following measures as a matter of national priority to:

- Raise general living standards;
- Accelerate savings, investments and economic growth;
- Ensure price stability and international competitiveness;
- Increase export of goods and services;
- Achieve social and economic stability;

Alternatively, from a global perspective, successful discourses surrounding Ireland's social partnership experience may have also been a factor influencing the development of the document as Collister (2005), drew analogies between Ireland's fiscal crisis which prompted its 'Programme of National Recovery 'in 1987 and Jamaica's fiscal challenges. This document was presented to Parliament, from where efforts were made to elicit a broad national social partnership. According to Goolsarran (2006), this process erred in that no consultations were held with the Jamaica Confederation of Trade Unions (JCTU) the Jamaica Employers' Federation (JEF) or the Jamaica Labour Party (JLP), as opposition members and civil stakeholders. This error was attributed to the reason why the 'social contract' was not endorsed and in the absence of a national consensus being derived, which reflects the divisiveness and bipolarity in the political culture of Jamaican society at the time.

The Partnership for Progress (PFP) Initiative

In 2003, the fear of financial crisis and concerns for the future direction of the economy led the Private Sector Organization of Jamaica (PSOJ) to make efforts towards building a better relationship with the unions from which the Partnership for Progress (PFP) initiative began. This collaboration initially between the Economic Policy Committees (EPC) of the PSOJ and the Jamaica Chamber of Commerce (CAPRI, 2009), was to be extended to include other societal stakeholders- union groups, non-governmental organizations and academia. This coalition's attempt at engendering social partnership was to support the restoration of the economy and encourage the trust and consensus needed to further coalescence around critical issues and engendering support and collaboration for deriving national solutions. They identified initiatives of national concern which included:

- Measures to address the fiscal deficit and reverse the growth trends in the national debt
- Mechanisms to support small and medium enterprises (SME) which stimulated employment
- creation
- The divestment of public sector assets
- Wage restraint
- Tax reform measures
- Crime reduction
- Improvement in the education framework
- Societal transformation towards more productive and constructive social values

The PFP initiative also sought to improve union and private sector relations, making it broader in scope than that of the 'Acorn Group', which was an initial collaboration between private sector and the union movement.

This approach to social partnership differed from those made previously, by being led from the 'bottom up' and according to Collister (2009), was the forerunner to a national debate within society on governance and the future direction of the country. The impetus was further bolstered by the PSOJ's seminar which incorporated representatives from Ireland who had been instrumental in crafting Ireland's first 'Programme of National Recovery' mentioned earlier. Dialogue with respect to the creation of a social partnership for Jamaica had intensified whereby a mission comprising of government, union and civil society representatives visited Ireland to study the Irish social partnership experience first-hand as well as the policy changes that were critical to Ireland's economic transformation. The resulting Draft 'social partnership' representing recommendations from the mission was presented to the Government of Jamaica in January 2004, which contained measures to:

- Ensure long term sustained fiscal responsibility;
- Contain growth in public sector non-interest expenditure
- Strengthen monetary policy independence and accountability in decision making;
- Accelerate the divestment of state-owned assets;
- Seek voluntary debt swaps in domestic instruments to improve the fiscal accounts
- consistent with monetary policy;
- Monitor the achievement of fiscal targets;

The discussions with respect to the concretization of the Partnership for Progress (PFP) social partnership on August 18, 2005, was not realized due to a lack of consensus (CAPRI, 2009). It was felt by some respondents that parties were not willing to cede or relinquish anything in the brokering of an arrangement. One union leader commented on the issue that.

'.simultaneously with the negotiations for the MOU, there were discussions going on with the private sector and government in what they call a Partnership For Progress, which is another name for social contract, and I attended some of these meeting. In fact, when we signed the MOU, I took a copy to one of these meetings at the PSOJ, and they were all so happy to see that the trade unions were able to sign and a many felt that this having been done, they were now in a better position, to come up with this Partnership for Progress'... Well, after months and months of discussions, when you look at what they

had on the table, there was nothing that the private sector was prepared to give up! Nothing! '(UN 6)

Meanwhile the Partnership for Progress (PFP) discussions were subsequently overtaken by the ensuing dialogue which resulted in the Public Sector Memorandum of Understanding (MOU) between the government and the trade unions. It is argued that the PFP informed the Public Sector Memorandum of Understanding (MOU) 2004-2006 as some of the union members involved (CAPRI. 2009) in its creation had been a part of the mission to Ireland and had 'appeared to be motivated by a spirit of shared sacrifice at a critical point in the finances of the country' (Collister, 2009).

THE ELUSIVE SOCIAL PARTNERSHIP: JAMAICA

In the case of Jamaica, it has been observed that a tripartite national social partnership remained elusive.

In comparing Jamaica's experience or lack thereof, with the social partnership outcomes of Barbados and the Caribbean, several authors (Brewster, 2007; Brown, 2002; CAPRI, 2009) sought to explain the differences. Barbados is considered to possess a historical legacy which has led to it being described as a homogeneous society, (Fashoyin, 2001) seemingly devoid of the ethnic cleavages of neighbouring states like Guyana, or divisions engendered by a fractious political culture, like Jamaica, influencing the fibre of their societies.

Brown (2002), states that Barbados had not experienced any serious ideological shifts with regards to its politics that has served to divide the society and its sectors and hence prevents consensus and cooperation. Other features of the society that have contributed to the success of the social partnership were: the absence of any serious conflict in relation to labour, commitment of the general population to the government and its policies and the small size of the country which has contributed to its homogeneity with regards to ideology.

The social partnership agreements of Barbados have become an intrinsic part of their National Development Strategy 2005-2025, and has ushered in, according to Farley (2000), a new era and indeed a paradigm shift in the concept and practice of governance. The preconditions from which a social partnership could be created existed in all cases, but it is felt that Barbados had a sufficiency of social capital (Brewster, 2007; Osei, 2004) which, given the context of impending crisis, has prompted the development of a cohesive partnership in the national interest than engendering division.

Stone (1985), highlighted divisions due to the existence of two counter prevailing ideologies in Jamaican society, that were at their peak in the 1970's, that split the country along political party lines. He noted that these ideologies created a climate of hostility between the PNP Government and the JLP supporters thus no consensus or partnership could be reached. This supports the view of Brewster (2007) and Osei (2004) concerning the social capital deficit and additionally that working together as one in Jamaica is further crippled by a climate of hostile industrial relations, anger and resentment over inequality and social injustice (Brewster, 2007).

One could argue that Caribbean societies each retain their own level of diversity, despite the many similarities of colonial legacy and history. There is no credibility to the view that the results would even be similar or be the same, if the successful models are replicated elsewhere, which mirrors Boyd's (2002) negative view of importing and transplanting social partnership models them from one context to another.

Specific to the Caribbean experience of social partnership, academics (Brewster, 2007; Brown, 2002; CaPRI, 2009) have posited that the absence or presence of social capital is one of the key ingredients under girding social partnership arrangements. The importance of social capital to social partnerships in the Caribbean, (Brewster, 2007; Brown, 2002) has also been noted by Payne and Sutton (2007) who recall the commitment made by CARICOM Heads of Government to a 'greater engagement with social partners and the establishment of mechanisms for continuous dialogue; including civil society' at the 23rd Conference of Heads of Government held in Guyana, July 3-5, 2002. Another study (Brewster, 2007) compared the social capital in Barbados, which has had five social partnerships from 1993-2007, against that of Jamaica arguing that the low stock of social capital (Osei, 2004) was a brake on development in the latter and there needed to be mechanisms to mobilize it for development.

Furthermore, in the absence of any serious conflict concerning labour, the commitment of the general population to the government and its policies and the small size of the country has contributed overall to its ideological homogeneity.

This strengthens the propositions of Brewster (2007) and Osei (2004) concerning the social capital deficit. Meanwhile working together as one in Jamaica has been further crippled by a hostile industrial relations environment,

(Cowell, 2006; Goolsarran, 2005, 2006; Munroe, 2000) anger and resentment over inequalities and social injustice (Brewster, 2007). Certain preconditions from which a social partnership could be created have existed in all cases. With respect to lessons from the Caribbean experience, social capital (Brewster, 2007; Osei, 2004), is an added dimension of value, that when combined with impending crisis yielded a cohesive partnership in the case of Barbados, compared to states where social capital was deemed low or absent.

However, the discourse of the International Labour Organization, has captured and made popular the pursuit of governance structures centered upon social dialogue and partnership, and its hegemony in establishing standards of operationalizing social partnership and co-opting support from other global governance institutions. I consider the authority it exercises in consolidating, disseminating the social dialogue discourse and conventions adopted by states. I weigh elements of the evidence presented in the social world and experiences of several states and regions worldwide, in terms of types of tripartite and bipartite arrangements which reveal the benefits and value held and the rationale and insight as to why the course of social dialogue is pursued.

The experiences of states have shown that traditional union discourse has been modified, which is a theme within this study, being molded along the lines of a neoliberal, democratic ethos which brings to the fore controversies in terms of traditional union discourse, labour practice, credibility and trust.

Three key elements have been identified that drive the development of social partnership agreements, namely, globalization, a weak state and crisis conditions that have interacted together in various country contexts with differing historical, cultural socio economic and political backgrounds to yield different forms of social partnership, albeit with these three elements being constant in them all.

Moreover, there is the implicit suggestion that the three main elements are interdependent and are mitigated by other factors of context- namely institutional, cultural, political and socio economic and perhaps the more intangible dimensions such as trust, leadership, social capital and mutual need which may play a greater role in the formation and duration of partnerships than the tangible.

The inclusion in the Caribbean of the type and role of leadership that militates with contending and diverse interests is highlighted in the case of the Barbados Social Partnership and the Bauxite Memorandum of Understanding. Several authors have argued (Brewster 2007) that in Jamaica, the key conditions for a tripartite social partnership have been apparent but has never materialized on a national scale because of the lack of social capital. Gourevitch (1986) notes that the role and nature of the threat of crisis could be so compelling, that normal politics are abandoned and former combatants may rally around a shared cause. One could also argue that the need for self-preservation, (Kelly, 2004) to survive and minimize the risk of loss, could become the doors that entertain power sharing overriding social capital deficiencies, producing instead an imperative of need to negotiate at all costs and agree at all costs, as demonstrated in the case of the Bauxite MOU.

CONCLUSION

In the context of Jamaica, the key conditions for social partnership have been apparent over the years but such an arrangement has never been realized on a national scale, despite several lesser sectoral MOU arrangements being negotiated, such as for the Bauxite industry and the National Water Commission, etc.

Attempts to build a national consensus has met with limited success, despite the recognition by all parties that there are benefits, yet a common meeting ground had not been ascertained.

On the part of the Government and their interaction with international financial institutions, there is value placed on dialogue that is inclusive and engaging in joint consultations with societal stakeholders. Correspondingly, the trade unions had ILO accords to uphold and pursue, linked to the hegemonic discourse of the ILO and labour relations genre. Contextually, one can infer that other dimensions intervene - cultural and historical context, the past relationship between the parties, as well as the qualitative aspects of the process to influence or colour the processes of dialogue. Outcomes will be influenced by intangible attitudes and motivations as well as the needs of the partners, their individual and joint capacities, the effectiveness of the mechanisms of dialogue and the resources committed to it, alongside clarity of roles and functions within the prevailing power constructs.

These conceptualizations parallel the nature of the multiple interactions within social partnership and network relations relevant to the application of the theoretical framework of Actor Network Theory (ANT) in analysis. Actor Network Theory to be discussed in chapter 3, possesses an ontology that confers agency on all the actors that converge within the network of relations. This ontology is unique in that inanimate objects are also included as well as the subjects or social actors. ANT also explains the mechanics of and power relations within networks becoming a lens through which to analyze the nature of the linkages and interface within the network, which I denote as being discursive, between the actors.

Critical discourse as another intervening dimension and used as a unit of analysis, traverses and integrates multiple focal points facilitating the integration of cultural and historical context, the past and characteristics of current relationship between the parties, qualitative aspects of structures, social processes and outcomes. Critical discourse analysis also provides for an exploration of dimensions of the nature of relationships of power and the influence of intangibles- such as attitudes and motivation of need, mutuality between partners, capacities, roles and functions within prevailing power constructs, to create a kaleidoscope of inputs and interactions for consideration.

Limitations of Social Partnership

Several studies demonstrate that dialogue (Alby et al., 2005; Etukudo, 1995) and the participation of multiple stakeholders in support of policies to ameliorate challenges, (Buhlungu, 2005) due to crisis, or initiated in the aftermath of post structural adjustment programmes (Gallin, 2000; Kreiger, 1989 ; Trebilcock, 1996 ; Tokman, 2007 ; Weeks, 1999*)* have made positive contributions, more so within the context of dislocations of labour and political instability (Cook, 2000).

Social partnership serves as a strategic approach towards reconstituting relationships between the state, market and civil society (Jones & Schoburgh, 2004). Governance is thus viewed as self- organizing and inter organizational networks (Rhodes, 1997) consisting of state and non-state actors resting upon relations of exchange and trust rather than on informal institutional roles and boundaries. The state emerges as leading a hierarchy of societal groups in new emerging relationships founded upon a social contract. The growth of epistemic communities through the increased need for multi-dimensional approaches to issues and common concerns have created new alliances through risk sharing, information exchange and developing cohesiveness through new consistent discourse. Therefore, as explained by Hertin, Scoones, and Berkhout, (2000, p. 22)

governments have become nodes for communication and decision-making, constantly interacting with concerned groups. Policymakers must acknowledge the need for complex and simultaneous processes of bargaining involving several policy areas, in order to improve efficiency between levels. Barriers to co-operation and questions of competency, transparency and legitimacy need to be recognized and overcome.

Social dialogue and forms of social partnership are not without their challenges. They have become the governance pathway chosen in response to globalization's effect, conditionality and pending crisis or instability in varied forms- whereby states become vulnerable, threatened or unstable, economically and or politically and thereby seek preservation of control. There are implications for the economic, political, cultural and social relations of states and state actors, particularly, with regard to governance and the exercise and sharing of power. Treating with power inequalities, as powerful partners seek to maintain status amidst being compelled to treat with multiple stakeholders, creates power differentials which are not easily managed. Successful governance at this frontier of interaction presents the potential for partnerships to be transformative.

Going Forward: Social Partnership as a Governance Response

From the explorations undergone it is observed that social partnerships - forged from within contentious arenas of negotiation for the establishment of new and the changing of traditionally held power relations within the state and between its actors - are political. The rationale driving the process is one of actors minimizing losses in the face of changing relative power positions and maximizing the possibility of benefits and maintenance of position, through reciprocity and compromise in the new arrangements

The literature positions social partnership as a governance response to crisis conditions, examining outcomes and effects in terms of institutions – labour and the state, political economic and socioeconomic contexts, the types and models of partnership relationship employed and from leadership perspectives and processes. In global discourses, it is positioned as a solution to the resolution of conflict, measured as deliverables from labour and social policy making within conciliatory governance regimes which promotes nation building.

These perspectives all signal gaps in the research on social partnerships and present the opportunity to legitimize alternative approaches, to facilitate greater introspection and unearth other dimensions of partnership arrangements. I draw upon networks of relations that uphold social partnership arrangements and governance, as well as the role of discourse in the interactions between actors, which have implications for partnership outcomes.

The state employs strategies (Jones, 2004) that are selective, forming arrangements and involving relationships between inherited and emergent state structures, which harness these institutions towards a particular socio-economic project, such as social partnership. The relational power of the state (Jessop 1990b, 2008) and the selectivity employed is consequently not a structural feature of the state but is as a result of the dialectic of strategic interaction and socio-political contestation within and beyond state institutions that shapes them, as well as the states' mode of socioeconomic interventions towards hegemonic projects. Jessop (1990b, 2008) makes reference to network aspects of the state (Bevir, 2006; Nettleford, 2002) in that he believes that;

the state as such has no power – it is merely an institutional ensemble. It has only a set of institutional capacities and liabilities that mediates that power. The power of the state is the power of the forces acting in and through the state. (Jessop 1990, p. 270)

Furthermore, that;

the legacy of past struggles are structurally inscribed, ... strategic selectivity, ... once accumulation regimes and modes of regulation have become relatively stable, they comprise a specific strategic terrain on and through which particular forms of struggle take place. ... Since there is no institutional guarantee that struggles will always be contained within these forms, the stability of the accumulation regime or mode of regulation is always relative, always partial, always provisional. (Jessop, 1990, p. 309)

Given its root, representation and expression within global space, social partnerships have been used as devices in relation to changing governance. In supporting the neoliberal philosophies that undergird the process of globalization, social partnerships have been a vehicle with respect to the labour movement, in support of a shift towards social governance models and industrial relations practices that are participative and democratic.

Regardless of the challenges in operationalizing social dialogue and the different forms taken as a function of country history and context, the process has proven to be valuable. Benefits from tripartite arrangements vary within developing countries where the degree of transformation is dependent upon the state context, culture and capacity to respond. From country experiences of social partnership, the benefits realized will be conditioned and vary in scope, depth of success and duration, according to hard tangibles such as structure, institutions, resources etc., but also by the soft intangibles, such as the character of leadership, attitudes and engendering of trust.

Social partnership therefore, emerge as forms of governance, that alters or adjusts the way societies are organized to treat with pending forces of destabilization, leading to either the preservation of existing balances and or alterations in the distribution of power relations within the network of the state towards a new equilibrium or consensus.

REFERENCES

Acosta, A. M., & Alleyne, D. (2006). *The policymaking process in Jamaica.* Washington, DC: Inter-American Development Bank.

Alby, P., Azam, J. P., & Sandrine, R. (2005). *Labour Institutions, Labour Management Relations and Social Dialogue.* Unpublished ILO Report.

Alexander, R., & Parker, E. J. (2004). *A history of organized labour in the English-speaking West Indies.* Westport, CT: Praeger.

Auvergnon, P. (2006). Some lessons drawn from a comparative approach to the issue of the effectiveness of labour law. *Managerial Law, 48*(3), 288–302. doi:10.1108/03090550610674653

Bernal, R. (1984). The IMF and class struggle in Jamaica, 1977-1980. *Latin American Perspectives, 42*(11), 53–82. doi:10.1177/0094582X8401100304

Boyd, S. (2002). *Partnership Working: European Social Partnership Models.* Scottish Trades Union Congress (STUC). Retrieved from http://www.scotland.gov.uk/Resource/Doc/25954/0028681.pdf

Brewster, H. (2007). *Understanding development challenges of the Caribbean.* Prepared for World Bank Forum for parliamentarians on 'Shaping A Trade Agenda to Promote Regional Integration and Competitiveness for CARICOM,' St. Lucia.

Brown, D. (2002). The private sector as a social partnership: the Barbados model. In R. D. Selwyn & A. M. Bissessar (Eds.), *Governance in the Caribbean. Sir Arthur Lewis Institute of Social and Economic Studies (SALISES)*. University of the West Indies.

Buddan, R. (2006, April 2). A Statesman Departs. *Sunday Gleaner*, p. G3.

Buhlungu, S. (2005). Union-party alliances in the era of market regulation: The case of South Africa. *Journal of Southern African Studies, 341*(4), 22.

Caribbean Policy Research Institute (CaPRI). (2009). *A new social partnership for Jamaica*. Kingston, Jamaica: Author.

Collister, K. (2005, August 28). Looking for a better Jamaica. *Sunday Gleaner*, p. 8.

Collister, K. (2009). *Mapping of Public-Private Dialogue in Jamaica: Issues and Options for Jamaica*. Inter-American Development Bank.

Cook, M. L. (1998). Toward flexible industrial relations? neo-liberalism, democracy, and labour reform in Latin America. *Industrial Relations, 37*(3), 311–336. doi:10.1111/0019-8676.00090

Cowell, N. (2006). Industrial relations theory and practice with reference to Jamaica. In *Industrial Relations in the Caribbean: Issues and Perspectives*. Port of Spain, Trinidad: Caribbean Office, ILO.

Dean, J. W. (1998). Can financial liberalization come too soon? Jamaica in the 1990s. *Social and Economic Studies, 47*(4).

Department For International Development. (2001). *Jamaica: Country Strategy Paper.* Author.

Djuric, D. (2002). Social dialogue, tripartism and social partnership in the South East European countries, including recommendations for Serbia and Montenegro. *Europe Review for Labour and Social Affairs, 3*, 87-100. Retrieved from: www.ceeol.com

Etukudo, A. (1995). Reflections on the role of African employers' organizations in tripartism and social dialogue. *International Labour Review, 134*(1).

Farley, R. (2000). *The Social Partners Experience of Barbados*. Speech given at the Caribbean Regional Ministerial Consultation: The State in the Third Millennium, Trinidad and Tobago. Retrieved from http://unpan1.un.org/intradoc/groups/public/documents/caricad/unpan008604.pdf

Fashoyin, T. (2001). *Fostering economic development through social dialogue*. Geneva: ILO.

Fashoyin, T. (2004). Tripartite Cooperation, Social Dialogue and National Development. *International Labour Review*, *143*(4), 341–372. doi:10.1111/j.1564-913X.2004.tb00553.x

Gallin, D. (2000). *Trade unions and NGOs: a necessary partnership for social development.* Civil Society and Social Movements Programme, 1/2000.

Ghellab, Y., & Vylitova, M. (2005). *Tripartite social dialogue on employment in the countries of South Eastern Europe*. International Labour Organization.

Goolsarran, S. J. (2002). *Caribbean labour relations systems: an overview*. Port of Spain, Trinidad: Caribbean Office, ILO.

Goolsarran, S. J. (2006). *Industrial Relations in the Caribbean, Issues and Perspectives*. International Labour Organization.

Hertin, J., Scoones, I., & Berkhout, F. (2000). *Who governs the global environment? ESRC Global Environmental Change Programme*. Brighton, UK: University of Sussex.

Hethy, L. (2001). *Social Dialogue and the expanding world. the decade of tripartism in Hungary and in Central Europe 1988-1999*. Brussels, Belgium: European Trade Union Institute.

Hodgett, S., & Johnson, D. (2001). Troubles partnerships and possibilities - a study of the 'Making Belfast Work' initiative in Northern Ireland. *Public Administration and Development*, *21*(4), 321–332. doi:10.1002/pad.181

Hughes, W. (2006). *Strategic structural transformation*. Paper presented at the Conference on Globalization and the Problems of Development, La Asociacion Nacional de Economistas y Contadores (ANEC), Havana, Cuba.

International Labour Organisation. (1999). *Country employment policy review, employment policy in a small island economy: Barbados*. Trinidad: ILO Sub regional Caribbean Office.

International Labour Organisation. (2002). *Governing Body Resolution GB.285/7/1, adopted by the International Labour Conference at its 90th Session concerning tripartism and social dialogue*. Geneva: ILO.

Johnson, C. (1980). The emergence of political unionism in economies of British colonial origin: The cases of Jamaica and Trinidad. *American Journal of Economics and Sociology*, *39*(2), 151–164. doi:10.1111/j.1536-7150.1980.tb01624.x

Jones, E., & Cruickshank, I. (2004). Forging Institutional Convergence Between Labour Policy & Public Sector Reform: The Case of The Ministry of Labour and Social Security, Jamaica. *Social and Economic Studies*, 89–124.

Jones, E., & Schoburgh, E. (2004). Deconstructing policy-making and implementation issues in a Caribbean context. *Social and Economic Studies*, 35–61.

Keohane, R., & Nye, J. (1989). *Power and interdependence*. Harper Collins Publishers.

Kernaghan, K. (1993). Partnership and public administration: Conceptual and practical considerations. *Canadian Public Administration*, *36*(1), 57–77. doi:10.1111/j.1754-7121.1993.tb02166.x

Krieger, J. (1986). *Reagan, Thatcher, and the politics of decline*. New York: Oxford University Press. Retrieved from http://socialistregister.com/socialistregister.com/files/SR_1987_Krieger.pdf

Kuruvilla, S. (2003). *Social Dialogue for Decent Work, Education Outreach Programme*. Geneva: International Institute for Labour Studies.

Lado, C. (2000). The state and civil society: Transition and prospects of labour geographies in an era of economic globalisation in Nigeria and South Africa. *Singapore Journal of Tropical Geography*, *21*(3), 295–315. doi:10.1111/1467-9493.00083

Manley, M. (1991). *A voice at the workplace: reflections on colonialism and the Jamaican worker*. Washington, DC: Howard University Press.

Martinez-Lucio, M., & Stuart, M. (2004). Swimming against the tide: Social partnership, mutual gains and the revival of "tired' HRM. *International Journal of Human Resource Management*, *15*(2), 410–424. doi:10.1080/0958519032000158581

McCartan, P. (2002). Towards social partnership– or cooperative industrial relations? *Irish Journal of Management*, *23*(1), 53.

Munroe, T. (2000). *Voice participation and governance in a changing environment: the case of Jamaica. Caribbean Group for Cooperation in Economic Development (CGCED)*. Washington, DC: World Bank.

O' Donnell, R., & O' Reardon, C. (1996). Ireland's Experiment in Social Partnership 1987-96. In G. Fajertag & P. Pochet (Eds.), *Social Pacts in Europe*. Brussels: European Trade Union Institute.

Osei, P. D. (2004). Tripartite social partnership in small states: Barbados and Jamaica a comparative perspective. In A. Bissessar (Ed.), *Globalization and Governance: Essays on the Challenges for Small States*. Jefferson, NC: McFarland &Company.

Payne, A. (2007). *Repositioning the Caribbean within globalisation*. Caribbean Working Paper (1).

Peart, K. (1995). Financial reform and financial sector development in Jamaica. *Sir Arthur Lewis Institute of Social and Economic Studies*, *46*(2&3), 131–167.

Rhodes, R. A. W. (1997). *Understanding governance: policy networks, governance, reflexivity and accountability*. Buckingham, UK: Open University Press.

Stephens, E. H., & Stephens, J. D. (1986). *The Political movement and social transformation in dependent capitalism*. London: Macmillan. doi:10.1515/9781400886074

Stone, C. (1985). *Class, state and democracy in Jamaica*. Kingston: Blackett Publishers.

Tokman, V. E. (2007). The Informal economy, insecurity and social cohesion in Latin America. *International Labour Review*, *46*(1-2), 81–107. doi:10.1111/j.1564-913X.2007.tb00045.x

Trebilcock, A. (1996). Structural adjustment and tripartite consultation. *International Journal of Public Sector Management*, *9*(1), 5–16. doi:10.1108/09513559610693233

Webster, E. (2005). *Trade unions, social movements and left parties: governing in a globalising world. Sociology of Work Unit (SWOP), University of the Witwatersrand: Congress of South Africa Trade Unions*. COSATU.

Weeks, J. (1999). Wages unemployment and workers' rights in Latin America 1970-98. *International Labour Review, 138*(2), 151–169. doi:10.1111/j.1564-913X.1999.tb00064.x

Woods, N. (2000). The political economy of globalization. In *The political economy of globalization* (pp. 1–19). London: Palgrave. doi:10.1007/978-0-333-98562-5_1

Chapter 5
Actor Network Theory (ANT)

ABSTRACT

Actor network theory (ANT) or the "sociology of translation," is introduced, being a systematic way to explain the mechanics and dynamics of relational interactions, within networks. The unique ontology of ANT equates human and non-human systems thereby conferring the MOU social partnership agreement with the status of an actor. The text within the MOU Agreement as an intermediary becomes the inscription, enabling the agreement to obtain having a discourse of its own and the capacity to attain a "black box" status within the network of relations that it creates for itself. ANT's strengths and weaknesses, critiques and value are highlighted as well as its suitability to be used to analyse network relations partnering with critical discourse analysis methodology.

INTRODUCTION

The literature positions social partnership as a governance response to crisis conditions, examining outcomes and effects in terms of institutions – labour and the state, political economic and socioeconomic contexts, the types and models of partnership relationship employed and from leadership perspectives and processes. In global discourses, it is positioned as a solution to the resolution of conflict, measured as deliverables from labour and social policy making within conciliatory governance regimes which promotes nation building.

DOI: 10.4018/978-1-5225-8961-7.ch005

Other dimensions that also need consideration in the analyses of social partnerships, include past legacies, leadership attitudes to dialogue, a lack of knowledge and information and other relational aspects, contributing to weaknesses in the institutionalization of social partnerships, some of which have been highlighted by Djuric (2002, 43).

institutionalization of social dialogue and new legislation alone are insufficient to offset the legacy of negative, often anti-unionist practice in the countries of this region. There are examples that tripartite institutions, although formally established, are actually hollow, ineffective, faced with the problems such as lack of willingness for dialogue, lack of knowledge for resolution of complex social, economic and general developmental problems. (Djuric, 2002, p. 43)

Other authors, Ghellab and Vylitova (2003) have identified the need to consider the attitudes of parties who should demonstrate in word and deed, the willingness to cooperate and reach a consensus and find common responses, both in times of crisis and economic prosperity. Several general and idiosyncratic factors contribute to differentiated results in social partnerships, such as the nature of the politics, the political culture, the vibrancy of the trade union movement, the immediate circumstances of each country before the introduction of the policy style and state capacity for policy management, which have also been identified by Osei (2004). These perspectives all signal apertures in the research on social partnerships and opportunities presented to legitimize alternative approaches, to facilitate greater introspection and unearth relational dimensions of partnership arrangements through Actor Network Theory.

Actor Network Theory to be discussed, possesses an ontology that confers agency on all the actors that converge within the network of relations. This ontology is unique in that inanimate objects are also included as well as the subjects or social actors. ANT also explains the mechanics of and power relations within networks becoming a lens through which to analyze the nature of the linkages and interface within the network, which is denoted as being discursive, between the actors.

Critical discourse as another intervening dimension and used as a unit of analysis, traverses and integrates multiple focal points facilitating the integration of cultural and historical context, the past and characteristics of current relationship between the parties, qualitative aspects of structures, social processes and outcomes. Critical discourse analysis also provides for an exploration of dimensions of the nature of relationships of power and the influence of intangibles- such as attitudes and motivation of need, mutuality between partners, capacities, roles and functions within prevailing power constructs, to create a kaleidoscope of inputs and interactions for consideration.

ANT Origins

Actor Network Theory (ANT) arises from the works of Bruno Latour, (1986, 1987, 1991, 1996, 1999), Michel Callon (1998) and John Law (1987, 1991a, 1991b, 1992, 1993; 1999a, 1999b; 2001, 2007) which describe how actor networks are created, held and disintegrate through networks of social relations. ANT views the world as consisting of networks of relations (Law, 1991b, p. 166; Law & Hassard, 1999; Watson, 2007) and is a distinctive approach (Law, 2007) to social theory and research.

Originating as a socio technological framework, ANT (Callon, 1986; Latour, 1986; Law, 2007) was concerned with the process by which scientific ideas became closed, the methods accepted and how issues became 'black boxed'. ANT asserts that science involves the management and reconstruction of social contexts within a laboratory environment. Scientific results were embedded in what scientists do at the sites of knowledge production such as in laboratories (Couldry, 2004), where the natural and technical are linked in heterogeneous networks of social relations.

Knowledge, then, is embodied in a variety of material forms. But where does it come from? The actor-network answer is that it is the end product of a lot of hard work in which heterogeneous bits and pieces -- test tubes, reagents, organisms, skilled hands, scanning electron microscopes, radiation monitors, other scientists, articles, computer terminals, and all the rest -- that would like to make off on their own are juxtaposed into a patterned network which overcomes their resistance (Law, 1992).

ANT rejects the binary separations (Watson, 2002; Castree, 2002) of normal Western conceptual thinking and rejects epistemological convictions of essential distinctions for example, subject/object or local /global etc., (Williams-Jones & Graham, 2003) of how categories are created. ANT however is dualist (Watson, 2002) in that material objects are deemed just as important as human beings. In his book 'Aramis: Or the Love of Technology,' which traces the failed attempt to create an innovative public transport system in Paris, Latour (1996) demonstrates the view that machines and humans should be negotiated equally, recruited, made allies and mobilized in the formation of 'continuous chains of translation' (Law, 2002). Latour (1996) notes;

The only way to increase a project's reality is to accept socio-technological compromises. The pertinent question is not whether it is a matter of technology or society, but only, what is the best socio-technological compromise. (Latour 1996, p. 99 - 101)

In one of his seminal studies 'Science in Action', Latour (1987) utilized the two-faced Roman God Janus as a metaphor, to reflect a 'two-faced' perspective in assessing science and the nature of scientific facts as presented. One of the two-faced perspectives or 'science in the making' represents a researcher looking at controversies, while the other face is retrospective, re-examining those facts that have already gained acceptance or science that is 'ready-made' (Latour, 1987). These rules of method identified 'follow the study of science in action' tracing controversies before they become 'factual' or fixed. When this stage has already been reached, then science is re-opened and controversies are followed anew.

The term 'follow the actors' (Latour, 1987) was coined to emphasize that the 'study of science in action' (Latour 1987) necessitates examining the various transformations of actors and controversies prior to settlement as well as those that reopen them, in determining the efficiency or perfection of a mechanism or objectivity or subjectivity of a claim (Latour, 1987). In essence, looking at the actions of scientists alone before facts and artefacts have become 'black boxed' (Latour, 1987) and emphasizing the process of transformations.

The actors are followed, to trace all the transformations they undergo and those later in the hands of others, setting aside the objectivity or subjectivity of a claim, the efficiency or perfection of a mechanism as well as their intrinsic qualities (Latour, 1987). This results in the actors being followed without preconceived judgments or determinations of what 'structure of society can explain the distortion' (Latour, 1987, p.258) so whether the actors are human or non-human, they would be considered symmetrically.

To examine all of the heterogeneous transformations and associations of the actors (Lowe, 2001) necessitates delineating networks and following their construction through weaker and stronger associations (Law 1999a). In this manner, there is the identification of the case mix of human and non humans (Lowe, 2001), in the network, enabled by the ways in which inscriptions are gathered, combined and tied together and 'sent back' (Latour, 1987). In order to truly appreciate ANT, there are key concepts critical to understanding the development and dynamics of the actor network and the nature of the interactions.

Actant/Actor and Their Characteristics in ANT

An 'actor' is any system element, which influences others in the network, be it a human being, a text, or an artefact (Garson, 2008) that bend space around themselves to make other elements dependent upon them. The term 'actant' (Law & Hassard, 1999) also coined in ANT, is oxymoronic and seeks to capture the tension between the centered actor and decentered network, as well as to stress the incorporation of material and human actors as determinants of social interactions and outcomes (Garson, 2008).

Effectively, actors translate other wills into their own, (Callon & Latour 1981, p. 279) and impose their view of the world upon others. Actors demonstrate different potentials in influencing other members of the same network, by building networks (Callon, 1986) around themselves and incorporating those networks associated with the actors that they influence. Actors are unequal, macro or micro actors, depending on the size of the network that each can assemble and put in place for a particular purpose, which in turn relates to the networks of the actors or intermediaries being commanded (Latour, 1992). Actors form alliances to strengthen a position and incorporate others in the process of seeking to achieve individual or collective objectives (Williams-Jones & Graham, 2003). Outside of the relations that catalyses instances of action such as negotiation, (Shaikh & Cordello, 2006) actors do not possess action or the potential for action, in and of themselves.

A coin, for example, within an economy, is vested with an attributed value, standard and mechanism of exchange, which gives it a defined competence and independence which enables it to be an actor (Stadler, 1999) shaped by the network and interacting with human actors (Garson, 2008). Coins mobilize and network heterogeneous allies together in transactions, forming closed connections within the network of coin users, where transactions are simplified based on its unquestioned value (Stadler 1997, p. 5).

Network/Actor-Network

A network of actors (Callon, 1993), is conceptualized as a group of unspecified relationships with an undetermined nature, composed of animate and inanimate or heterogeneous elements (Callon, 1987; Law, 1991; Watson, 2007; Hunter & Swan, 2007) linked in limited time and space. The actor networks created are heterogeneous, by having relations and interactions that are both material involving people, ideas and technologies, being hybrids of the social technical and personal (Latour, 1993; Williams-Jones & Graham, 2003). It is reducible neither to an actor alone, nor to a network (Law, 2007) as the heterogeneous networking allows the network to be able to redefine and transform itself. Heterogeneous networks of the social (Law, 1987) involve the heterogeneous alignment and networking of interests (Latour, 1987). The example is given by De Jong, (2007) of a computer keyboard which mediates communication, redirected by networks and objects such as the computer, paper, printer as well as persons within a system (Law, 1992).

However, the inclusion of human and non-human actors convey a 'precariousness' (Williams-Jones, & Graham, 2003) where stability resides in the commitment to the network as well as the performance of actors, which may and can be reversed (Latour, 1991). All the components of a network are causally important in ensuring that it holds together and endures (Hajer, 1995). ANT enables an appreciation that, 'It is not the Boeing 747 that flies us but the airline itself, with its entire ensemble of willing actants' (Ahkbar and Gopal 2005, 1). Actor and network are mutually constitutive, (Stadler 1997, 2) whereby an actor cannot act without a network and a network consists of actors which both constantly redefine and shape each other and are dependent upon the other in terms of the 'network', which is termed 'semiotic relationality' (Law, 2007).

The performative character of the network resides in the 'continuous relational interplay' (Shaikh and Cordello, 2006) and translation of interests whereby actors are 'performed in, by and through relations' (Williams-Jones & Graham, 2003). The actors are in a continuous state of mutation, as they emerge and retreat from interplay, (which defines the characteristics of the interplay) as they themselves influence and dialogically influence. As a shifting open alliance system (Williams-Jones & Graham, 2003), the network consists of social groups, people, artefacts, devices and objects, where each plays a role to influence one another (Shaikh & Cordello, 2006; Law, 2007) in the alignment and networking of interests. For example, a lecturer uses a Power Point presentation that together, becomes a 'collective' or partnership endeavour (Murdoch, 2006) assisting to communicate to students and becomes a means to define the social relations between the lecturer and the students. Another example is where a machine operator loses the role of being an autonomous decision maker when operating machinery, as the boundary between operator and machine becomes blurred. Once the action of the machine is initiated, subsequent actions of the operator are defined or determined by the machine, which may also incorporate other objects into the actor network, to the point where further action is not dictated by either party (Hernes, 2007) as they become 'hybrids of the social technological and personal' (Latour, 1993).

An actor can also be a network in its own right - an actor-network, composed of intermediaries which have been accepted by the actor which in turn transforms them, to carry the actor's signature of authorship (Law, 1991) towards being black boxed. Where there is the incorporation of a new actor into a network, or convergence, this entails taking over the alignment that the newcomer has with other networks in the transference of wills (Callon & Latour, 1981) which successively becomes more challenging and involves mutual shaping (Stadler, 1997). Network elements are linked with elements internal and external to it, becoming enlarged (Latour, 1992) by additional associations and hence requiring more effort to hold and sustain the original meaningful relation, despite appearances of stability over time. Networks characterized by a high level of convergence, demonstrate agreement, being highly aligned and coordinated (Ritzer, 2006). Network persistence is a function of role repetition by actants (Garson, 2002). Actors are allowed to translate their objectives through many vehicles, such as choice, by adding other actors' powers to their own, or by the prescription of an object (Stadler, 2000).

Intermediary

Intermediaries pass between actors in the course of 'relatively stable transactions' (Law & Bijker, 1992) and is construed as a language, a text, a product, or service, that assists in communication. Actors form networks by circulating intermediaries among themselves, thus defining the respective position of the actors within the networks and in doing so, constituting the actors and the networks themselves. Despite the actor and the intermediary overlapping at certain junctures, the former is distinguished by the ability to circulate the intermediaries that carry messages of the networks in which they are inscribed (Law, 1991). Heterogeneous actors build networks of intermediaries that are accepted by other actors through negotiations. Once these actors are inscribed they are transformed by that actor, bearing its signature of authority and becomes reliant on the now 'macro social' actor, to define its role. This, in turn, redounds to transform the heterogeneity of the actor network and its characteristics (Callon, 1991).

Inscription

Actor Network Theory acknowledges the use of text as a means of inscription, as one of the many material forms which includes artifacts, work routines, legal documents, prevailing norms and habits, written manuals, institutional and organizational arrangements and procedures, within which patterns can be inscribed (Montiero, 2000). When network negotiations are complete, certain interests are held and carried forward while others become obsolete. These specific interests held, captured as inscriptions represent what has to be achieved in order to maintain the overall translation of interests within the new network ascribing to it a difference than that of the past. The translations become more permanent and tangible, being inscribed in material form, to become the history circulated within the ontology of the network (Kaplan, 2004), strengthened by the adding and superimposing of inscriptions.

Child resistant closures on medicine bottles, for example, represent an inscription whereby technologies and objects are networked to define a framework of action. Based on research determining small children's' inability to perform two different motions of pushing and turning simultaneously, it was expected, that they would be unable to open bottle tops inscribed to open, combining these actions (Knight & Willmott 2007).

The strength of this inscription, meant to protect children however, can also be contested by the elderly and infirm who may have difficulty in this regard. The latter can respond by transferring medicines previously held in these "child proof" bottles to ones which they can access more easily, but unfortunately so can the small children meant to be protected (Knight & Willmott, 2007). Monteiro (2000) identifies four dimensions of inscriptions, which include;

- The identification of explicit anticipations, scenarios of use, and standardizations held by the various actors.
- How these anticipations are translated and inscribed into the materials of the inscriptions.
- Who inscribes them.
- The strength of these inscriptions, that is, the effort required to oppose or work around them.

Network Dynamics

With regard to network flexibility, 'irreversibility' relates to the degree of difficulty to make changes once resistance accumulates, given the strength or weakness of the inscription undertaken. Given that links and nodes in the network are not permanent fixtures and guaranteed, effort must be exerted to maintain them.

The degree of 'reversibility' therefore, according to Callon (1991), is dependent upon the feasibility of going back to the point where the translation was only one amongst others and the extent to which subsequent translations are determined by it and shaped. In essence, it factors the longevity and predetermination of the connections (Callon, 1991). A case is referenced by Latour (1988b), of the early privatization attempts of the Parisian metro system that was thwarted by a radical government which constructed subway tunnels that could not accommodate railway coaches owned by the commercial operators, as a deterrent. The ability to reverse the subway network has declined overtime with the proliferation of the subway network being viewed as an 'irreversible technical construct' (Knight & Willmott, 2007) being able to resist alternative translations. When the shifting alliances of actors (networks) that are interacting by the entry of new actors, the desertion of existing actors or changes in alliances, becomes stabilized (Tatnall & Gilding, 1999, p. 958).

The absence of a monopoly by any actor allows the network to be always contestable and despite the one voice or macro social actor, there is no inflexibility such that another network could not emerge. The durability of actor-networks depends upon the commitment of the objects to the network, moving from place to place without changing, termed, 'immutable mobiles,' (Law, 2007) that hold their shape physically, geographically, functionally and relationally (Law & Singleton, 2005). Networks that are translated result in a degree of simplification, while retaining difference or heterogeneity to the point of becoming 'black boxed'.

The Macro Social Actor/"Black Box"

A 'black box', is described solely in terms of its inputs and outputs (Bijker et. al., 1987) and contains 'that which no longer needs to be considered, or contents that have become a matter of indifference' (Callon & Latour, 1981). The coin mentioned earlier as an actor can, in many ways, be considered a black box, for when it is opened, it is seen to constitute a whole network of other, complex, heterogeneous associations (Callon, 1986). The law can also be conceptualized as a collection of black boxes that in the formative legislative stage, has its shape influenced by the forging of consensus between various interests and alliances around the text. Once legislation has been passed, the law becomes largely uncontested as black boxes with their elements sealed in fixed stable relationships (Stadler, 1997).

THE 'SOCIOLOGY OF TRANSLATION': THE NETWORK DYNAMICS OF ACTOR NETWORK THEORY (ANT)

ANT, as the 'sociology of translation' emerged from a seminal study by Callon (1986) on scallops and the fishermen of St. Brieuc Bay (Callon 1991, 1994; Latour 1987), which traces the attempts of marine biologists to develop a conservation strategy to govern the farming of scallops in that region. The term 'translation,' (Callon, 1986) was coined to encapsulate the shifting, making equivalent, linking and de-linking of actors in network relations and the glue that holds independent actors capable of resistance or accommodation, or participation (Williams-Jones & Graham, 2003). Translation has also been considered a process of social ordering (Lowe, 2001) whereby continuous translation at varying levels, generate institutions, governments organizations and agents that exist over time (Williams-Jones & Graham, 2003). The analysis of ordering struggle is central to ANT, (Law & Hassard, 1999) where each actor has their own interests and the stability of the network will be a function of an effective, translation process, where interests are negotiated, involving 'intrigues, calculations, acts of persuasion and violence' (Callon & Latour 1981, p. 279).

The process of negotiation creates critical nodes or 'Obligatory Points of Passage' or 'OPP' which ensure that communication attains a certain uniformity by passing through a single domain, often established by the primary actor, thereby becoming indispensable to the network (Garson, 2008). The openness of the network facilitates actors having their individual objectives agreed to by other actors, which in being co-opted, defines the network. Actors also bring in characteristics from other actor-networks of which they are a part of (Shaikh & Cordello, 2006), resulting in new emergent characteristics being introduced and recursively being re proposed back into the other actor networks creating 'circularity' (Shaikh & Cordello, 2006). Translation essentially becomes a circular process of interpretation being the definition that each actor makes of other actors in the network (Callon, 1991). The more relations an actor has through translation, the bigger the actor grows and has more relations to put in a 'black box' (Callon & Latour, 1981; De Jong, 2007). The more elements placed within the box and the multiplicity of associations the actor has inscribed causes it to act like a 'single man', (Callon & Latour 1981, p. 285) like-minded, and stable, forming a macro social actor or becoming a black box (De Jong, 2007).

'Translation' Deconstructed: *'Problematization,' 'Interessement,' 'Enrollment,'and 'Mobilization'*

Callon (1986) identified four moments or theoretical constructs in the process of translation namely; problematization, interessement, enrollment and mobilization, to be discussed in chapter 6, in more detail. Within these four moments, the identities of actors, the possibility of interactions and the margins of maneuver are negotiated and delimited. At the end of the process of translation a constraining network of relationships exists whereby 'truth lies in power and power emerges from within networks. Some issues are organized into politics while others are organized out' (Schattschneider, 1960: Murdoch, 2006).

Concepts of Power in Actor Network Theory (ANT)

Power is not conceptualized as being monopolistic (Callon, 1986), nor possessed, nor exerted from a single centre or social system. In ANT, the actor network gains power over and through those enrolled in the network (Whittle and Spicer 2005) so power is derived socially where the entire network is implicated in power relations. This reflects a perspective held by Foucault, where power is not determined or possessed, in this case, by any one actor, being exerted on others, or used as a tool of domination of constraint, but is a productive and relational product of the network itself (Akbar & Gophal, 2005).

As a relational shared capacity between social and natural actants, thoroughly decentered in different heterogeneous networks (Castree, 2002), power is based upon the positions that actors hold within the network as an outcome of their relationships with the heterogeneous elements in the network (Cordello & Shaikh, 2006). There is a focus upon interdependencies and networks rather than individual, independent decisions and actions of sovereign actors (Newton, 2002).

In his book 'The Whale and the Reactor,' Langdon Winner (1986) argued that artefacts were not passive and demonstrated how they could be used politically, embodying specific forms of power and authority (Gooding & Tilly, 2008). He argued that the low underpasses designed by Robert Moses for suburban highways in New York, kept busloads of African-American day-trippers away from white residential enclaves, alluding that social exclusion was built into the design of urban infrastructure (Whiteside, 2002). As an outcome of 'all the struggle' (Law, 1992, p. 5), power is generated relationally until stability becomes evident when a black box configuration has been achieved, denoting the cessation of controversy and an equilibrium of social meaning established (Bijker et al., 1987). Power is derived by the ability of the actor to enroll, enlist and convince other actors to allow the initial actor to represent them (Murdoch, 1995). However, translation and the structuring of power relations are a dynamic process and never a completed accomplishment (Latour, 1986)

The study of marine biologists' attempts to develop a conservation strategy, to govern or black box the restocking and sustainability of the farming of scallops for fishermen at St Brieuc Bay, (Callon, 1986) as aforementioned, is a classic case in point. The fishermen in the actor network were represented as seeking to sustain, farm and cultivate the local scallop beds, which was accepted, being a potentially viable enterprise. The scientists and their experiments were positioned as being a valuable source of expertise with the farmers acceding to their research in order to achieve their goal. It was assumed that the farmers would demonstrate support by accepting the scientists' world view and position as well as the relationship and roles assigned to them inclusive of investing and trusting in the scientists' expertise. However, the fishermen acted outside of their given role in the network, by 'breaking ranks and prematurely trawling the bay,' (Galvin, 2009) effectively over harvesting the scallop beds to the point of no recovery. This undermined the position of the scientists and it was no longer feasible for them to claim to represent the interests of the fishermen (Law, 1991a). The maintenance of the power relations or black box of stability within the actor network being furthered by the scientists, was dependent upon the actors' adherence to the defined roles that they were given and the positioning of the scientists themselves as the OPP, without which the actors could not realize their goals. As Latour (1986) explains,

Power is the illusion people get when they are obeyed... people who are obeyed, discover what their power is really made of when they start to lose it. It was made of the wills of all the others.' (Latour, 1986, pp. 261-269)

Actor Network Theory (ANT): Applications and Limitations

ANT has been applied in various kinds of research where its ontology, symmetry and equating human, non-human systems and artefacts has been influential in providing insight in analyzing sociological, behavioural and organizational research outcomes. Apart from the studies on St Brieuc Bay (Callon, 1986) and others mentioned previously, Latour and Vickers (2007) note additional cases, including studies on the Toyota Motor Company (Ahkbar and Gopal, 2005), hotel keys (Latour, 1991) and a 250 tonne engine (Lindahl, 2005). Diverse research on themes, such as door grooms (Latour 1992), self-coupling carriages (Latour, 1996) in economics, the agency of the market (Callon, 1997), the narration of childbirth in medicine (Akrich & Pasveer, 1998), studies on muscular dystrophy (Callon & Rabeharisoa, 1998) and gender issues (Singleton, 1993) have been undertaken. ANT has been used in accounting studies (Lowe, 2001) and to explore the political dimensions of artefacts, such as, low underpasses (Winner, 1986) as well as to examine how power is implicated within organizational studies by Whittle and Spicer (2005).

Like many theories, ANT has been criticized by some authors who have argued that, it has limitations and self-imposed constraints (Couldry, 2004; Lowe, 2001) which make it more a 'sociology of networks' than a 'sociology of action'. The network epistemology of ANT presumes that a given actor's network configuration will define or predetermine the actions of humans in the network (Newton, 2007) and that actors will adhere to their given role and assigned position overall, obscuring the role of independent choice and agency by the human actors in network relations. ANT is criticized for not addressing issues of time adequately (Couldry, 2004) in that, the long-term effect of networks on the distribution of social power equalities and inequalities are neglected. According to Couldry (2004), time is dynamic and networks can be transformed even after they have been created and this is not considered in processes of how networks become either stabilized or changed. The significance of the social is downplayed in ANT, according to Newton (2007, 32) as in the case of the hotel keys discussed earlier, in that there is no consideration of how the keys became the property of the hotel manager or the social etiquette of the guest that would guide the returning of the hotel keys outside of that prescribed.

This reflects limitations in the exploration of human agency, independent action and the historical construction of objects. Neither does the power of an actor automatically confer the ability to cause change, unless other actors are persuaded to perform the appropriate actions for this to occur (Tatnall & Gilding, 1999). The inability to examine the stabilization of an object as a constructed achievement within ANT reduces power in networks to the effects of a reality impermeable to social analysis (Mutch, 2002).

Regarding ANT's ontology, Castree (2002) argues that the relegation of humans downwards to a non-human status and lifting non-humans to a human status in ANT, is not a true reflection of reality as everything is not equal and there is a 'value emanating from difference rather than a homogeneity' (Watson 2007, 18). Similar areas of concern were posited by McLean and Hassard (2004) within the context of heterogeneous engineering, regarding the inclusion and exclusion of actors, treatment of humans and non-humans, nature of privilege and status, handling of agency and structure and the nature of politics and power.

Grint & Woolgar (1997) noted that Callon (1986) cited the failure of the catalyst in the fuel cells in his treatise on the French electric vehicle as being part of the reason why the network failed. However, this rests upon the action or a defined, inherent essential property of the catalyst, which inadvertently, relies on the essential or real property or nature of technology to explain the power relations of the network. While ANT stresses that actors do not have fixed boundaries and attributes (Callon & Law, 1997), it actually relies upon these same assumptions when dissecting the world, for example, aircraft, text, social groups etc., reflecting a fundamental division of labour as every distinction between human and non-human is a social act. In a sense, there is the re-creation and reinforcement of the very dualism that is being deconstructed (Whittle & Spicer, 2005).

Concerning the methodology of ANT, Stern (1998) is critical of Latour's 'rules of method' indicating the failure to distinguish between the context of discovery and that of justification in terms of the epistemological assessment of the reasons for the findings that occur in scientific studies. It has proven even more challenging to define a methodology for ANT, especially when one of the major proponents Bruno Latour, has 'recalled ANT,' indicating that all the main terms, namely 'actor,' 'network' and 'theory,' are flawed and misunderstood, suggesting that ANT should be conceptualized as a theory of space or circulation in a non-modern context (Latour, 1999). By an unwillingness to be specific about its own internal and external boundaries, Lee and Hassard (1999) argue that ANT is a 'sliding over methodology', lacking explanatory powers (Martin, 1998) and is at its best when used for descriptive purposes, the ordering of observations and the alignment of interactions.

CONCLUSION

Despite its critics, ANT provides an ontological and epistemological perspective useful for understanding the development of the MOU actor network as an emerging mode of governance revolving around the text of the Agreement and the network of actors and their respective networks converging around it. As 'the sociology of translation' (Callon, 1986; Latour, 2005; Law & Hassard, 1999) and a 'new approach to the study of power,' (Callon, 1986) ANT is represented as an analytical framework to study the role played by science and technology in structuring power relationships and as a mechanism by which the social and natural worlds progressively take shape (Callon, 1986)

As a systematic way to explain the mechanics of the interactions, ANT's unique ontology, ascribes symmetry or equity of treatment to the human and non-human actors, within the dynamics of network relations. In ANT, the MOU Agreement, a 'material object common in organizational life' (Hunter & Swan, 2007), is afforded the status of an 'actant' or 'actor' in its own right, with equal status with human actors within the network of relations of the social partnership.

As a theoretical mechanism to analyse networks Actor Network Theory (ANT), was used to explore the creation of this social partnership and to trace the chronology of the development of the MOU actor network. Actor Network Theory (ANT) has a unique ontology, being termed a distinctive approach to social theory (Law, 2007) as actors or actants in the network are conceptualized as being heterogeneous, unique in incorporation and considered as equals, both the human and non-human actants (Michael, 1996) and possess symmetry in the formation of chains of associations (Law, 1991a; Latour, 1991). According to Latour (1986) one of the proponents, ANT as an approach to social theory has no 'social' dimension, but rather 'the social' is always already 'technical' just as the 'technical' is always already 'social,' (Couldry, 2008) as we are 'faced with chains which are associations of humans and the non-humans.' (Latour, 1991). ANT entails the interweaving of the technical and human (Callon, 1991) and convergence (Bowker & Leigh Star, 1996) has produced 'hybrids' or 'imbroglios of human and non-human' (Michael, 2000) that populate and proliferate (Law & Hassard, 1999) within the structures of everyday life. Thereby suggesting that society, organizations, agents and machines are all effects generated in patterned networks of diverse and not simply human, material. (Law, 2007).

ANT provides an explanation and a means to explore the development of the MOU social partnership ontologically construed as an actor network as well as the MOU network's mechanism and relations, being "a social construction of social relations" (Lowe 2001, p. 345) and the dynamics operable within it. ANT also reveals some theoretical and methodological limitations which reside in its ontological framework which precludes its sole use as a critical research methodology for the analysis of discourse. According to Whittle and Spicer (2005), ANT concentrates on the networks of the powerful (Ritzer, 2006) and simply describes and legitimizes established power relations. *The unique ontology and epistemology of ANT, enables the MOU Agreement to be conceptualized as an actor network, having a discourse of its own and capable of attaining a 'black box' status within the network of relations that it creates for itself.* ANT is fused as a theoretical framework, with the methodological approach of Critical Discourse Analysis (CDA) which has its foundation in Critical Theory to analyse the discourses of the actor networks surrounding the MOU Agreement actor network. The following chapter builds upon the latter by explaining the tenets of Critical Discourse Analysis (CDA) methodology used to analyse the discourses within the network relations, in conjunction with ANT.

REFERENCES

Bijker, W. E., Hughes, T. P., & Pinch, T. J. (Eds.). (1987). *The social construction of technological systems: New directions in the sociology and history of technology*. MIT Press.

Bijker, W. E., & Law, J. (1992). *Shaping technology/building society: Studies in sociotechnical change*. MIT Press.

Callon, M. (1986). Some elements of a sociology of translation: domestication of the scallops and the fishermen of St Brieuc Bay. In Power, Action and Belief (pp. 196-223). London: Routledge.

Callon, M. (1991). Techno-economic networks and irreversibility. In A Sociology of Monsters: Essays on Power, Technology and Domination. London: Academic Press.

Callon, M. (1998). Introduction: The embeddedness of economic markets in economics. *The Sociological Review*, *46*(S1), 1–57. doi:10.1111/j.1467-954X.1998.tb03468.x

Callon, M. (2003). Some Elements of a Sociology of Translation: Domestication of the Scallops and the Fishermen of St. Brieuc Bay. In J. Law (Ed.), Power, Action and Belief: A New Sociology of Knowledge? Routledge.

Callon, M., & Latour, B. (1981). Unscrewing the big Leviathan: how actors macro-structure reality and how sociologists help them to do so. *Advances in social theory and methodology: Toward an integration of micro-and macro-sociologies, 1*.

Castree, N. (2002). False antitheses? Marxism, nature and actor-networks. *Antipode*, *34*(1), 111–146. doi:10.1111/1467-8330.00228

Couldry, N. (2008). Actor network theory and media: do they connect and on what terms? In A. Hepp, F. Krotz, S. Moores, & C. Winter (Eds.), *Connectivity, Networks and Flows: Conceptualizing Contemporary Communications* (pp. 93–110). Cresskill, NJ: Hampton Press, Inc.

De Jong, B. (2007). *Shedding Light on the darkness: Using the Actor-Network theory to analyse the distribution of power*. Paper for the 47th Europe Regional Science Association.

Galvin, R. (2009). *Modifying actor-network theory to analyse the German project of photovoltaic electrical energy generation* (No. 09-02). CSERGE working paper EDM.

Garson, G. D. (Ed.). (1999). *Information technology and computer applications in public administration: issues and trends*. IGI Global. doi:10.4018/978-1-87828-952-0

Goodin, R. E., Goodin, R. E., & Tilly, C. (Eds.). (2006). *The Oxford handbook of contextual political analysis* (Vol. 5). Oxford Handbooks of Political. doi:10.1093/oxfordhb/9780199270439.001.0001

Grint, K., & Woolgar, S. (1997). *The machine at work: technology, work and organization*. Cambridge, UK: Polity Press.

Hajer, M. (1995). *The politics of environmental discourse*. Oxford, UK: Oxford University Press.

Hernes, T. (2008). *Understanding organization as process. Theory for a tangled world*. London: Routledge.

Hunter, S., & Swan, E. (2007). Oscillating politics and shifting agencies: Equalities and diversity work and actor network theory. *Equal Opportunities International*, *26*(5), 402–419. doi:10.1108/02610150710756621

Kaplan, B., & Shaw, N. T. (2004). Future directions in evaluation research: People, organizational, and social issues. *Methods of Information in Medicine*, *43*(03), 215–231. doi:10.1055-0038-1633862 PMID:15227551

Knight, D., & Willmott, H. (2007). *Introducing organizational behaviour and management*. Cengage Learning EMEA.

Latour, B. (1986). The Powers of Association. In J. Law (Ed.), Power, Action and Belief. A New Sociology of Knowledge? (pp. 264-280). London: Routledge.

Latour, B. (1987). *Science in action: How to follow scientists and engineers through society*. Cambridge, MA: Harvard University Press.

Latour, B. (1991). *Technology is society made durable. In Sociology of Monsters: Essay on Power. Technology. and Domination*. London: Routledge.

Latour, B. (1992). Where Are the Missing Masses? The Sociology of a Few Mundane Artefacts. In W. Bijker & J. Law (Eds.), *Shaping Technology/ Building Society: Studies in Sociotechnical Change*. Cambridge, MA: MIT Press.

Latour, B. (1996). *Aramis, or, The love of technology*. Cambridge, MA: Harvard University Press.

Latour, B. (1999). On recalling ANT. *The Sociological Review*, *47*(1_suppl), 15–25. doi:10.1111/j.1467-954X.1999.tb03480.x

Law, J. (1987). Technology and heterogeneous engineering: The case of Portuguese expansion. In W. E. Bijker, P. Hughes, & T. J. Pinch (Eds.), *The social construction of technological systems: New directions in the sociology and history of technology*. Cambridge, MA: MIT Press.

Law, J. (1991). *A sociology of monsters: essays on power, technology and domination*. London: Routledge.

Law, J. (1991a). Strategies of power: power, discretion and strategy. In J. Law (Ed.), *A sociology of monsters: essays on power, technology and domination*. London: Routledge.

Law, J. (1992). Notes on the theory of the actor-network: Ordering, strategy, and heterogeneity. *Systems Practice*, *5*(4), 379–393. doi:10.1007/BF01059830

Law, J. (1993). *Materialities, Spatialities and Globalities*. Lancaster, UK: Centre for Science Studies, Lancaster University. Retrieved from www.lancs.ac.uk/fass/sociology/papers/law-hetherington-materialities-spatialities-globalities.pdf

Law, J. (1999a). *Heterogeneities*. Lancaster, UK: Centre for Science Studies: Lancaster University. Retrieved from http://www.comp.lancs.ac.uk/sociology/papers/Law-Heterogeneities.pdf

Law, J. (1999b). *Traduction / trahison: notes on ANT*. Lancaster, UK: Centre for Science Studies, Lancaster University. Retrieved from http://www.comp.lancs.ac.uk/sociology/papers/Law-Traduction-Trahison.pdf

Law, J. (2001). *Notes on the Theory of the Actor Network: Ordering, Strategy and Heterogeneity*. Lancaster, UK: Centre for Science Studies, Lancaster University. Retrieved from http://www.comp.lancs.ac.uk/sociology/papers/Law-Notes-on-ANT.pdf

Law, J. (2007). *Actor Network Theory and Material Semiotics*. Centre for Science Studies and Department of Sociology. Retrieved from www.heterogeneities.net/publications/Law-ANTandMaterialSemiotics.pdf

Law, J., & Hassard, J. (1999). *Actor network theory and after*. Oxford, UK: Blackwell.

Law, J., & Singleton, V. (2005). Object lessons. *Organization*, *12*(3), 331–355. doi:10.1177/1350508405051270

Lindahl, M. (2005). The little engine that could: on the managing qualities of technology. In B. Czarniawska & T. Hernes (Eds.), *Actor-Network Theory and Organizing*. Copenhagen, Denmark: Copenhagen Business School Press.

Lowe, A. (2001). After ANT: An illustrative discussion of the implications for qualitative accounting case research. *Accounting, Auditing & Accountability Journal*, *14*(3), 327–351. doi:10.1108/EUM0000000005519

McLean, C., & Hassard, J. (2004). Symmetrical absence/ symmetrical absurdity: Critical notes on the production of actor-network accounts. *Journal of Management Studies*, *41*(3), 493–519. doi:10.1111/j.1467-6486.2004.00442.x

Michael, M. (1996). *Constructing Identities: The Social, the Nonhuman and Change*. London: Sage. doi:10.4135/9781446279182

Monteiro, E. (2000). Actor-Network Theory. In C. Ciborra & T. Jellasi (Eds.), *From Control to Drift. The Dynamics of Corporate Information Infrastructure*. Oxford, UK: Oxford University Press.

Munroe, T. (1992). *The industrial relations culture: perspectives and change*. Paper prepared for the Conference: Planning Institute of Jamaica.

Murdoch, J. (2005). Post-structuralist geography: A guide to relational space. *Sage (Atlanta, Ga.)*.

Mutch, A. (2002). Actors and networks or agents and structures: Towards a realist view of information systems. *Organization*, *9*(3), 477–496. doi:10.1177/135050840293013

Ritzer, G. (2006). *The Blackwell encyclopedia of sociology* (Vol. 36). Maidenhead, MA: Blackwell Publishers. doi:10.1111/b.9781405124331.2006.x

Saeed, A. M., & Gopal, A. (n.d.). *Immutability, Inimitability and Autonomy: The 3 little paradoxes of the Toyota (Re) Production System CMS4 Stream 27: Technology and Power*. Retrieved from https://www.mngt.waikato.ac.nz/ejrot/cmsconference/2005/proceedings/technology/Saeed.pdf

Schattschneider, E. E. (1960). *The Semi sovereign people*. New York: Holt, Rinehart and Winston.

Shaikh, M., & Cordello, A. (2006). *From epistemology to ontology: challenging the constructed truth of ANT*. London: London School of Economics and Political Science.

Stalder, F. (1997). *Latour and actor-network theory*. Available online at http://amsterdam. nettime. org/Lists-Archives/nettime-l-9709/msg00012. html

Stalder, F. (1999). Fluid Objects: Reconfiguring Money and the Limits of Actor-Network Theory. Sociality/Materiality Conference.

Stalder, F. (2000). Beyond constructivism: Towards a realistic realism. A review of Bruno Latour's Pandora's Hope. *The Information Society, 16*(3), 245–247. doi:10.1080/01972240050133698

Stern, D. (1998). *Rhetoric, narrative and argument in Bruno Latour's "Science in Action"*. Paper presented at the 16th Philosophy of Science Association, Kansas City, MO.

Tatnall, A., & Gilding, A. (2005). Actor-Network Theory and Information Systems Research. *Proceedings of the 10th Australasian Conference on Information Systems.*

Watson, G. (2007). *Actor network theory, after ANT and enactment: Implications for method.* Academic Press.

Whiteside, K. H. (2002). *Divided natures: French contributions to political ecology.* MIT Press. doi:10.7551/mitpress/2470.001.0001

Whittle, A., & Spicer, A. (2005). Why Organization Studies Should Resist. In EGOS 2005 colloquium in Berlin (pp. 1-26). Academic Press.

Williams-Jones, B., & Graham, J. E. (2003). Actor-network theory: A tool to support ethical analysis of commercial genetic testing. *New Genetics & Society, 22*(3), 271–296. doi:10.1080/1463677032000147225 PMID:15115034

Winner, L. (1993). Upon opening the black box and finding it empty: Social constructivism and the philosophy of technology. *Science, Technology & Human Values, 18*(3), 362–378. doi:10.1177/016224399301800306

Chapter 6
Convergence:
Actor Network Theory (ANT) and Critical Discourse Analysis (CDA)

ABSTRACT

Actor network theory as the "sociology of translation," is used as a lens to examine the chronology of the development of the MOU Agreement, which provides insight into the mechanics of its formation and network of relations. Translation uncovered dimensions of the network's development: why associations between the actors were created, the factors that mobilized these heterogeneous parties to come together. Further, it also uncovered how their functions were ascribed and how stability or "black box" status was achieved. Critical discourse analysis (CDA) is positioned as a moment in ANT facilitating the analyses of the network linkages of the MOU actor network assist to identify the interactions at various levels of the MOU social partnership actor network. The two worldviews complement each other within an interpretivist framework revealing the potential to analyse network interactions through the lens of discourse.

INTRODUCTION

Critical Discourse Analysis enables an understanding and analysis of the dialectic interactions involved that shape systems of discourses as well as how these in turn have shaped social practices and structures with transformative and reproductive capacity, in relation to the MOU in Jamaica.

DOI: 10.4018/978-1-5225-8961-7.ch006

On using discourse as the unit of analysis, Fairclough's CDA approach facilitates the deconstruction and exploration of the discourses surrounding the MOU as a network through which the research questions are answered. Its usefulness also resides in being able to facilitate "multiple points of analytic entry" (Janks 1997) as well as being a vehicle to investigate, describe, interpret and explain patterns within the interactions within the study.

BACKGROUND

The utility of Actor Network Theory (ANT) or the sociology of translation as an appropriate theoretical framework to understand the MOU, resides in the possibilities that it presents to trace the linkages and interactions between actors and to explain how the network of social partnership converges, diverges, stabilizes or disintegrates. Furthermore, it allows an exploration of the dynamics of network construction, the mechanics of how alliances (Williams-Jones & Graham 2003, p. 273) are built and to identify the interactions at various levels of the MOU social partnership as a "lens", to "follow the actors" (Latour, 1987, p. 176).

THEORY OF TRANSLATION

This involves the application of ANT as a 'Theory of Translation" to derive the MOU chronology, that exhibits usefulness in providing an explanation of the mechanics of the interactions. ANT also serves as a "lens" to facilitate the use of a network perspective which is of value for exploring the MOU partnership, even as an emerging relational network and mode of governance, affecting the structure, human relationships, interactions, and associations amongst and between the Partners of the alliance. This chapter 'follow the actors', in developing a chronology of the formation of the MOU partnership and ANT provides an explanation as to the MOU actor network of relations, being "a social construction of social relations" (Lowe, 2001, p. 345) and the dynamics operable within it. The utility of Actor Network Theory (ANT) or the '*Sociology of Translation*' as an appropriate theoretical framework to understand the MOU, resides in the possibilities that it presents to trace the linkages and interactions between actors and to explain how the network of social partnership converges, diverges, stabilizes or disintegrates. Further, the ways that the networks of relations are composed, how they emerge and come into being, how they are constructed and maintained, how they compete with other networks, and how they are made more durable over time. (Tatnall & Gilding, 2005).

BACKGROUND

Actor Network Theory demonstrates mechanically through different steps how an actor (De Jong, 2007) becomes the macro social actor, conferred with the 'authority to speak or act on behalf of another actor or force' (Callon & Latour, 1981, p.279) within the context of dependent network relations (Law, 1991a). Furthermore, which actors become intermediaries because of the compromise and mutual adjustment.

Emerging from the relational effects between actors and their social asymmetry, ANT is perceived as a 'theory of the mechanics of power.' (Ritzer, 2006; Law 1992; Tatnall & Gilding, 2005).

The Public Sector Memorandum of Understanding (MOU) or Memorandum of Understanding (MOU) social partnership agreement was created between the Government of Jamaica and the Jamaica Confederation of Trade Unions (JCTU) as the Partners in response to pending macroeconomic crisis

Using the assumptions and terminologies associated with ANT as well as the chronologies and discourse as text obtained, 'translation' leading to the formation of the MOU network, was explored by examining,

What mobilized the parties to the MOU to come together and why were the associations between actors created? Further, what caused their alignment and coalescence to become stabilized and in terms of the process of *translation,* what drives it so that it has the potential to proliferate or destroy the network?

To begin, there is an assumption of two pre-existing networks represented by the Government as actor in the Government of Jamaica Network (GJN) and the Jamaica Confederation of Trade Unions or (JCTU) as actor in the Trade Unions' Network (TUN). These would each consist of a large number of heterogeneous actors, according to ANT, for example in the GJN to include the diverse ministries, departments and statutory bodies that make up the public sector network, with each possessing its own set of relations, internal towards their clients within the Government network and through external relations within the wider economy.

The unions similarly would be represented by individual union groups within the Trade Union Network (TUN). Each network would be positioned relative to each other as actor networks, with network linkages between to each other, within their own network, as well as possessing other relationships, experiences, events, externally, across and between other networks. Such as members of the TUN having relations with public sector ministries and agencies at the level of labour and industrial relations activities or the Government having inter- ministerial relationships.

What Mobilized the Parties to Come Together?

The process of *translation* involves four moments called, *problematization, interessement*, *enrollment*, and *mobilization*. In *problematization,* according to (De Jong, 2007) a focal actor has a problem, and determines a set of actors to be involved to remedy it, soliciting their interest to form an alliance of mutual benefit. In this case, the Ministry of Finance and Planning (MoFP) as part of the GJN, made representation of a multi-dimensional problem that had its roots in a number of factors and circumstances.

The historical analysis of the context of the Government as actor and a glimpse of its discourse and practice is reflected in the dimensions of the macroeconomic conditions of the state. One may recall that the contextual issues foregrounded, included, the lingering state and economic vulnerabilities of the past, that overshadowed the policy making thrusts into liberalization and deregulation in the present and the commensurate outcomes on the economy. These vulnerabilities were compounded by the financial crisis in the 1990s, low productivity and the trend of real wages increasing amidst declining inflation. The context of the Government as actor were aptly described as being one of low economic growth. There was significant liberalization of the exchange rate and deregulation with inflation.

In the context of the period leading up to the MOU, the economy of Jamaica went through a very challenging period. It had experienced significant policy reforms, liberalization and deregulation, while real wages were increasing. Circumstances were exacerbated by the financial crisis of the mid-1990s towards the end of the decade. In the sense that productivity was not growing, and real wages were growing, Jamaica's global competitiveness was being eroded in a period of great volatility while the exchange rate was changing and depreciating very rapidly. Government allowed wage increases in the public sector and it was apparent that the movement of real wages in the public-sector was out of sync with productivity.

Overall, the rate of increase in wages and salaries and allowances, had far outstripped the rate of increase of revenues. Along with the precursors described, there were long periods of high inflation and adversarial bargaining between employers and employees, coupled with Government's difficulty to borrow both domestically and externally, to address growing expenditures, specifically wages and salaries.

These challenges experienced by the Government actor network are encapsulated as the macro linkages of fiscal challenges which prompted the MoFP to respond by taking measures to stem the rate of growth of the wage bill. The issuance of 'Circular 21: Operation of Posts' by MoFP, sought to halt employment, by instructing the cessation of all new employment, but if urgent, there were stipulated conditions and processes to seek permission to do so. However, from the perspective of the Union actor network, there were also events taking place, revealed at the operational level within the public sector, which strongly signalled severe fiscal challenges. There were widespread micro challenges, such as, salaries and allowances not being paid in a timely fashion and contractual obligations entered into with suppliers for Government services, which were not being honoured reported by members in the public sector.

Public servants were also being told that the salaries' accounts had not been funded on arrival at the bank to collect their salaries on pay day. Added to that, people who were involved in the procurement of goods and services were reporting to the Unions that they were having a very difficult time satisfying the commitments and obligations of their respective organizations. After engaging the services of contractors on behalf of their entity, when the time came for payment to be made, they could not honour the obligations to pay them. Hence rumours started to swirl that Government indeed had no money to meet basic obligations and there was going to be a cut in the size of staff. The promulgation of Circular 21 by the MoFP, that capped public sector employment, was the Government's response to curtail a growing wage bill that was unsustainable, given government's fiscal accounts and policy, linked to the number of persons employed in the public-sector. This was received negatively by the Union movement causing a "hue and cry' and interpreted by them as an 'outrage.'

In the ensuing consultations, held at the Jamaica Confederation of Trade Unions (JCTU), the Unions decided to write, requesting a meeting to outline their objections and discuss their concerns. This represented the inner processes involved in ANT *problematization*. The Government thereafter, put forward a number of proposals motivated by the acknowledgement that obtaining the JCTU's support for the process was necessary against the background concern of an apparent growing militancy within the public service. The Government engaged the JCTU in dialogue because there was a recognition that such a policy could not be implemented without them being involved. Further, the Government could not afford any strikes or disruptions, given the belief that the JCTU had seemingly become more militant, in their agitation for wage increases which the government could not afford.

Why Were Associations Created Between Actors?

In *problematization* according to De Jong (2007) the focal actors of the GJN and the TUN became the MoFP and the JCTU respectively, that determined the set of actors to be involved to address the problems or the issues, that provided the nexus that was shared. The *problematization* process and explicit dimensions of it was represented by the issues that brought the network actors together and drove the ensuing dialogue. Namely, the inability of the economy to sustain rising recurrent expenditures from the public sector wage bill, within the context of a vulnerable and unstable macroeconomic legacy. This also linked to and included the proposed capping of employment emerging from the inability of the Government to pay a rising public sector wage bill, compared to the rate of growth of revenues.

Other issues and options included, the proposed cutting of fifteen thousand (15,000) public sector jobs by the Government seeking to solve its fiscal challenges. The trade unions were not in support of this due to the social implications, even moreso, as the job market was limited and those being made redundant had little labour mobility. These issues cumulatively became the 'Obligatory Passage Point' (OPP) in *problematization,* reflected and representing interests that must be satisfied or treated with, as determined by the focal actors - MoFP and JCTU- which were, in turn, also the points of interaction for all other actors from their respective networks. These focal actors became indispensable and central to the OPP dialogue without which the other actors or networks in turn could not act or obtain what they needed by themselves.

What Caused Their Alignment and Coalescence to Become Stabilized?

In *problematization*, the focal actors worked to form an alliance around the OPP or problem to address it, as all sides had a vested interest in achieving a resolution. Therefore, a mutual convenience or coincidence of interest between the Government and the JCTU was derived from looking rationally and analyzing the situation and coming to an identical conclusion, that what existed was not sustainable and an alternative or adjustment needed to be found.

Regarding the second moment of *interessement*, Callon (1986) posits that actors in the network do not have equal access to each other hence there are nodes in the network which are necessary conduits through which each link in the network must pass, in maintaining and attaining the dynamics of it. The MoFP and the JCTU as focal actors, stabilized the identities of the other actors defined during problematization (De Jong, 2007) and dialogue on the OPP, providing a focus and direction for the other actors (Stalder, 1997) locking them into position in the network. These nodes would work to actively solidify the engagement of other related actor networks around the problems and determine their interest. The *interessement* or locking into position in ANT involved a recognition that actors in turn cannot obtain what they want alone outside of the OPP and must either choose to change direction or remain with the focal actors to attain their objective.

Enrollment is the moment whereby a set of interrelated roles are defined and attributes accepted by the actors through the process of negotiation, building upon the moment of *interessement*. This process allowed other actors the option of exercising choice to either reject or accept these interrelated roles, terms and attributes being defined. Callon (1986, p. 10) describes this process as involving 'trials of strength and tricks' while De Jong (2007, p.7) adds 'persuasion, seduction, consent without discussion, intrigues, propaganda, violence, transaction, interpretation and even physical violence.' The *enrollment* becomes materialized in the creation of the MOU Agreement and associated institutions where the negotiated text becomes an intermediary. This moment would relate to the creation of the text of the MOU Agreement and the related Provisions and commitments agreed in the consensus and the text as a means of inscription .

The MOU Agreement emerged as a focal actor of its own network in which it formed direct relationships with the MoFP and the JCTU that became key network nodes. These still remain as focal points in each of their own

Figure 1. Event State Network: Negotiations Leading to the Public Sector Memorandum of Understanding (MOU)
Adapted from (Miles & Huberman, 1994)

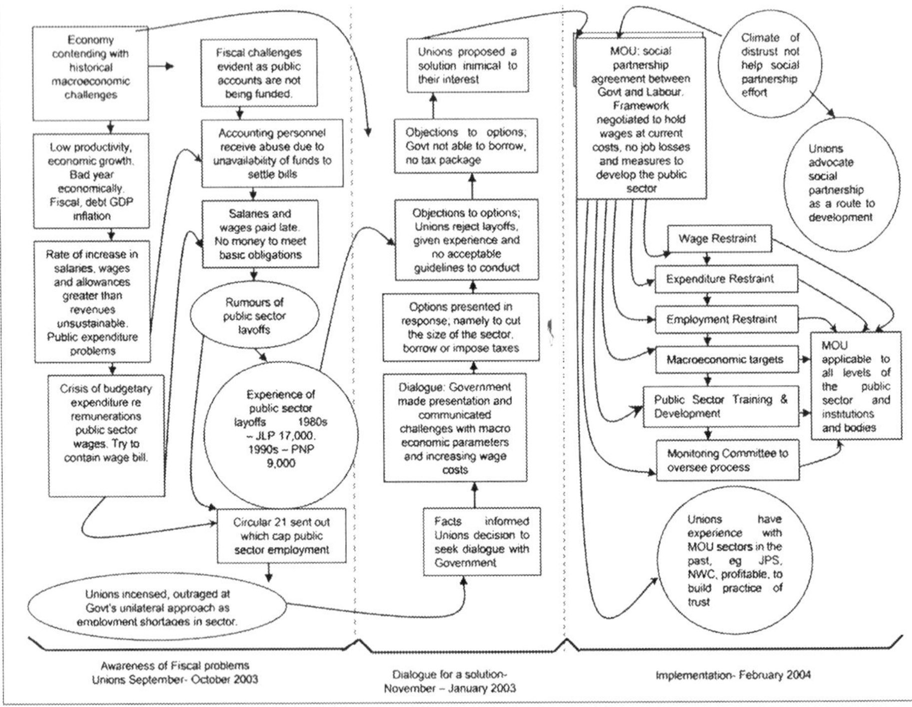

networks but in interacting with the MOU network, became key conduits through which each entity in their respective networks must pass through to link and keep the dynamics of the MOU network going.

In mobilization, the MOU Agreement emerges as a sole macro-social (De Jong, 2007, p. 5) spokesperson through the progressive mobilization of actors around the OPP of the GJN and TUN networks into an MOU network, which renders interessement credible and through enrollment, created alliances (Callon, 1986). This process involves expansion and the engendering of more actor networks around the MOU. It is through the intermediary (Bijker & Law, 1992) or text of the MOU that the actors became locked into the processes of the network. Other actors - namely the ministries and government entities with specific roles - through the cohesion provided by the intermediary, interface with the focal actors of their own networks- MoFP and JCTU, as nodal points for the MOU network of relations.

The text of the MOU Agreement served to inscribe the actors in the MOU network and their cohesion to the process. In addition, it becomes the new discourse of the MOU network and the provisions encapsulate its perspective, being the lens through which all the actors in its network view the world and benchmark their exchanges and network connectivity.

There was a direct relationship between the size of the actor and the size of the network it commanded which conferred status, as well as the number of actors associated with them (Latour, 1992) as the process is replicated. The MOU Agreement acquired a macro social credential (De Jong, 2007) having aligned several actors and their networks into its MOU network, by virtue of them behaving in accordance to its vision of the world with which they have all been successfully inscribed.

Further inscription and institutionalization of the discourse and practice of the MOU network of relations enabled it to attain its true macro social form, which permeated throughout all the ancillary networks of which it was composed, coalescing into a black box (Pinch & Bijker, 1987; Winner, 1993). The actors in the black box became punctualized actors according to Law (1992, p. 385) with a unified voice, as they were subjugated and were no longer able to be considered individually as separates.

The black box defined the margin of manoeuvre enjoyed by the other actors, their desires, position, knowledge and abilities and unified voice (Callon & Latour, 1981) which persisted at various levels throughout adjoining networks. The MOU Agreement became a 'macro social actor seated on black boxes' (De Jong, 2007, p. 9) which evidenced a level of stability, representative of a shared meaning and diminished controversy throughout the entire network of relationships. The MOU Agreement therefore had the authority to 'speak on behalf of those translated elements' (De Jong, 2007, p. 10) having implications for their respective discourses and industrial relations practice in the public sector.

In ANT, power is relationally generated, not monopolistic in character, so each union member and government body had the potential to influence, although it was also embedded in another network of relations and institutions. Furthermore, there was no monopolistic power exerted by any one actor in the network, although there was one voice amongst them. The network was therefore subject to instability driven by 'shifting alliances' (Tatnall & Gilding, 2005, p. 4; Williams-Jones & Graham, 2003, p. 273) which needed constant maintenance. ANT conceptualizes power as being shared, demonstrated in the

MOU network by the modality of the partnership dialogue within the MOU institution of the Monitoring Committee which operated through consensus decision making.

What Drives Translation So That It Has the Potential to Proliferate or Destroy the Network?

The actors in the MOU network are in constant motion relationally, changing continuously, influencing and reflexively shaping operations processes and performance accordingly, so that power is considered to be generated, relationally and distributively (Law & Hassard, 1999). The heterogeneous nature of the network with inanimate and animate actors engenders 'semiotic relationality' (Law, 2007, p. 7) as the network elements define and shape one another with 'continuous relational interplay' (Shaikh & Cordello, 2006, p. 7). The actor-networks are in constant interaction, as 'immutable mobiles', (Law & Singleton, 1995, p. 6) and as 'social order' (Williams-Jones & Graham, 2003, p. 5) develops through these continuous translations that occur at various levels, various institutions are generated and associated with the MOU within the network of relationships.

However, the *enrollment* of actors is not guaranteed due to the possible interference by alternatives, external interactions or other competing concerns. By divergence, translation incorporates a new actor into a network, which involves capturing the alignment of the newcomer with respect to its location in the network of which it is coming from. The additional network elements are then linked and brought in, in addition to the effort to sustain the existing relations. Convergence on the other hand, represents the reverse of this. In translation, the inscription from the MOU network as the external network, is being undertaken (Shaikh & Cordello, 2006) and at the same time is being represented in the other actor networks recursively, creating a type of circularity as each actor interprets and defines for itself, other relations in the network (Callon, 1991). An example of this, is where the provisions of the MOU Agreement become inscribed in different ministries with their own network relations, such as the Ministry of Health, which began to capture or align the Regional Health Authorities within their own network of relations, appropriating its position and into relations and interactions at various levels, in turn recursively influencing the process at its origin. The actor has a choice to decide whether to enroll in the network, or as a result of interference by other actors or competing concerns and beliefs or opt to diverge and not to enroll.

In the case of discontinued translation, an example of divergence occurred in the MOU network when the Nurses Association of Jamaica (NAJ) which initially was enrolled in the JCTU and subsequently the MOU network, chose to disassociate itself from the JCTU and witdraw its membership from the organization. ANT interprets this as an incomplete *enrollment* in translation, contested within the NAJ, a member union of the JCTU network which, due to other external concerns, decided to diverge, opting to reject the locking into position process of *interessement* towards *mobilization*. Divergence in terms of losing the NAJ as a member, was attributed to the lack of cohesiveness or unity of the JCTU and the feeling that the MOU might not serve their interests. It was noted that the MOU precipitated a new approach to collective bargaining which would result in taking away the opportunity for all union groups to be at the bargaining table which was a challenge for them.

The Discourse Dimension of the MOU Actor Network

The text of the MOU Agreement, as a component of the discourse of the MOU can be viewed as an intermediary, which is communicated (Bijker & Law, 1992) throughout the MOU network and becomes the inscription that adds cohesion to the multiple interactions and assists the growth, development and grounding of it. The MOU, having a discourse of its own, is capable of attaining a 'black box' status and stability within the network of relations that it creates for itself. Having followed the actors and explored the mechanics of the network infrastructure behind the black box (De Jong, 2007) of the MOU social partnership, Critical Discourse Analysis (CDA) facilitates an exploration of discourse included as a moment in the network relations of power, using discourse as the unit of analysis to explore the inner workings of network connectivity revealed in text.

Social partnerships can be conceptualized as actor networks, which presents the need to identify or prescribe an approach that can adequately explore and extract insights useful for understanding the development of the networks within social partnership. As the sociology of *translation,* ANT provides a tool to explore the dynamics of network construction, how alliances are built and to trace the interactions at various levels of the MOU network, revealing the implications for its durability over time. Through the ANT construct, the MOU Agreement as an actor can represent its own discourse, having implications for the characteristics of the translations of the network, the discourses of the other participating actor-networks and the nature of the interface with pre-existing discourses, institutions and social processes.

The theoretical framework of ANT assisted to construct how the MOU developed, clarify the interplay and interactions of the network, its dynamics and how various actors coalesced. The MOU Agreement became an actor in its own right, enlarging in scope and the ability to enrol and solicit actors and represent them (Murdoch, 1995) as an indicator of its power, which was derived relationally (Callon, 1986). The MOU Agreement within the ANT framework is not deemed passive, but has, through its provisions and as an actor has influenced the discourses of institutions, cultural change and furthered human relationships, interactions, and associations amongst and between the key partners of the alliance as well as throughout the public sector and trade union networks.

Having applied ANT to the development of the MOU Agreement as a network, the agreement reached in text, represents a negotiated discourse, fixed or inculcated within the Agreement, which gives the network its anchor. It is through the discourse emanating from the text provisions which infiltrates, coopts and integrates other actors within the MOU network of relations that the network is sustained and used as a vehicle to enlarge it through the four moments of Problematization, Interessement, Enrollment, and Mobilization

As an independent actor within ANT with its own discourse, the MOU Agreement interfaces with existing actor networks, their discourses, institutions and social processes, to create a new network around the MOU. Giving rise to contests of power in the realm of discourses, institutions or human agency, the MOU Agreement emerges from this interface as the macro social actor, having attained the equilibrium of a black box throughout the MOU network of relations.

These contests of discourse also contribute to the fluidity and dynamics of the network which although settled, is circular and open to new translations, so that MOU discourse becomes inscribed or inculcated within the network, giving it its anchor. The ANT approach affords an examination of the power relations in the MOU network created at the interface of the actors and translated into the numerous social processes involved in the implementation of the Agreement. With respect to the interplay of the actors and their discourses, the modality as to how one discourse is able to interface and exert influence, with sufficient power to affect the practices identified with another discourse, also comes to the surface and can be expressed in discursive outcomes.

Beyond ANT, the MOU Agreement then represents its own discourse as an actor, with the intermediary of text as the discourse of the MOU, seeking to inscribe other actor-networks into the MOU network, to achieve black box and macro social status. The positioning of discourse as a moment in the network allows the use of discourse as the unit of analysis and CDA methodology, to explore in depth the nature of the actor interactions and connectivities during the process of translation, portrayed in dimensions of discourse.

Discourse and Language

Several authors have rendered their own perspective on what discourse and language means. Foucauldian tradition (Jorgenson & Phillips 2002, p.14) viewed discourse as systems of knowledge (Wodak & Meyer, 2001, 9; Gee 1996, 101; Fairclough Gee, J. P. (2004). *An introduction to discourse analysis: Theory and method* (2nd ed.). United Kingdom: Routledge. 2001) which informed the social and constituted power. Harvey (1996) echoed similar views by focusing on how words and actions frame and represent spaces based on power relations (Richardson and Jensen 2003). Habermas (1984) regarded discourse as communicative action and as ideological practice while Thompson (1984) related structures of discourse with structures of society (van Dijk 2001).

These perspectives also have synergies with Frow (1985, p. 200) for whom the discursive, socially constructs and distinguishes reality and the symbolic. Discourse (as the study of talk and text) and language are routes into the study of meaning (Wetherall, et.al., 2001) and Gee (1996, p. 26) is of the view that discourse uses language to identify and position oneself with and within a "socially meaningful group" (MacKay, 2007). There is the merger of "ways of talking, listening, writing, and reading," with "acting, interacting, believing, valuing, and feeling," into patterns associated with a recognizable social network or affinity group (Gee, 1996, p. 131).

From all these perspectives, discourse as text and language provides data and affords the theorizations of that data, to interpret, explain and analyze social behaviour. Language conceptualized as a form of social practice and the "critical" dimension of discourse analysis, attempts to make human beings aware of the reciprocal influences of language and social structure of which they are normally unaware (Fairclough 1989; Van Dijk 1993; Wodak 1989).

Discourse: Norman Fairclough

The concept of discourse advocated by Norman Fairclough includes the properties of text, their production distribution and consumption, the socio-cognitive processes of producing and interpreting them, social practice in various institutions and the relationship of this practice to power relations and hegemonic projects at the societal level (Fairclough,1992).

Discourses constitute one moment of the social alongside other moments, for example, inter personal relationships which internalize each other and are dialectically related (Fairclough 2003). Discourse shapes society and culture from the perspective that every single instance of language use reproduces, shapes or transforms society and culture, including power relations. The boundaries of social life result in different domains for the social use of language. The subsequent interactions and fluidity between them emerges as a hybridism that involves dialectic shaping, commensurate with struggles in the construction of identity in discourse and in reflecting ways of representing the world and oneself (Chouliaraki & Fairclough, 1999).

Fairclough (2003) describes discourse as consisting of the following elements described below:

- **Representation:** How things are or have been.
- **Imaginaries:** How things might or could be.
- **Social Practice:** Social practices and networks of social practices. Synthesis of activities, subjects, social relations, instruments, objects, space-time, values, forms of consciousness. Imaginaries enacted as actual networks of practices becoming real activities, subjects, social relations etc.
- **Enactments:** Materialization of discourses-economic discourses, materialized in instruments of economic production "hardware" and "software" management systems etc. Discoursal/semiotic discourses become enacted as genre.
- **Discourses:** As imaginaries inculcated as new ways of being new identities, people coming into their "own" discourses to position themselves inside them, to act, think and talk, seeing themselves in terms of "new discourses."
- **Inculcation:** Discourses are dialectic and inculcated as material aspects, not only in styles and ways of using language, but are also materialized in bodies, postures, gestures ways of moving and so forth.

- **Dialectical:** Reflexivity- for those enactments and inculcation in social life, as people act and interact with networks of social practices interpret and represent to themselves and each other what they do and these interpretations and representations shape and reshape what they do.

In the study of discourse, every text is seen as being embedded in a context which in turn, requires the study of differential relations to the social, political or other context from which the basis of interpretation is derived (Titscher, et.al., 2000, p. 24). Fairclough and Chouliaraki (1999) also emphasize that the analysis of a particular discourse, as a piece of discursive practice, focuses upon text production, consumption and distribution. These social processes require embedding in the economic, political and institutional contexts from within which the discourse originated and which may explain the social constructions of responses in text production.). Based on these conceptualizations, Fairclough (1992) espouses the use of texts as units of analyses and forms of social activity within the operations in the network that can reveal relations of power. In the process of analyzing discourse and the influences involved in the production and consumption of language, verbally and in text, there is an intrinsic connection between how language is used in its context - historical, cultural, political and social, in time and space - the nature of the social interaction and how this in turn influences social relations, practices - discourse.

Text and Discourse

Text is defined as a communicative event by Titscher, et.al. (2000) and consists of material objects as an outcome of representational practices, using a variety of signifying actors which contribute individually to the specific meaning of text (Kress & Van Leeuwen, 1996). Text also refers to any product whether written or spoken that is simultaneously constituting and representing, relations and identities (Fairclough, 1992).

Language is conceptualized as a form of social practice and there is a reciprocity of influence between language and social structure (Fairclough, 1989; Van Dijk, 1993; Wodak, 1989). The boundaries of social life result in different domains for the social use of language that has formative and transformative effects on culture and society and relations of power (Fairclough, 2003). Language is conceptualized as a form of social practice and attempts to make human beings aware of the reciprocal influences of language and social structure of which they are normally unaware (Fairclough 1989; Van Dijk 1993; Wodak 1989).

The concept of social practice facilitates the oscillation between the perspective of social structure, social action and agency (Chouliaraki & Fairclough, 1999).

In the study of discourse, every text is seen as being embedded in a context which in turn, requires the study of differential relations to the social, political or other context from which the basis of interpretation is derived (Titscher, et.al., 2000, 24). Text refers to any product whether written or spoken that is simultaneously constituting and representing, relations and identities (Fairclough, 1992). Fairclough and Chouliaraki (1999) also emphasize that the analysis of a particular discourse, as a piece of discursive practice, focuses upon text production, consumption and distribution. These social processes require embedding in the particular economic, political and institutional context from within which the discourse originated and which may explain the social constructions of responses in text production.

Based on the conceptualization of discourse, Fairclough (1992, 2001) espouses the use of texts as units of analyses and forms of social activity within the operations in the network that can reveal relations of power. The MOU text is semiotic, as it has redefined levels of relationships between the partners to the Agreement, affecting various networks of practices, with tangible and intangible outcomes. The concept of social practice facilitates the oscillation between the perspective of social structure, social action and agency (Chouliaraki & Fairclough, 1999).

Discourse shapes society and culture dialectically, from the perspective that every single instance of language use reproduces shapes or transforms society and culture, including power relations.

These perspectives also have synergies with Frow (1985) for whom the discursive, socially constructs and distinguishes reality and the symbolic. Discourse (as the study of talk and text) and language are routes into the study of meaning (Wetherall et.al., 2001) and Gee (1996) is of the view that discourse uses language to identify and position oneself with and within a 'socially meaningful group' (MacKay, 2007). There is the merger of 'ways of talking, listening, writing, and reading,' with 'acting, interacting, believing, valuing, and feeling,' into patterns associated with a recognizable social network or affinity group (Gee, 1996). Discourse as a form of social behaviour, is multidimensional, (Fairclough, 1992, p. 5) and dialectic, (Harvey & Braun,

1996) being shaped both by the structures within which the developments take place and also by the agency of the actors seeking to influence them.

Discourse as a form of social behaviour, is multidimensional, (Fairclough, 1992) and dialectic, (Harvey & Braun, 1996) being shaped both by the structures within which the developments take place and by the agency of the actors seeking to influence them (Fairclough, 2005). From all these perspectives, discourse as text and language provides data and affords the theorizations of that data, to interpret, explain and analyze social behaviour.

Norman Fairclough's Critical Discourse Analysis (CDA) methodology amalgamates some of the aforementioned aspects, as well as examines discourse, text, language and their manifestation in the realm of the social, social theory and critical linguistics. This multidisciplinary understanding of discourse is merged with a critical dimension, which has its base within Critical Theory.

The concept of discourse advocated by Fairclough (1992; 2000; 2001; 2003; 2003a) includes the properties of text, their production, distribution and consumption, the socio-cognitive processes of producing and interpreting them, social practice in various institutions and the relationship of this practice to power relations and hegemonic projects at the societal level (Fairclough, 1992). Discourses constitute one moment of the social alongside other moments, for example, inter personal relationships which internalize each other and are dialectically related (Fairclough, 2003). Discourse shapes society and culture from the perspective that every single instance of language use reproduces, shapes or transforms society and culture, including power relations. The boundaries of social life result in different domains for the social use of language.

CRITICAL DISCOURSE ANALYSIS (CDA)

Critical theory has implications for a social theory of modernity related to new modalities of power, characteristic of globalization. Nowlan (2001), highlights the transformative aspect of critical inquiry, emancipating the old and entrenching new social facts which transform the agents, their ideals and institutional forms, as it is 'practically' necessary for one to effect change using institutional means (Roderick, 1983). Critical social theorists have positioned language in their theories and dialectical views of society, being concerned with the social constructs- material and cultural- as revealed in the discourse. Other authors have stressed discourse in the analysis of power interests, encouraging self-reflection and criticism on the part of the researcher and in the undertaking of social research (Toolan, 2002; Chouliaraki & Fairclough, 1999; Foucault, 1980).

Four key attributes of critical theory (Alvesson & Deetz, 2000, p. 8) have been determined to which CDA relates accordingly, in that:

- History, culture and societal position influence beliefs and actions;
- All inevitability, sole claims to truth (Alvesson & Deetz, 2000, p. 8) and alternative knowledge should be viewed with scepticism and be challenged;
- All normative and ordinary conventions, cultural traditions and methods of perceiving, conceiving and acting and the accepted assumptions underlying them, should be identified and challenged 'encouraging productive dissension' (Alvesson & Deetz, 2000, p. 9); and finally,
- Alternatives should be explored and imagined even though they may disrupt routines and overturn established orders.

Influences from Critical Theory are reconstituted within CDA, which represents an amalgam of concepts and theories which introduces tensions (Chouliaraki & Fairclough, 1999) between them, being drawn from multiple philosophical approaches and disciplines. Fairclough's CDA gains a distinction as it marries discourse analysis with critique (Wickham & Kendal, 2008) and uses a multidisciplinary ensemble of techniques for the study of textual practice and language use, - as social and cultural practices (Fairclough, 1992). CDA provides theory and method to study the relationship between discourse, social and cultural development in different social domains (Wodak & Fairclough, 1997).

Contributions to CDA include Volosinov's (1973) work, that the complexity and quality of social interactions and social structure depends upon ongoing instantiation and structures that are contested. Other contributions interwoven into CDA include, Mikhail Bakhtin's 'intertextuality' and the 'texture of texts'. Hallidayan functional systemic linguistics theory (Fairclough, 2003, p. 24; Halliday, 1978) and its "ideational" function which is "contained in every text through its representation of experience and the world" (Titscher et al., 2000, p. 148) is also interwoven.

Discourse

The concept of discourse based on Norman Fairclough's CDA methodology, is Foucauldian, merging the importance of the textual and social within a critical epistemological examination of discourse. Fairclough (2003) describes discourse as involving representation –as how things are or imaginaries- as they could be, social practices, enactments- (as materializations of discourse or enacted as genre) as discourse- of imaginaries being inculcated as new ways of being and identities).

Discourse therefore does not just reflect or represent social entities and relations, they construct or constitute them...historical change, different discourses combine under particular social conditions to produce a new, complex discourse... any discursive event (or instance of discourse) is seen as being simultaneously a piece of text, an instance of discursive practice and instance of social practice.

The 'text' dimension attends to the language analysis of texts. The 'discursive practice' dimension, like 'interaction' in the 'text -and- interaction' view of discourse, specifies the nature of the processes of text production and interpretation...and how they are combined. The 'social practice' dimension attends to issues of concern in social analysis such as the institutional and organizational circumstances of the discursive event and how that shapes the nature of the discursive practice and the constitutive constructive effects of discourse (Fairclough, 1992, p.4).

The subsequent interactions and fluidity between them emerge as a hybridism that involves dialectic shaping, commensurate with struggles in the construction of identity in discourse and in reflecting ways of representing the world and oneself (Chouliaraki & Fairclough, 1999). These elements and their relationships within discourse as explained by Fairclough (2001) reveals the linkages, interactions between elements and the complexity of the relationships, within networks that are dialectical in nature.

The overriding objective of discourse analysis, on this view, is not simply the analysis of discourse per se, but analysis of the dialectical relations between discourse and non-discourse elements of the social, in order to reach a better understanding of these complex relations (including how changes in discourse can cause changes in other elements). There is the internalization of moments without any reduction or loss of their identity (Fairclough, 2003).

But if we are to analyze relations between discourse and non-discourse elements, we must obviously see them as ontologically (and not just epistemologically, analytically) different elements of the social. They are different, but they are not discrete – that is, they are dialectically related, in the sense that elements 'internalize' other elements, without being reducible to them (Fairclough, 2005). Broadly speaking, text becomes just one part (Fairclough, 1989) of discourse and social practices that incorporate dialectically, ways of acting and actions, ways of being and representation and ways of identification in terms of the personal and in relation to societal position (Fairclough, 2001). More comprehensively, the language of texts also includes the systems and regulations that govern the text and processes which the text itself governs (Fairclough, 2003).

Society and culture are shaped and dialectically related to discourse, from the perspective that every single instance of language use reproduces shapes or transforms society and culture including power relations. According to Fairclough (2000) discourse is connected with social practices in three ways. Firstly, it is a part of the social activity within the practice which involves the use of language in a particular way. Secondly, discourse is a part of representation, as social actors produce representations of other practices as well as their own in the course of the activity within a particular practice. As these in turn, are incorporated into their own practices, different social actors will again represent them differently, depending on how they are positioned within the practice. Hence representation is the social construction of practices including reflexive self-construction, by also entering and being shaped by other social processes and practices. Thirdly, discourse is entailed in 'ways of being' by the constituting of identities which are partly semiotically constructed (Fairclough, 2000). The constructive effects in relation to social identities, subject positions, and inter personal relationships knowledge and belief systems, relate to language which has interactions within discourse according to the three moments or functions of language, which relate to, identity", are "relational", and "ideational in character.

These moments combine corresponding to three functions of language and dimensions of meaning which coexist and interact in all discourse namely the, "identity", "relational" and "ideational" functions of language (Fairclough 1992) reflecting the constructive effects in relation to social identities, subject positions and relationships between people and systems of knowledge and belief. This multidisciplinary understanding of discourse is merged with a critical dimension which has its theoretical base within Critical Theory of a Marxist tradition.

Four key attributes of critical theory (Alvesson & Deetz, 2000, p. 8) have been determined to which CDA relates accordingly, in that:

1. History, culture and societal position influence beliefs and actions;
2. All inevitability, sole claims to truth and alternative knowledge should be viewed skeptically and challenged;
3. All normative and ordinary conventions, cultural traditions and methods of perceiving, conceiving and acting and the accepted assumptions underlying them, should be identified and challenged, "encouraging productive dissension" (Alvesson & Deetz, 2000, p. 9); and finally,
4. Alternatives should be explored and imagined even though they may disrupt routines and overturn established orders.

Critical social theorists have positioned language in their theories and dialectical views of society, being concerned with the social constructs- material and cultural- as revealed in the discourse. Other authors have stressed discourse in the analysis of power interests, encouraging self-reflection and criticism on the part of the researcher and in the undertaking of social research (Toolan, 2002; Chouliaraki & Fairclough, 1999; Foucault, 1980).

Critical Discourse Analysis (CDA)

These influences from Critical Theory are reconstituted within CDA, which represents an amalgam of concepts and theories which introduces tensions (Chouliaraki & Fairclough, 1999) between them, being drawn from multiple philosophical approaches and disciplines. Fairclough's CDA gains a distinction as it marries discourse analysis with critique (Wickham &Kendall, 2007) and uses a multidisciplinary ensemble of techniques for the study of textual practice and language use, (as social and cultural practices) (Fairclough, 1992). CDA provides theory and method to study the relationship between discourse, social and cultural development in different social domains (Fairclough & Wodak, 1997).

Contributions to CDA include Volosinov's (1973) work, that the complexity and quality of social interactions and social structure depends upon ongoing instantiation and structures that are contested. Other contributions interwoven into CDA include, Mikhail Bakhtin 'intertextual' approach (Fairclough, 1992), Hallidayan functional systemic linguistics theory (Fairclough 2003, 24; Halliday, 1978) and its "ideational" function which is "contained in every text through its representation of experience and the world" (Titscher et al. 2000, p. 148). CDA however goes beyond linguistic study to analyze language itself not the constituent units (Mills, 2004) which according to Fairclough (2003, p. 2), "is an irreducible part of social life, dialectically interconnected with other elements of social life, so that social analysis and research always has to take into account language."

Therefore language, as discussed in the work of Michel Foucault (Fairclough, 2003, p. 2), is an irreducible part of social life, being dialectically connected with other elements of social life and this is foundational in the considerations of language in social analysis and research. Within CDA constructs, language is conceived of as a social force and a vehicle through which ideological dominance is sustained and established legitimizing relations of organized power and inequities of social power relations (Fairclough 2003, 9; Weiss & Wodak, 2002, p.14).

There is a role for discourse in capturing the interactions between and within social structures inclusive of social action and agency (Mills, 2004, p. 127), in "ways of representing" social life (discourses), enacted in specific "ways of acting" (genres or social practices) and inculcated in certain "ways of being" (certain styles) Fairclough (2003). Discourses then, are "potent causal agents in their own right" (Mills, 2004, p. 10) enacted and developed within a social context (which determines, contributes and sustains its existence), which is then circulated as a function of institutions and social context.

The CDA model has incorporated Foucauldian functions of discourse specifically in areas such as the:

- constitutive nature of discourse, which includes the social and "objects" as social subjects;
- primacy of interdiscursivity and intertextuality (See appendix A) which defines a discursive practice by its relations with others and extracting them in complex ways;
- discursive nature of power;
- political nature of discourse, as there are power struggles in and over discourse (Fairclough 1992, p. 56); and the
- discursive nature of social change by changing discursive practices which are important elements in that change. (Fairclough 1992, p. 56: Mills, 2004).

Critical discourse analysis sees discourse-language used in speech and writing as a form of social practice with a dialectical relationship, where the discursive event is shaped by situations, institutions and social structures, but in return, it also shapes them (Fairclough & Wodak, 1997, P. 55).

CDA also draws on Gramsci's concept of hegemony in that, the way power operates is by dominating and shaping the consciousness and the oppressive aspects. There are also the reproductive aspects which seek to empower marginalized groups and encourages the consideration of the socio-political role (Zou & Trueba, 2002), central in critical theory and useful as a framework for conceptualizing and investigating political and ideological dimensions of discursive practice. Hegemony as a political concept can be used to analyze orders of discourse (Fairclough 1992). According to Weiss and Wodak (2002), CDA positions and methodology, synthesizes both linguistic and sociological concepts to better analyze and explain complex interactions and interrelations between and amongst the communicators of social life. Fairclough's Critical Discourse Analysis.

As a methodology that deconstructs discourse, CDA has gained in popular usage to expose and also contend with hidden power relations as reflected in the relationship between talk and text, discourse practice and their sociological manifestations in context. By providing an associated set of methods to explore perceptions sensitive to context, CDA is 'fluid' enough (Waller, 2009) to be used in conjunction with other types of flexible theories and methodologies and ANT represents one of these.

Fairclough's methodology is based on three components - description, interpretation and explanation and these three interrelated processes of analyses are tied to three inter related dimensions of discourse of which language represents just one level of analysis. The dynamics of the discourse according to Waller (2006), lies in the comparative analysis of the other co equals in the system, that of discursive practices and socio-cultural practices. Together, these dimensions provide an understanding of the social relations and actions derived through continuous movement between the various levels with each requiring a different kind of analysis as the dimensions are interdependent (Janks, 1999).

However, Fairclough (1992) notes that there are socio cognitive dimensions of text production and interpretation which are constrained by available resources – internalized social structures, norms, orders of discourse, conventions, constituted through past social practice, as well as by the specific nature of the social practice itself. These elements determine what resources are drawn upon and how, whether in a normative, creative, acquiescent or oppositional manner.

In the process of analyzing discourse and the types of influence involved in the production and consumption of language, verbally and in text, CDA reveals an intrinsic connection between how language is used in its context - historical, cultural, political and social, in time and space - the nature of the social interaction and how this in turn influences social relations, practices and discourse.

The role of discourse in hegemonic struggles between strategies, their successful implementation and the development, promotion and dissemination of them for social change, is captured by "strategic" critique (Waller, 2006). This can relate to how strategies are pursued by groups of social agents, in this case the Partners to the MOU Agreement and the strategic content and direction, employed to, for example, move the public sector away from its customary practice and behavior to embrace MOU discourse and practice.

REFERENCES

Alvesson, M., & Deetz, S. (2000). *Doing critical management research*. Sage Publications. doi:10.4135/9781849208918

Callon, M. (1986). 1986: Some elements of a sociology of translation: domestication of the scallops and the fisherman of St Brieuc bay. In J. Law (Ed.), *Power, action and belief: a new sociology of knowledge* (pp. 196–232). London: Routledge.

Callon, M., & Latour, B. (1981). Unscrewing the big Leviathan: how actors macro-structure reality and how sociologists help them to do so. In K. Knorr-Cetina & A.V. Cicourel (Eds.), Advances in social theory and methodology: Toward an integration of micro-and macro-sociologies (pp. 277-303). Boston: Routledge.

De Jong, B. (2007). *Shedding Light on the darkness: Using the Actor-Network theory to analyse the distribution of power*. Paper for the 47th Europe Regional Science Association.

Fairclough, N. (1992). *Discourse and Social Change*. Cambridge, UK: Polity Press.

Fairclough, N. (2001). The dialectics of discourse. *Textus, 14*(2), 231–242. Retrieved from http://www.ling.lancs.ac.uk/staff/norman/2001a.doc

Fairclough, N. (2003). *Analysing discourse: Textual analysis for social research*. London: Routledge. doi:10.4324/9780203697078

Gee, J. P. (1996). *Social linguistics and literacies: Ideology in discourses* (3rd ed.). London: Routledge.

Gee, J. P. (2004). *An introduction to discourse analysis: Theory and method* (2nd ed.). Routledge.

Habermas, J. (1984). *The theory of communicative action* (Vol. 1). Boston: Beacon Press.

Halliday, M. A. (1978). *Language as social semiotic: The social interpretation of language and meaning*. London: Arnold.

Latour, B. (1992). Where Are the Missing Masses? The Sociology of a Few Mundane Artefacts. In *Shaping technology/building society: Studies in sociotechnical change*. MIT Press.

Law, J. (1991). *A sociology of monsters: essays on power, technology and domination*. London: Routledge.

Law, J. (1992). Notes on the theory of the actor-network: Ordering, strategy, and heterogeneity. *Systems Practice*, *5*(4), 379–393. doi:10.1007/BF01059830

Law, J., & Hassard, J. (1999). *Actor network theory and after* (1st ed.). Oxford, UK: Blackwell.

Law, J., & Singleton, V. (2005). Object lessons. *Organization*, *12*(3), 331–355. doi:10.1177/1350508405051270

Lowe, A. (2001). After ANT: An illustrative discussion of the implications for qualitative accounting case research. *Accounting, Auditing & Accountability Journal*, *14*(3), 327–351. doi:10.1108/EUM0000000005519

MacKay, T. (2007). *Gee's theory of D/discourse and ESL research in teaching English as a second language: Implications for the mainstream*. University of Manitoba.

Murdoch, J. (2005). *Post-structuralist geography: a guide to relational space*. London: Sage Publications.

Pinch, T., & Bijker, W. J. (1984). The social construction of facts and artefacts: Or how the sociology of technology might benefit each other. *Social Studies of Science*, *14*(3), 399–441. doi:10.1177/030631284014003004

Richardson, T., & Jensen, O. B. (2003). Linking discourse and space: Towards a cultural sociology of space in analysing spatial policy discourses. *Urban Studies (Edinburgh, Scotland), 40*(1), 7–22. doi:10.1080/0042098022008013l

Ritzer, G. (2006). *The Blackwell encyclopedia of sociology*. Maidenhead, MA: Blackwell Publishing. doi:10.1111/b.9781405124331.2006.x

Shaikh, M., & Cordello, A. (2006). *From epistemology to ontology: challenging the constructed truth of ANT*. Working Paper Series 143. London: London School of Economics and Political Science. DOI: doi:10.13140/RG.2.1.1546.5367

Stalder, F. (1997). *Actor-network-theory and communication networks: toward convergence. Paper for discussion*. University of Toronto.

Tatnall, A., & Gilding, A. (2005). Actor-Network Theory and Information Systems Research, *Proceedings of the 10th Australasian Conference on Information Systems*.

Thompson, J. B. (1984). *Studies in the Theory of Ideology*. University of California Press.

Van Dijk, T. A. (1993). Principles of Critical Discourse Analysis. *Discourse & Society, 4*(2), 249–283. doi:10.1177/0957926593004002006

Volosinov, V. N. (1973). *Marxism and the Philosophy of Language*. Cambridge, MA: Harvard University Press.

Waller, L. G. (2006). *Introducing Fairclough's critical discourse analysis methodology for analyzing Caribbean social problems: going beyond systems, resources, social action, social practices and forces of structure or lack thereof as units of analysis*. Retrieved from: https://www.academia.edu/28963268/Introducing_Faircloughs_Critical_Discourse_Analysis_Methodology_for_Analyzing_Caribbean_Social_Problems_Going_beyond_systems_resources_social_action_social_practices_and_forces_of_structure_or_lack_thereof_as_units_of_analysis

Waller, L. G. (2009). *The role of discourse in ICT for development: Lessons from Jamaica*. VDM Publishing.

Weiss, G., & Wodak, R. (Eds.). (2002). *Theory and interdisciplinarity in critical discourse analysis*. Palgrave Macmillan.

Wetherell, M., Taylor, S., & Yates, S. J. (2001). *Discourse theory and practice: A reader*. London: Sage Publications Ltd.

Williams-Jones, B., & Graham, J. E. (2003). Actor-network theory: A tool to support ethical analysis of commercial genetic testing. *New Genetics & Society*, *22*(3), 271–296. doi:10.1080/1463677032000147225 PMID:15115034

Winner, L. (1993). Upon opening the black box and finding it empty: Social constructivism and the Philosophy of Technology. *Science, Technology & Human Values*, *18*(3), 362–378. doi:10.1177/016224399301800306

Wodak, R. (Ed.). (1989). *Language, power and ideology: Studies in political discourse* (Vol. 7). John Benjamins Publishing Company. doi:10.1075/ct.7.11wod

Wodak, R., & Meyer, M. (Eds.). (2009). *Methods for Critical Discourse Analysis* (2nd ed.). Sage Publications.

Chapter 7
MOU Convergence:
Public Sector Discourse and Practice

ABSTRACT

The origin and elements contributing to the emergent characteristics of "traditional" public sector discourse and practice are explored contextualized to the Jamaican state. Dimensions of these traditional characteristics are subsequently altered and contested in the process of the public sector actor network being translated through convergence into the MOU actor network of relations. Text, representative of struggle, and discoursal contests emerge, reflective of the rigour of the convergence process. Texts reveal outcomes in terms of governance for the sector as the public sector responds to the inscription as well as embracing new genres and social practices with the operationalization and inculcation of MOU discourse and practice. CDA is valued as an approach to examine and probe the nature of the connectivity in and between actor networks of the MOU social partnership and reveal the implications for the traditional discourse and practice of the public sector.

INTRODUCTION

In exploring the MOU construed as an actor network, ANT provided an explanation as to the MOU network's mechanism and relations, being 'a social construction of social relations' (Lowe, 2001) and the dynamics operable within it. The MOU Agreement, given ANT's ontology is enabled to represent its own discourse as an actor, with the intermediary of text as

DOI: 10.4018/978-1-5225-8961-7.ch007

the discourse of the MOU, seeking to inscribe other actor-networks into the MOU network, to achieve black box and macro social status.

The MOU actor network emerged as black box consisting of "punctualized actors" according to Law (1992, p. 385) to the point of having one voice by means of accession to the dominant discourse, whereby authority is given for the macro social focal actor to "speak or act on behalf of another actor or force" (Law, 1991, p. 151). Winner (1993, p. 365) indicates that the term black box 'in both technical and social science parlance is a device or system that, for convenience, is described solely in terms of its inputs and outputs, and one need not understand anything about what goes on inside such black boxes'.

Moving Forward

Discourse as a unit of analysis, has value by its use to reveal, deconstruct and examine relationships and the practice of power in the connectivity of the MOU network and within the black box that are now brought to light and by which the nature of the inner fabric of social partnership power relationships can be observed. The nature of the struggle between the different discursive practices and discursive endowments of the actors, have to become engaged in the derivation of consensus, modulated and encapsulated within the 'black box' of network interactions. This has implications for the durability of arrangements made. The positioning of discourse as a moment in the actor network provides for the use of discourse as text, as a unit of analysis and CDA methodology, to explore in depth the nature of the actor network interactions and connectivities during the process of translation, portrayed in dimensions of discourse and text.

Within the formation of the MOU network of relations, translation and network strategies for change required discourse and narratives that would be operationalized, enacted or inscribed as new ways of being, new identities and materialized as new ways in space and time (Fairclough 2005).

Several themes and implications arise, in probing the black box of network interaction revealing the nature of the interface between the traditional public sector discourse and that of the MOU discourse.

The MOU emerging as the macro social actor influences representation, social practice, enactments, identities, etc., all played out in the realm of the struggle and inner dynamics of the connectivity or the discoursal linkages, that determine whether the traditional actor networks converge or diverge or become stabilized within the MOU black box of network interaction.

The contextual development, institutional and structural determinants of the 'traditional' public sector discourse are discussed which became contested in convergence within the MOU actor network. Several themes were foregrounded with implications for public sector structures and institutions in response to the imperatives of the discourse of the macro-social MOU Agreement actor network.

CONSTRUCTING TRADITIONAL PUBLIC SECTOR DISCOURSE

Many scholars and academics have studied various dimensions of the public sector of Jamaica, (Isaacs, 2002, 2004, 2004a ; Jones, 1974, 1992, 1996 ; Mills, 1970,1997 ; Munroe, 1987, 1992 ; Nettleford, 2002 ; St Hill, 1970, 1990) and these outcomes will not be restated. However, some of these studies connect intertextually and interdiscursively with the findings to strengthen the scope of understanding and deductive positioning implicated by the context.

The Public Service

Regarding government administration, the Jamaican Constitution defines the Public Service as the service of the Crown in a civil capacity which includes all agencies that are part of the Civil Service, public enterprises established by Acts of Parliament and companies incorporated under the Companies Act, where the state or one of its agencies has a majority or controlling interest and which by law, execute policy. Despite being unable to divorce Jamaica's institutional endowment in the post-independence period from its pre-independence and colonial experience (Schobergh, 2006), in the 21st century, the Public Service remains responsible for government's administration, service delivery and to fulfill expectations of good governance in policy implementation. The Westminster legacy has left a discourse and has framed mechanisms and institutions that have influenced the society's perception and acceptance of standards of good governance while, establishing norms based on democratic principles.

The Civil Service

The Civil Service formed within the colonial dispensation were seen as "colonially conditioned bureaucracies', efficient as far as they serviced requirements of a 'law and order' oriented government (Mills, 1970). The civil servant was regarded as having skills in paper passing, assembling papers for decisions, producing long literary minutes to be filed (Mills & Robertson, 1990) but was traditionally not involved in policy formulation being the arm of a remote benevolent master (St. Hill 1970,1990) extending favours to society as instructed. After Jamaica's independence, there was a shift in bureaucratic emphasis from the requirements of the overseas official to that of the Minister or local politicians who now occupied positions of unquestionable supremacy in matters of decision-making. There emerged the challenge of transforming the traditional system of administration and legacy of the former colonial administration into a new proactive system of government (Bissessar, 2002) supporting administration for development (Stone, 1993) and representative bureaucracy under national political control (Mills & Robertson, 1990). There arose difficulties in that the civil servant, formally insulated from the politician, would now be required to contribute to the policy making process (Isaacs, 2002) and face the challenge of maintaining non- partisanship and an apolitical civil service structured on a triad of principles, namely neutrality, anonymity, and impartiality (Mills, 1997).

Several writers, (Stone, 1993; Mills, 1970; St Hill, 1990) believed, that a reconceptualization of the role of the civil servant was necessary, as they assume tasks to become the efficient dedicated servant of a developing society charged with the delicate responsibility of managing the changes required for development and for the continuous promotion of national well-being. Policies would now be articulated by the mass of the people through their political representative (St Hill, 1970). St Hill (1970) goes further to indicate that what is required is a capability to generate, accept, and implement new ideas processes and services, adapting and changing with the capacity to innovate. The civil servants' new role would be that of formulators, executors, monitors and advisors of public policy programmes and projects, putting aside attitudes which exhibit a lack of commitment, distance from reality, a lack of urgency, creativity and ideological weakness.

Public Sector Reform

During periods of structural adjustment continued efforts were made to reform the Public Service led by the Cabinet Office as one of its major functions. Other aspects of the public sector reform process included privatizing or contracting out Government services and the reformation of the Government procurement system to improve transparency and efficiency. Over the years, the scope of the reform efforts has changed, being focused on administrative and regulatory functions in the 1950s, towards being more developmental and then more service oriented - towards clients and customers within the framework of good governance. Consequently, initiatives have been taken to improve the Public Services, under projects such as the Administrative Reform Programme (ARP) and more recently the Public Sector Modernization Programme (PSMP). For example, within the context of structural adjustment undertakings ARP 1 was implemented in 1981, which implanted new systems of human resource planning, pensions administration, training in accounting, auditing and job classifications. ARP II initiated in 1988, focused on new accounting systems and Human Resource Management Information Systems (HRMIS) among other improvements (Isaccs, 2002).

The 1992 Nettleford Report on Government Structure in Jamaica, recommended on pages 22-23, that useful public entities should be strengthened and their management improved and that the rest should be disposed of. A process of privatization began with World Bank assistance as well as the contracting out of facilities and services in an effort to facilitate fiscal savings, with a renewed focus on Government's core competencies and the improved efficiency and effectiveness of the service.

Traditional Public Sector Discourse

Several Caribbean academics have suggested that the imposition and the persistence of structures and cultures of colonial administration have hindered the efforts to reform the public sectors (Jones, 1974; Mills, 1970; St Hill, 1970). It is noted by Schobergh (2006), that there is also a role played by the norms and values underlying and bred from the colonially transplanted institutions which affect political, judicial, and administrative operations. But in addition, these effects, (which have implications for discourse) are made more complex in turn by their interaction within the local environment.

Debates concerning the progress of reform efforts and the development of the public sector pivot on the negative influence of the colonial, historical legacy and some of the cultural remnants that have weakened the service. They persist, are sustained and even perpetuated by interactions and relationships with other institutions and practices of government which have themselves been influenced in a similar way, resulting in patterns that seem cyclical, reciprocal and dialectic.

The discourses on structural and cultural impediments are diverse, relating to the size of the sector, the adequacy or inadequacy of the establishment in terms of posts and functions and their sufficiency or adequacy to respond to public demand. There are recruitment issues and challenges concerning the absence of established methodologies for effecting redundancies, autocratic bureaucratic practices, low productivity (Downes, 2003) inefficiency, waste and corruption (Ryan, 2002). Concerning bureaucracies, one could argue that the trajectory of the pattern of the socio economic and political development of the state over the years, coupled with the effect of globalization in the post- independence era, have also played an influential role in shaping the public sector as it responds to these effects domestically, as translated through Government's structural and policy changes and external imperatives.

If we consider institutions to include the system, norms and socially constructed rules socially sanctioned over and above the juridical-political institutions (Polantza, 1973, p.115), there are challenges which affect the successful implementation of policy and service delivery. According to the 1992 Report of the Committee of Advisors on Government Structure, concerns about the functioning of government had centered mainly on how decision making was concentrated, consigning the rest of the community to a largely peripheral role in the management of affairs. Also, the low quality of the Civil Service and the over-bureaucratization of working methods, leading to compliance rather than a service orientation in its dealings with the public.

Ryan (1972) notes the reluctance to delegate, that led junior officers to become less responsible or involved and more prone to paper passing, as an underlying fear of rebuke, paralyzed their willingness to act. He intimates that, notwithstanding efforts at structural reform, the administrative climate needs to encourage initiative, become more permissive and reduce the tendency to rely on the security of the rules, (the hallmarks of the civil service). Reflections on the attitudes of bureaucracies made by participants suggest the persistence of such trends. Specific behaviours and practices have been socially constructed and conventionalized in identifying the persona of the civil servant over the years however, there are critical attitudes and behaviours essential to managers. Isaacs (2002) observed that there are increasingly more persons with degrees in the public sector which has not resulted in more effective management as there is little correlation between academic brilliance and effective management skills. There is the inference that management of human and social relations requires attributes of tolerance, humility, earned respect, and effective communication skills (Isaacs 2002) and I would add, bolstered by a culture of concern or a "human face" within organizations.

Challenges exist towards effective implementation despite the able provision of legislative authority and capacity to execute policy. The challenges are seemingly more intrinsic and intangible in character, relating to ethics, culture and behavioural issues, long entrenched in some cases. Hood (1986) suggests that the lack of responsiveness by public sector leadership could be attributed to emotional conservativism, vanity, groupthink, lassitude, vested interest or rule structures, that do not provide effective incentives for change. In so much as the public sector holds the position of being the key infrastructure to achieve national development goals, (Davis, 2001) as agents of social change they must first change their own behaviour (Weiss, 1966). The characteristics and genre of the traditional public sector discourse has been labelled the "old civil service mode" and compared, with that of the emerging "modern" mode of operation within the civil service as represented in the text.

Wage Restraint

The provision of Wage Restraint had the outcome of foregrounding some of the systemic issues within the public sector network of relations. One of these was the structural disparities between salaries of Central Government in the public sector and that of the private sector and statutory bodies. One adverse effect was the public sector finding it difficult to attract quality staff and unable to compete with the private sector in terms of recruiting the best and retaining them. It was acknowledged that the public sector traditionally had low salaries compared to the private sector and quasi-public sector from "medieval' times and this did not change, moreso with a wage freeze. In terms of intertextual links to the broader context of the public sector, authors such as Bissessar (2002) and Isaacs (2004) have asserted that the Civil Service has over the years been plagued with the difficult task of recruiting and retaining suitably qualified staff to perform the complex operations of government primarily due to the low levels of pay in the service. Furthermore, that underlying the network of relations, the salaries of public servants were far below that of their private sector counterparts and once they acquired the relevant training, they opt for more lucrative positions in private companies. Thus, Government was challenged to provide revenue to raise the levels of compensation to retain competent staff at the technical and administrative levels in order to enhance productivity. Staff also sought to compensate their earnings elsewhere as "salaries are perceived not to be generally competitive and … are often motivations to seek additional income through overtime or jobs outside of the service," according to Isaacs (2004, p. 227).

This feature of traditional public sector discourse has also been recognized by the World Bank since the 1980's, whereby loan conditionality has stipulated that the salaries and allowances of public sector managers should be brought to 85 per cent of that paid to Statutory bodies and Public Companies within five years. Two pay adjustments were made to Civil Servants under the Administrative Reform Programme in the mid to late 1980's (Ministry of Finance, 2003). Additionally, intertextual links can also be made regarding the 1992-94 wage and fringe benefits negotiations with the Jamaica Civil Service Association (JCSA) where it was agreed that, the Civil Service was to be redeveloped or restructured over the period 1992-95 to bring the emoluments and conditions of service of civil servants to within 20 per cent of that obtained in statutory bodies and the private sector. A subsequent agreement in 2000 - 02 with the Jamaica Civil Service Association (JCSA) provided for the implementation of the market adjustments under certain conditions and for the implementation of pay adjustments over the period 2000 to 2005. It was also expected that the total cost of moving civil servants to 80 per cent of market by 2005 would have been J$2.4bn spread over four (4) years (Ministry of Finance, 2004). However, the activities to bring the public-sector salaries more in line with that of the private sector were put in abeyance in the main, with the signing of the Memorandum of Understanding in 2004. The MOU essentially capped salaries and sealed new employment, (conditional upon approval) in addition to the normal challenge of recruiting persons, which was evident before the MOU.

The persistence of structural salary disparities between the public and private sector, was not alleviated by the MOU in fact, one could argue that the employment ceilings in the MOU accentuated it. The MOU cap on salaries led to the continued lack of competitiveness of the sector, staff losses for better job offers and prevented upward mobility in employment. A 2005 Report from the Permanent Secretaries Review Board noted that the majority of resignations were from the technical, middle and upper management groups and the main reason cited for this was the receipt of better job offers.

One example given was that a complement of about 47 persons in one division had left within the space of about four months, of which 30 of them had left for better employment. Claims were also made that during the period that there were a number of deterrents to staff attrition such as allowances and the moratorium on loans, bonding and contract arrangements and the availability of motor vehicle concessions. Some participants held that the granting of an increase in salary would be insufficient to address the inflationary cost of living effects and there was no guarantee that increasing salaries would have encouraged a more positive attitude and behavioural change on the part of workers. The issue of wage levels has also played a mediating role connecting private sector social practice with that of the public sector. There is an inference that the private sector social practice is one that should be emulated as it is under girded by good salaries and wages and was being used as a benchmark of mediation for public sector salary deliberations.

In considering a broader contextual perspective, intertextual links can be made with historical administrative reform measures, for example, the adoption of New Public Management (NPM) techniques, which could be interpreted as an effort to substitute elements of public sector discourse and practice with elements of private sector discourse and practice. Furthermore, the failures associated, interpreted from an ANT perspective, would have been attributed to incomplete *interessement, enrollment* and inscription in the process of *translation* into the network of NPM.

The text of the JCSA Heads of Agreement infers, in the context of public sector reform, that if wage increases trend towards that of the private sector, and if these were granted, this would have a commensurate positive influence on the discourse culture and behavioural attitudes of public sector workers. However, other assertions were that civil servants were not solely motivated by economics, money and wages but still possessed a work ethic and commitment to public service, with voluntarism, placing value on a job of work and that it should be well done. Other discoursal comparisons can be made in terms of comparing the functions and assessments of the value of work undertaken across private and public sector.

This overflows into the realm of social identities and representation across discourses (Fairclough, 1992; 2003) where, if private sector culture and practice as an order of discourse is to be emulated, (as reforms attempted through the adoption of tenets within Public Sector Modernization and NPM this represents the exertion of a "power over" (Hyman, 1975, p. 90) the public sector in terms of image and social representation (Fairclough, 1989).The former is deemed superior in discoursal terms to the latter's discursive practice and "ways of being" Gee (1990, p. 7) which also reflects power dimensions underlying wider societal relations.

Employment

Complacency in the pursuance of appointing persons to posts within the Public Service had become accepted over the years and inculcated within the culture and discursive practice of the public sector as a norm or convention. Persons were being temporarily employed or acting almost 6 months, in some cases, in vacant positions, despite possessing the requirements and being suitable for the post. The Employment provision of the MOU drove an intense scrutiny of the human resource practices of managers which eventually increased the output with respect to number of appointments. The public sector was deemed to have a serious issue with respect to several public sector workers acting in clearly vacant posts for many, many, years without being appointed to these posts, even after the incumbent had left or had retired from the post without any replacement. The discourse of the MOU challenged this practice by stipulating that if an employee was acting in a clear vacancy for six months, then they should be a review towards appointment. It appeared to have been a deliberate strategy to address this aspect of the traditional public sector practice, in the face of failing to *enroll* managers and engender compliance using the traditional method of authority of the Staff Orders, which were the operational guidelines of conduct for the sector.

From an ANT perspective, it suggests that public sector managers enrolled to the point of aligning themselves (Ritzer, 2006) with the MOU network and discourse towards convergence, on this particular issue. This contrasts with unsuccessful attempts at obtaining compliance through conventional methods of invoking the Staff Orders. If power is derived from the ability to *enroll,* enlist and convince others in the network (Shaikh & Cordello, 2006, p. 9) then it would appear in this instance, that the relative power position of the MOU discourse was superior, being at a level which elicited compliance with the Provisions. Conversely, this also implied that the relative power position of the conventional Staff Orders had diminished in some way in comparison to that of the MOU Provisions, in terms of effectiveness and in terms of eliciting the *enrollment* and convergence of managers towards compliance, around it. It was felt that there was a degree of "lethargy' in the appointments of persons and the MOU 'put persons on their toes' in relation to human resource management policy.

One may recall that the discourse and text surrounding the MOU partially emerged from the crafting of a joint GOJ and JCTU response to the imperatives of Circular 21, and from the context of attempts to curtail the wage bill by capping employment. The MOU militated against this concern by providing for employment approvals subject to a process of justification, through examination and proper scrutiny. However, some of the managers portrayed a reticence with the increased level of scrutiny and were averse to initiating such measures as they were now not able to employ persons on their own cognizance.

Overall, management was deemed unresponsive to issues concerning human resource management which was reflected in their not exercising the option, afforded by the MOU mechanism, to make representation for additional employees or posts, although the need existed. There are several inferences that managers, subject now to the rigour of preparing submissions and defending and justifying any employment requests, were reluctant to do so. Managers were not subject to this level of rigour before or if so, not in the manner now required under the MOU dictates. Subsequently, they had to become more responsive and extend themselves above the norm. Prior to 'Circular 21', some participants went as far as to label employment at that time as being 'willy nilly' implying that effecting employment in the Civil Service at that time was easier than before the MOU was created and with less scrutiny.

Non-compliance was thus exhibited in the stance taken that it was the MOU that precluded management from employing persons, intermingled with personal narratives, whereby the MOU was deemed to be the reason why staff were also not promoted. As public sector managers' margins of manoeuvre or discretionary freedom were curtailed, in the area of employment, there was a correspondingly diminishing of their normal exercise of authority and power in this regard. In respect of the network relations and decisions on convergence, (enlarging the network through additional staff within institutions with their associated networks in alignment) management no longer became the Obligatory PP for employment decisions which authority which had now been conferred upon the MOU institution of the Monitoring Committee (MC).

There are two inferences that emerge from this, one of which is connected to broader socio-economic and political discourses surrounding the issues of the size of the public sector and the other regarding public sector reform and development globally. The size of the public sector has been debated within Government and intertextually especially within the private sector as well as within the context of the programmes of international financial and development institutions, where there still resides the general perception, that the size of public sector is in fact too large and needs to become leaner and smaller (Isaacs, 2002). According to the Public Service Establishment Division, in 2005, the Government was the largest employer with a staff complement of approximately 95,000 persons. The issue has in turn been influenced by extra discursive practices within international development discourse and economic, socio-political, cultural and historical issues in the wider Jamaican context. The structural downsizing of the public sector and reducing the numbers employed, has been a part of the development discourse of the international financial and development community for several years in their interface with developing countries, (Macgregor, et al., 1998) being a condition for loan financing (Bissessar, 2002) as well as a part of public sector reform and privatization efforts.

Macgregor, et al., (1998, p.1) stated that:

In recent years, more and more calls are being heard in a growing number of developing, countries to downsize their civil services. It is argued that downsizing is needed because of the increasing shortfalls in government recurrent and development budgets. This situation results in underutilized, underfunded staff and often in the siphoning-off of donor funds in the development budget for recurrent expenditure.

A process of privatization had begun with World Bank assistance, as early as 1981, as well as the contracting out of facilities and services to enable fiscal savings. In 1991, there were over 300 statutory bodies and public entities, which were largely a drain on fiscal operations (Tindigarukayo & Chadwick, 1999).The Nettleford Report (1992, p. 22) on Government Structure in Jamaica recommended that useful public entities should be restructured and the management improved, but that the rest should be disposed of. There was a renewed focus on Government's core competencies and the improved efficiency and effectiveness of the service. Efforts to downsize the employment numbers of the service have been undertaken, albeit in a seemingly ad hoc manner in response to economic and fiscal imperatives, by both political parties in Jamaica. These considerations have brought into focus the debate as to what is the right size of the public sector? In relation to the functions of government and its needs, how can improvements, efficiency and productivity, ensure the development of the public sector?

Other accounts have identified corruption as a contributor to the increase in the size of the sector in other developing countries. Similarly, corruption has occurred in various forms in the public sector, (Acosta & Alleyne, 2006; Goolsarran, 2005, p. 396; Rajbansee, 1972; Ryan, 2002) revealed in clientelism and bribery to receive public services and in the form of political employment, appointments and promotions within the Civil Service. Employment pressure had also been placed upon the political directorate by the unions, according to Stone (1993), coupled with acts that represent a conflict of interest (Mills, 1997) that altogether have contributed to an increase in the size of the public sector. This gives increased credence to the perception that the public sector is oversized. The growth of wage increases as a percentage of GDP has grown from 7 per cent of GDP in the mid-nineties to approximately 12 per cent in 2004. It was observed by Acosta and Alleyne (2006) that total government expenditure grew from 25 per cent of GDP in 1992 to 45 per cent of GDP in 1996. Consequently, there was no surprise that this longstanding issue became one of the main catalysts for negotiations that formulated the MOU.

Development of The Public Sector

Efforts at institutionalizing a new public sector culture commensurate with the development of the public sector has been an agenda item for various government administrations as evidenced by the several modernization programmes pursued over the years. The institutionalization of public sector reform and modernization was the remit of the Cabinet Office of the Government of Jamaica, with it being the focal point of implementation for the programmes and the corresponding social processes, practices and orders of discourse within the public sector. The identification, representation, inculcation and enactment of public sector reform and modernization remained largely the functions, discourse and practice of the Cabinet Office. From an ANT perspective, the Cabinet Office would therefore have the responsibility of effecting the public sector modernization network of relations, translating the interests and discourse of public sector reform initiatives. In following the processes of *translation*, this would involve "negotiation, intrigues, calculations, acts of persuasion and violence" (De Jong, 2007, p.7) towards acceptance of them.

Conversely, roles and attributes being translated by Cabinet Office would also be subject to contests, and "trials of strength and tricks" (Callon, 1986, p.10), with actor networks of other public sector entities in response to Cabinet Office's efforts to advance *interessement* around public sector modernization, resulting in them not being enacted and inculcated effectively in the sector.

Training

Specific areas for training were identified in the text of the MOU, such as for the Ministry of Health which was undertaken, as well as effort made to capitalize on ongoing projects such as the training of teachers in the Ministry of Education and new programmes for training members of the fire services in the Ministry of Local Government. Training was underscored as a critical and important mechanism to further the development of the sector and the provisions of the MOU emphasized the genre of training, and Government's responsibility to undertake the activity. Government had a role to play in improving the capacity of the human resources in the sector to deliver required services. It was opined that the budgetary support for material resources and assistance was needed to deliver quality services, without which the sector would be unable to respond to the needs of the public.

In several cases it was alluded to, that the MOU was used as a tool by some negotiators to resurrect public sector training, formerly left dormant, against the backdrop of stymied training efforts in the public sector because of economic and fiscal constraints. Several comments were made that training catalyzed by the MOU, would either not have happened or if it did happen, would have occurred very slowly and or with a 'contest' or 'tussle.' So, the MOU was seen as an accelerator of training programmes and a catalyst for training plans that had been left dormant, with the onus on managers to specify the direction of these plans.

There was a clear valuation made by participants that the training imperatives within the MOU provided an impetus for public sector wide training programmes to be revitalized, by compelling or prodding ministries to clearly define their training programmes and execute them. This aspect of training as a provision in the text of in MOU and part of its discourse, was embraced by traditional public sector discourse as it already formed a part of and complemented its discourse although activities had been dormant due to fiscal constraint.

Cross Training

The text of the MOU provided for "cross training" to be undertaken, across public sector entities and between public and private sector. It was believed that benefits could be derived from enhanced mutual learning experiences and synergies being built between the public and private sectors. All participants acknowledged and appreciated the benefits of a reciprocal relationship of experience and exposure between private and public sectors and also between members and entities within the service. However, two major concerns arose;

Firstly, it was felt that the exercise of cross training between the public and private sector, would afford increased marketability for public workers. There were fears that once public sector workers became empowered and more marketable after the exposure, that they would then leave the service.

Secondly, the younger persons in the service could take advantage of the cross-training opportunities and then leave, as they are assumed to be less loyal to the sector, compared to the career or mature civil servant with length of service. Overall there was an increased potential for the public sector to lose its best personnel or those better trained with skills.

From an ANT perspective, one could infer that the inscription of public sector workers into the genre and discoursal network of the private sector was something to be desired. As power relations are derived through the social, where it gains power over and through those enrolled in the network (Whittle & Spicer, 2005), this has implications for those, however transient, who become aligned in the private sector network of relations as compared to the public sector, through that inscription process.

Despite public sector workers producing representations of other practices including their own in the discourse of private sector alignment and interaction, there was the fear that they would be shaped by the latter social processes and practices (Fairclough, 1992), defining and deriving power relations. The interaction would have reconstructive effects in relation to the public sector social identities, subject positions, relationships and even systems of knowledge and belief towards realignment with or being inscribed with those of the private sector.

In *enrollment,* there would be a co-opting of the public sector worker into a network of private sector relations and discourse where they would be inscribed to the loss of the public sector network and institution. This also highlights the political nature of discourse as there are power struggles in and over discourses (Chouliaraki & Fairclough, 1999) towards the preferred private sector discourse as alluded to, in the Provision on Wage Restraint and the translation of wills and alignment.

Public Sector Discourse and Entrepreneurialism: The 'Summer Programme'

Under the Provision of the "Development of the Public Sector" in the MOU Agreement, the Cabinet Office introduced an initiative nicknamed the "Summer Programme," because it commenced in the Summer of 2005, however, it was continued outside of this season and throughout the year for several years after. An episodic narrative (Flick, 2006) from one of the participants later corroborated by others, explained that the Programme was not originally envisioned by the Partners nor specified within the text of the Agreement. The Programme, which was free of cost to staff in the public sector, was focused on training staff at the lower levels of the Civil Service emoluments system in entrepreneurial skills, such as drapery, tiling, culinary arts, masonry and basic computer skills, in its first phase. This was undertaken, to give them opportunities to acquire additional skills, as it was felt that they were the ones who had the tendency to be affected first, in terms of potential job losses in the future.

The Programme earned its relevance and justification by all participants and the civil service community as a critical vehicle to prepare persons, or to provide a transition period of preparation, for those in the lower ranks of the service who would possibly be made redundant or undergo retrenchment during the exercise of right- sizing the sector. However, all participants admitted that the Programme was not directly consistent with the remit of the public sector, the Public Sector Modernization Programme or Vision.

However, the Programme was significant by encouraging the introduction of a genre and practice into public sector discourse which was formerly alien to it as the texts suggests. The approach to training in the public sector has been one to address the immediate training needs of the sector, strengthen human resource capacity and upgrade the capabilities to fulfil the human resource component or requirements to directly benefit the sector itself. The training given did not fit into the core training or established development strategy of the Government, being more of the genre of skills training, such as, cooking, drapery, cosmetology etc., which was outside the types of training normally afforded the sector. The Programme became indicative of a spontaneous shift in conceptualization, application and remit of public sector training and its normal discursive focus, to embrace entrepreneurialism. The Programme enabled the public sector to be inscribed and entertain genre mixing of public sector discourse and entrepreneurialism, which together gained acceptance within conceptualizations of the framework of a modern public sector discourse.

Another unexpected outcome of the Programme was the heightening of the prominence and value benefit of training within labour /union discourse. The text infers that the utility of training has increased as an independent benefit to be leveraged within the context of wage negotiations, equitable in value, or commensurate with that of monetary or salaried benefits being negotiated.

The Cabinet Office inadvertently, introduced an additional dimension to the discourse of the MOU and into public sector discursive practice by institutionalizing entrepreneurialism and the idea of a transition period and entrepreneurial training in preparation for possible worker retrenchment, which the MOU Agreement had effectively forestalled.

Furthermore, the Programme embraced entrepreneurialism in the broader vision of training to prepare workers for the wider job market, enhancing their job mobility external to the public sector, which is alien to traditional public sector discourse. This created intertextual and discoursal linkages to labour / trade union discourse and practice, also being inculcated within public sector discourse.

From the texts, the Programme became a signal to workers that there was unfinished business with respect to the issue of the size of the sector and claims for the need for retrenchment in the public service to obtain efficiency, recognizing that this was one of the issues that triggered the MOU initially.

It was opined that the MOU bought some time, in terms of the Government being able to "put its economic house in order' and would have to come back to address the issues that triggered the MOU in the first place, which was the relative size of the public sector and the wages, visa-vee the resources available to the public sector for salaries. The temporary respite given would have to be revisited.

Outcome: Lack of 'Buy In' by Public Sector Managers Towards the MOU

The attitudes of managers to the changes required of them in the domain of their traditional public sector discourse and practice affected the balance of the existing human resource management practices and the culture in the sector. This was brought to the fore in several dimensions such as in staff relations and in responding to public sector workers who sought to access benefits afforded by the MOU Agreement. Various descriptive and figurative language was used to describe the MOU from the perspective of the management of the public sector. Examples of the language used by public sector managers to describe the MOU, such as, 'a noose around their necks', 'holding a gun to their heads,' or 'a big stick over their heads,' suggests that they considered the MOU to represent a danger to their lives or that it exerted a menacing threat or control over them or in other words a resultant overturn of the status quo or power status. Others held the MOU as a taskmaster, 'putting them on their toes,' being 'dictatorial' giving them no choice, or limiting their freedom to act in certain respects in certain areas. On a more positive note, the MOU was also seen as "a wake-up call,' compelling action to refocus attention on the work at hand or to follow through on matters left in abeyance.

The descriptive and graphic terms used in the texts reflect various degrees of force and the way in which the power in the network of relations being constructed by the MOU translation process was interpreted. It would appear, that the managers felt threatened with the MOU seen as analogous to "a noose," "a big stick," or a "gun," at the point of *interessement* as a moment of translation.

The MOU process was interpreted as robbing choice and the freedom to operate as usual, being compelled by force to act against the norm and ones will. All of the terms used involved a contest of wills with considerations of degrees of consequences in the absence of compliance. What is represented discoursally in the network is clearly unwanted by the recipient managers for it to be represented and described in these terms. The attitudinal responses of management to the MOU were reflected in several ways, for example, some managers were dismissive and felt that the MOU was something that concerned human resources management and not them directly.

Public sector managers felt that they were under scrutiny, in terms of their performance in the management of human resources. There was a degree of resentment felt by some in that, the will of a small group was being imposed upon them. Some opposed because they felt that the MOU had taken away some of their rights as managers because so many things were submitted to the Monitoring Committee (MC) of the MOU. Formerly, some of the matters needing resolution were held to fall within the responsibilities and purview of the public sector manager but now these were removed and now being shared with persons who were not connected to the individual organizations but 'outsiders', namely the trade unions and very senior government officials who were on the MC. This reflects how management perceived the new authority of the MC, which you may recall, was an MOU institution consisting of union and ministerial persona, created by Cabinet to oversee and drive the implementation of the MOU provisions and to be a watchdog for breaches which they had to adjudicate on.

Such attitudes reflect interpretations of managements' response to the convergence with the emerging MOU network and discourse. The text is indicative of the network tensions as articulated within the discourse, expressed discursively in the language and in the seeming reluctance to follow through (or lack of) with the requirements of the new discourse. From an ANT lens, incorporating changes in the network involves the actor (management) being aligned (Callon & Latour, 1981) which necessitates the transference of wills in the formation of "continuous chains of translation." (Latour, 1996, p. 108; Law & Mol, 2002, p. 98). These responses indicate a range of attitudes to the intermediary of the text of the Agreement and inscription process. They also reveal how management interpreted and reacted to the hierarchical shift in their power position and resulting instability for them, as well as giving insight into the extent of the work in negotiations as part of the translation process towards them being recruited, made allies (Latour, 1996) and achieving their alignment.

Management therefore exercised "interpretative flexibility" (Bijke, 1994) by being hesitant and resisting divergence from the traditional public sector network and structure, towards convergence and acceptance of a new regime of authority and alignment as required by inscription into the MOU network of relations. Correspondingly there is demonstrated a degree of struggle in the power relations in the network between the discourses of the public sector and the MOU and public sector management and the MC..

This is internalized in the language of the text, which is essentially fought over (Chouliaraki & Fairclough, 1999) mirrored and contested between the orders of discourse and practices articulated in the existing human resources management practices of the public sector as against those represented in the MOU.

Other types of responses suggest that management demonstrated a partial 'buy-in' or *interessement* and *enrollment* into the MOU network, reflected in the extent to which they committed themselves and what motivated their convergence with and partial acceptance of, the alteration in their relative power position in light of the MOU provisions. Conversely, there is a simultaneous representation of the struggle in diverging from the traditional public sector network of relations in the dimension of behaviour and human resource management practices. Further, to the extent to which convergence was attained, demonstrated that the process of translation was mixed and not completely settled being militated by processes of *interessement* and *enrollment* and being motivated by the fear of being responsible for any breach or by being prodded.

Consequently, managers were also motivated by the fear of not wanting to be held responsible for undermining the MOU or for any breach of it or to 'put a spoke in the wheel' of the MOU Agreement. The repercussions they did not want to contemplate. Further, the onus to effect the obligations conferred by the MOU served to exert 'some amount of prodding,' thereafter managers 'stepped up' their performance. It was observed however, that in the haste to comply with the timeline of six months to appoint persons acting in clear, vacant posts, that persons were appointed to areas where they were not best suited which compromised the service qualitatively. Similarly, it was alluded that managers in the process of screening persons did not apply the attention required in their selection.

Power in the Actor Network

You may recall that from an ANT perspective, power was not something possessed hence the trade unions' new position became a productive and relational outcome of the network itself (Saad & Gophal, 2005). Their power was added and derived socially over and through all those enrolled in the MOU network (Whittle & Spicer, 2005) which had implications, for their relative power position within traditional public sector discourse and their alignment within the MOU network.

The resulting empowerment of the trade unions through the MOU network of relations was demonstrated in the effectiveness of union advocacy with regard to employment issues for public sector workers. In adhering or in the effort to comply with the 'letter of the law' of the MOU, appointments were speeded up which sometimes led to persons who were unsuited to certain posts being placed in them, putting "square pegs' into 'round holes.' However, management was overall deemed to be acting in good faith and taking the welfare of their staff into account.

CDA methodology was insightful in deconstructing the linkages and inner operations, helping to derive themes and discoursal roots that on analysis furthered an understanding of the implications for MOU outcomes materially, institutionally, relationally and discursively. The process of inculcation towards network stabilization from the perspective of discourse as a moment in the network was demonstrated in the varied contests between the traditional public sector discourse and the new discourse of the MOU Agreement seeking to establish itself. Management's authority and position was diminished within their own domain from the perspective of their constituents. This had implications for the governance of the sector and the dynamics of the relationship between management and staff. Additionally, this was relative to the extent to which their constituents felt they represented them and also in relation to where they felt they were positioned in hierarchies of power in the context of their relationship with Government.

CONCLUSION

Within the formation of the MOU network of relations, translation and network strategies for change require discourse and narratives that would be operationalized, enacted or inscribed as new ways of being, new identities and materialized as new ways in space and time (Fairclough 2005). A number of themes and implications arose, in probing the black box of network interaction and the nature of the interface between the traditional public sector discourse and that of the MOU discourse.

Within the public sector, stereotypical traditional "discourse, the management style, or genre was depicted as being unresponsive, which conflicted with that of the staff seeking to be emancipated and empowered or being 'enrolled' and 'mobilized'. By inculcating and being empowered by knowledge concerning the discourse of the MOU, staff agitated for benefits that were withheld or not delivered, although they were afforded some benefits through the MOU text, such as, an improved speed of appointment to vacant posts. The revelations concerning the challenges of the unresolved human resource functions within the service were brought into focus, presenting possibilities that the success in part of institutional reforms and structural change efforts, may be compromised by the lack of a similar, concomitant emphasis on the human resource component within the service.

There was a perceived diminishing of the scope of authority of some managers who felt that their autonomy to manage and make unilateral decisions was being eroded. The reluctance of management to become aligned through translation and resistance to inscription was reflected in their response to the MOU institution of the MC which, apart from curtailing the remit of management in certain dimensions, also relegated their position in the traditional hierarchical network as well as, within the MOU network of relations. The experience of fluctuations in their relative power positions in the newly emerging network of relations within their respective public sector bodies resulted in displays of uncertainty with respect to the MOU network in which the managers were being realigned with through translation.

The expected sustainability of the MOU discourse would be a function of the pace, depth and persistence of continued *interessement, enrollment* and *mobilization* by the focal actors within the MOU network of relations, which would engender the inculcation of the discourse. The effectiveness of the *enrollment* would be revealed in the inculcation into practice of the new discourse in the public sector to the detriment of the old. From the CDA analysis it is apparent that the process of inscription and inculcation of the new discourse from the MOU Agreement as an actor within the black box of network relations was not seamlessly undertaken. The implications for the traditional public sector and trade union discourse operationalised in practice, affected by the inscription processes of the MOU, engender change, distilling new forms of communicative interaction with new genres, dialogue and relations between genres and new communicative styles.

REFERENCES

Acosta, A. M., & Alleyne, D. (2006). *The policymaking process in Jamaica*. Washington, DC: Inter-American Development Bank.

Bijker, W. E. (1994). *Of bicycles, bakelites and bulbs. toward a theory of sociotechnical change*. Cambridge, MA: MIT Press.

Bissessar, A. M. (2002). The introduction of new public management in small states. In Governance in the Caribbean. Sir Arthur Lewis Institute of Social and Economic Studies, Jamaica, University of the West Indies.

Callon, M. (1986). Some elements of a sociology of translation: domestication of the scallops and the fishermen of St Brieuc Bay. In *Power, Action and Belief* (pp. 196–223). London: Routledge.

Callon, M., & Latour, B., (1981). Unscrewing the big Leviathan: how actors macro-structure reality and how sociologists help them to do so. *Advances in social theory and methodology: Toward an integration of micro-and macro-sociologies, 1*.

Chouliaraki, L., & Fairclough, N. (1999). *Discourse in late modernity-rethinking CDA*. Edinburgh, UK: Edinburgh University Press.

Davis, C. (2001). *The Role of the Public Service*. Paper presented at the Recruitment Ceremony: Recruits for the Immigration Division at the Police Academy, St Catherine, Jamaica.

De Jong, B. (2007). Shedding Light on the darkness: Using the Actor-Network theory to analyse the distribution of power. Paper for the 47th Europe Regional Science Association, Paris, France.

Downes, A. (2003). *Productivity and competitiveness in the Jamaican economy*. Economic and Sector Studies Series. Washington, DC: InterAmerican Development Bank. (RE3/OD6)

Fairclough, N. (1989). *Language and power*. London: Longman.

Fairclough, N. (1992). *Discourse and Social Change*. Cambridge, UK: Polity Press.

Fairclough, N. (2003). *Analysing discourse: Textual analysis for social research*. London: Routledge. doi:10.4324/9780203697078

Fairclough, N. (2005). Peripheral vision: Discourse analysis in organization studies: The case for critical realism. *Organization Studies*, *26*(6), 915–939. doi:10.1177/0170840605054610

Flick, U. (2006). An introduction to qualitative research. *Sage (Atlanta, Ga.)*.

Gee, J. P. (1990). *Social linguistics and literacies: Ideology in discourses*. London: Falmer Press.

Goolsarran, S. J. (2005). *Caribbean Labour Relations Systems: An Overview*. Port-of-Spain: ILO Caribbean.

Hood, C. (1986). *Administrative Analysis: An introduction to rules, enforcement and organizations*. Brighton, UK: Wheatsheaf Books.

Hyman, R. (1975). What is Industrial Relations? In *Industrial Relations* (pp. 9–31). London: Palgrave Macmillan. doi:10.1007/978-1-349-15623-8_2

Isaacs, H. (2002). *Evaluations of civil service systems: case study Jamaica*. Washington, DC: Inter American Development Bank.

Isaacs, H. (2004). *Short form for the institutional assessment of civil service systems: case of Jamaica. In Regional Policy Dialogue: Management and Transparency of Public Policy Network*. Washington, DC: The Inter-American Development Bank.

Isaacs, H. (2004a). The Allure of Partnerships: Beyond the Rhetoric. *Social and Economic Studies*, *53*(4), 125–134.

Jones, E. (1974). Some Notes on Decision-Making and Change in Caribbean Administrative Systems. *Social and Economic Studies*, *23*(2).

Jones, E. (1992). *Development administration: Jamaica adaptations*. Kingston: CARICOM Publishers.

Jones, E. (1996). Jamaica: a framework for managing the reform process. In M. Garrity & L. A. Picard (Eds.), *Policy reform for sustainable development in the Caribbean*. IOS Press.

Latour, B., & Porter, C. (1996). *Aramis, or, The love of technology*. Cambridge, MA: Harvard University Press.

Law, J. (1991). *A sociology of monsters: essays on power, technology and domination*. London: Routledge.

Law, J. (1992). Notes on the theory of the actor-network: Ordering, strategy, and heterogeneity. *Systems Practice*, *5*(4), 379–393. doi:10.1007/BF01059830

Law, J., & Mol, A. (2002). Complexities. Science and Cultural Theory. Durham, NC: Duke University Press.

Lowe, A. (2001). After ANT: An illustrative discussion of the implications for qualitative accounting case research. *Accounting, Auditing & Accountability Journal*, *14*(3), 327–351. doi:10.1108/EUM0000000005519

Macgregor, J., Peterson, S., & Schuftan, C. (1998). Downsizing the civil service in developing countries: The golden handshake option revisited. *Public Administration and Development: The International Journal of Management Research and Practice*, *18*(1), 61–76. doi:10.1002/(SICI)1099-162X(199802)18:1<61::AID-PAD988>3.0.CO;2-N

Mills, G. E. (1970). Public Administration in The Commonwealth Caribbean. St Augustine, Trinidad: Sir Arthur Lewis Institute of Social and Economic Studies, University of the West Indies.

Mills, G. E. (1997). *Westminster style democracy: The Jamaican experience. Paper prepared for the Grace Kennedy Foundation Lecture 1997*. Kingston, Jamaica: Stephenson's Litho Press.

Mills, G. E., & Robertson, P. (1990). The attitudes and behaviour of senior civil servants in Jamaica. In G. E. Mills (Ed.), *A Reader in Public Policy and Administration*. St Augustine, Trinidad: Sir Arthur Lewis Institute of Social and Economic Studies, University of the West Indies.

Ministry of Finance and Planning. (2003). *Budget Memorandum*. Kingston: Author.

Ministry of Finance and Planning. (2004). *Budget Memorandum*. Kingston: Author.

Munroe, T. (1987). Contemporary Marxist Movements: Assessing WPJ Prospects in Jamaica. Sir Arthur Lewis Institute of Social and Economic Studies, 1-35.

Munroe, T. (1992). *The industrial relations culture: perspectives and change*. Paper prepared for the Conference: Planning Institute of Jamaica.

Nettleford, R. (1992). *Report of the Committee of Advisors on Government Structure*. Ministry of Finance and Planning, Government of Jamaica. (unpublished)

Nettleford, R. (2002). Governance in the contemporary Caribbean: towards a political culture of partnership. In Governance in the Caribbean. St Augustine, Trinidad: Social and Economic Studies, University of the West Indies.

Rajbansee, J. (1972). Size and bureaucracy in the Caribbean. *Administration & Society*, *4*, 205.

Ritzer, G. (Ed.). (2006). *Encyclopedia of social theory*. Sage publications.

Ryan, S. (2002). We are all corrupt. In Governance in the Caribbean. St Augustine, Trinidad: Sir Arthur Lewis Institute of Social and Economic Studies, University of the West Indies.

Ryan, S. D. (1972). Race and Nationalism in Trinidad and Tobago: A Study of Decolonization in a Multiracial Society. Toronto: University of Toronto Press.

Saeed, A. M., & Gopal, A. (2005). *Immutability, Inimitability and Autonomy: The 3 little paradoxes of the Toyota (Re) Production System CMS4 Stream 27: Technology and Power*. Academic Press.

Schoburgh, E. (2006). *Presentation: Taking Responsibility; The Jamaican Economy Since Independence Institutional and Administrative Capacity*. IDRC Project.

Shaikh, M., & Cordello, A. (2006). *From epistemology to ontology: challenging the constructed truth of ANT*. London School of Economics and Political Science.

St Hill, C. A. P. (1970). Reform of the Public Services. *Social and Economic Studies*, *19*(1).

St. Hill, C. A. P. (1990). Towards the reform of the public services: Some problems of transitional bureaucracies in commonwealth Caribbean States. *Social and Economic Studies*, 135–145.

Stone C. (1993). Wages policy and the social contract. *Caribbean Labour Journal*, 3.

Tindigarukayo, J. K., & Chadwick, S. (1999). *Synopses of ten best practices in Jamaican Civil Service reforms, Project on "Case studies in best practices in civil service reforms," Millennium Development Goals project*. New York: UNDP.

Weiss, M. (1966). Some Suggestions for Improving Development Administration. *International Review of Administrative Sciences*, *32*(3), 193–196. doi:10.1177/002085236603200302

Whittle, A., & Spicer, A. (2005). Why Organization Studies Should Resist. In EGOS 2005 colloquium in Berlin (pp. 1-26). Academic Press.

Winner, L. (1993). Upon opening the black box and finding it empty: Social constructivism and the philosophy of technology. *Science, Technology & Human Values*, *18*(3), 362–378. doi:10.1177/016224399301800306

Chapter 8
MOU Convergence:
Trade Union Discourse and Practice

ABSTRACT

Several historical, sociocultural, and political dimensions have shaped the development and the discourse and practice of the trade union movement. The characteristics of "traditional" trade union discourse and practice are explored, providing a contextual understanding for the contest, challenge, and change evidenced by the process of translation into the MOU actor network. There are several implications for the "identity," "relational," and "ideational" aspects of trade union discourse and industrial relations practice by convergence with the MOU actor network. However, while relationships within the black box of network interaction affords the union movement prominence and access to the powerful halls of leadership and governance, the union constituency becomes contested in acceding to discoursal change and practice resulting in "boxing and dancing" within the new context of diminished adversarialism.

BACKGROUND

The trade union movement has been instrumental in advocating for and being the prime actors in, the development of social partnerships in Jamaica. Reflecting upon the traditional discourse and practice of the trade union movement, the political and socio-cultural context from which it emerged is

DOI: 10.4018/978-1-5225-8961-7.ch008

informative, moreso as the growth of the labour movement in Jamaica has been synonymous with the emergence of the two major political parties, the Jamaica Labour Party (JLP) and the Peoples' National party (PNP). As described by Acosta and Alleyne (2006), the Bustamante Trade Union (BITU) was formed in 1938 under the leadership of Alexander Bustamante, who was also the founder of the JLP and an advocate for several measures relating to worker rights and benefits. Bustamante's cousin, Norman Manley, was the founder of the National Worker's Union (NWU) in 1944 which was aligned to the PNP. These two unions were a central feature of the development of both political parties – the JLP and the PNP and memberships were 'mapped into political loyalties' (Acosta & Alleyne, 2006).

The roots of the affiliations of the two unions dictated the rivalry between them, described by Stephens and Stephens (1986) as being 'conflictual', which has been a persistent feature within the union movement, to the extent that unification of the union movement was never a possibility.

According to Johnson (1980), the rivalries, apart from being along ideological lines at one point in time as supported by Stone (1985), also stemmed from one union raiding the personnel and labour leaders of the other and them exhibiting a tough image, antagonistic stance and a readiness to fight, through threats towards each other and the taking of industrial action. The rise of trade unionism was underpinned by their formal legal recognition however the formal unity of the movement was always stymied by one group being antagonistic against the other. This was also in concert with the traditionally antagonistic relationship between workers and employees of the day, exacerbated by the authoritarian posture often taken by managers and employers mixed with racial and class overtones.

As part of the nationalistic posture and aspirations towards achieving independence in Jamaica, the union movement was integrally involved politically, which still has its effects in the contemporary dynamics of labour management relations (Goolsarran, 2006). The trade unions and their leaders were equal or dominant partners in the coalitions which ruled both the political parties and the governments (Munroe, 2000; Acosta & Alleyne, 2006). Acknowledgement of this feature, was also shared by Stone (1989) to the extent that the two seemed indistinguishable, causing political unionism (Cowell, 2006) to dominate industrial relations practice. This is consistent with Munroe (1992) who indicated that the unions became a vehicle to deliver political support, which had implications for the balance of power within industrial relations. It was also observed by Stone (1985) that in the 1980's, the dominance of the BITU and NWU, led to resentment amongst the smaller unions at that time such as the Jamaica Union of Public Officers and Public Employees JUPOPE, Union of Technical and Supervisory Personnel (UTASP) and the University and Allied Workers Union (UAWU).

Traditional Discourse of the Trade Union Movement of Jamaica

Traditional trade union discourse, behaviour and practice was reflected in 'ways of acting' in terms of the conduct of union representation as well as their 'being' and identity (Fairclough, 2003). The traditional discourse and practice characterised by the choice of language used by participants to describe trade union activities in terms of 'ways of acting', were words such as to 'lockdown the place' and 'sabotage the place' and put 'a spanner in the works' and ''mash up the place' and so on. There was the propensity to display disruptive behaviour as part of the discourse and practice, as described by participants' texts, to engender 'confrontation' and 'strikes.' These perceptions were universalized amongst all participants including the union participants themselves. The industrial relations climate was one demonstrated by the number of strikes being called without prior discussion or negotiations and was one that was in constant confrontation with Government. The traditional trade union discourse represented an aggressive behaviour and elements of a warring discourse overlapping with a militaristic discourse, always seeking for ways to demonstrate and exercise the threat of force or power, with intent demonstrated in particular ways, that they acted and interacted.

Industrial Relations Practice

The labour movement and industrial relations practice was fuelled by the depression of the 1930s, which produced deteriorating conditions for workers, in the post-colonial Caribbean, which lead to unrest and widespread disturbances in 1937 (Daniel, 1957).) On examining public sector industrial relations practice, this was intricately interwoven within the discourse of the trade unions, as part of their genre. There is a complementary dialectic between elements of both in terms of similar factors influencing their shape and form and each influencing each other without losing their identity. Over time industrial relations practice became more rules and procedural based which governed internal relationships in the workplace, while externally there was a focus on worker protection and conflict management. Industrial relations practice also exhibited the inherited British tradition of voluntarism, based upon fundamental freedoms, so that both worker and employer could respectively choose to form trade unions or employee associations (Mulvey, et.al., 2003).

There was a commensurate decline in power of the unions as the shift from voluntarism to a more regulated industrial relations system emerged to assert workers' rights (Goolsarran, 2006). Within the construct of voluntarism, (Goolsarran, 2006) legislative support to engender equity of treatment in the management labour relationship by the state became obsolete. This heralded a reliance upon parties to settle issues on their own usually resulting in skewed outcomes in favour of management and the maintenance of existing relations of power, to the disadvantage of the worker (Munroe, 1992; Mulvey, et.al., 2003).

Contributing to the development of industrial relations practice generally, there were attitudes and perceptions concerning the partners to the practice – labour and management - that were grounded in the structural. These emerged from the colonial legacy and relationships centered on the economic ordering of the factors of production and attitudes between plantation owner and slave or indentured servant, which persisted in the psyche between management and worker. Labour, as one of the factors of production, was organized to maximize profit, thereby diminishing the human factor to a sub human status, where the worker became a statistic, without identity except in relation to production outcomes and subordinated to the bottom of hierarchical authority structures. Fluctuations in economic performance over the years prompted conflicts to address inflationary pressures on the standard of living of workers and strikes in the 1980s were most often over public sector lay-offs (Goolsarran, 2006).

Poor worker management relations evidenced in industrial relations disputes and work stoppages from the 1970s to 1980s as reflected in Table 1, show that in the first half of the 1980s, Jamaica averaged roughly 600 industrial disputes a year, including 80 to 90 annual work stoppages with the latter declining during the mid-1980s (Downes, 2003).

Within these types of relations, adversarialism blossomed as the management and worker relationship was reduced to combative power struggles. Both sides held negative conceptualizations of each other, which was supported by the psychological acceptance of antagonistic relationships as the normal state of affairs

Table 1. Work Stoppages 1960-2001

Years	Total	Annual Average
1960-1963	250	63
1964-1967	257	64
1968-1971	316	79
1972-1975	568	142
1976-1979	702	176
1980-1983	(450)	112
1984-1987	216	54
1988-1991	252	63
1992-1995	251	62
1996-1999	165*	
2000	28	
2001	14	

*1999 data missing

Source: Economic and Social Surveys, Jamaica, PIOJ, ILO Websitehttp://www.ilocarib.org.tt/oldwww/digest/jamaica/jam23html

With respect to the industrial relations practice, this has been described as 'old school', and conceptualized as being a 'war' and 'a fight', involving strategic military preparations on the part of the unions, alluding to a militaristic discourse. So, 'old-school' industrial relations practice was pursued as against a more consultative way of handling disputes and controversies. This was consonant with the school of thought that industrial relations practice was a fight mindful that preparations had to be made for war. Discussions were held strategically, with the understanding that at some point in time, there would be a war to fight and one had to be planning how to win that war. The industrial relations culture and discursive practices had their genesis in the broader historical, socio cultural and political context, which interdiscursively and dialectically, influenced the shape and form of the institutions, structures and discursive practices within the genre of the trade unions.

One aspect of industrial relations practice included the institutional mechanism for the process of dispute resolution. There were institutional and procedural mechanisms that provide avenues for resolving disputes described as the 'three tier system' which was operable in the sector. An individual complaint between a worker and a manager would usually be dealt with by some disciplinary committee in a Ministry or Department. Similarly, the small disputes in the office environment, would normally be dealt with internally, however, at times, these could spillover into a major dispute. In such cases, that matter would then be referred to the Ministry of Labour. If reconciliation was still beyond reach, then the issue would be referred further to the Industrial Disputes Tribunal (IDT) for final arbitration whereby such cases, could be evidenced by industrial unrest, strikes and media reports.

For the public sector, the Ministry of Finance, namely, the Public Services Establishment Division, would be engaged, from the point of view of the line ministries or from the employee themselves. In some cases, there may be a need for Cabinet to take a position on the matter and would be referred through the required channels to Cabinet.

A key process within industrial relations practice, was that of collective bargaining which had been exercised by the unions since 1938 but over the years had progressively grown in intricacy. As a 'rich description' (Lincoln & Guba, 1985: Patton, 2002) of the individual bargaining practice, trade unions used the mechanism and instruments of collective bargaining and legal enactments as vehicles to advance industrial democracy (Farnham et al., 2003). This fuelled the need for educated persons with new skills and knowledge of companies, accounting practices and economics, to become involved as negotiation processes became more aligned, in response to the growing complexities of economic and market conditions within which entities operated. The demand for more highly skilled and educated persons in the collective bargaining process was such that a comment was made by a foreign official that 'the old days of banging on the table have passed' (Johnson, 1980). As part of the discourse practice of traditional trade unions', industrial relations practice for the public sector also had these challenges which warranted the finding of a solution.

Industrial relations practitioners highlighted the difficulties of negotiating with many different bargaining units. It was noted that there were about thirty (30) or forty-five (45) bargaining units with which negotiations had to take place, sometimes as much as seventy (70). And then, when an offer was made to one group, other groups heard about it and wanted to better the arrangement in their own negotiations that followed. Hence there were constant negotiations and it was a challenge to keep up with them as well as to keep the financial aspects of the contracts brokered, within the budgeted figure given by Government.

This situation was deemed onerous as there was a proliferation of bargaining units which made it more and more difficult for the Ministry to manage the process of negotiations. This occurrence coincided with the various negotiation cycles, approximately every two years.

These social practices and institutional imperatives demonstrated that the bargaining and wage negotiation process was a trying exercise due to the challenges of keeping within the fiscal limits prescribed by the Ministry, the proliferation of bargaining units and the management of the negotiating cycles as a result. Furthermore, there was the constant, competitive negotiating also between groups to better the offers received by their compatriots, leading to the multiplication and replication of processes. Consequently, the settlement process and the time between the settlements as well as the delivery of benefits was lengthy and retroactive. This was coupled with the characteristic cultural, traditional discourse aspects derived from internal rivalries fuelled along political partisan lines.

Trade Unions: Traditional Trade Union Discourse Versus 'MOU' Discourse

Social practices in the semiotic mode, consists of discourses, genres and styles. Where 'discourse' can be representational, consisting of a system of knowledge or belief and 'genres' involve action, and ways of interacting in social activities and relations, while 'styles' relate to identities and ways of being. In terms of the social practices within traditional trade union discourse and the MOU discourse, there were changes revealed in terms of new ways of interacting, (Fairclough, 2003). Firstly, interview data inferred through language and text, that the unions were being more responsible, mature, less antagonistic and subtly less aggressive in their social relations. Additionally, that the public perception and image of them had altered in contrast to the traditional trade union discourse and practice. The inculcation (Fairclough, 2003) of MOU discourse as against the traditional discourse, revealed itself in their 'new ways of being' demonstrated by the Unions described as now 'acting responsibly' and even working with the management to try to find a way forward. This type of behaviour changed the relatively negative perception of the unions from typically being 'antagonistic and always fighting' to a more positive perception, reflected in their new modus operandi.

The unions were ascribed as exhibiting maturity in terms of their undertaking informed deep analysis of the issues and a willingness to make adjustments on their part, for which they were commended. Their approach was described in militaristic parlance as representing tactical manoeuvres in that they recognized the problem and proposed a solution, which was less inimical to their membership.

The change in the social practices of the unions in their external relationships conveyed that they had appropriated 'new ways of being' (Fairclough, 2003, p. 26). Several participant discourses vested the unions with an improved image from how they were perceived before, giving them "new identities" as they exhibited a 'departure' from 'being 'antagonistic' and even with respect to them perceiving themselves differently. There was a departure from the concept that trade unions were there 'just to strike' as now, they seemed different, 'and not continuing to engage in actions which destroyed the country,' seemingly being more prone to reason and being rational in approach.

This suggests that the inscription process and mobilization into the MOU network had been successful to some degree where it could be considered that the unions had become 'black boxed' to the point of not contesting the MOU discourse and black box configuration entertaining a level of closure. The unions had become fully inscribed into the MOU actor network of relations and had become aligned and repositioned within it.

Another dimension in the way in which convergence with MOU discourse influenced the traditional trade union discourse is through institutional strengthening as it related to the umbrella institution, the Jamaica Confederation of Trade Unions (JCTU). The JCTU was a focal point in the trade union network of relations, with its leadership vested with authority at the 'highest level' in terms of being on the Monitoring Committee within the MOU network of relations, that could make commitments binding upon all members. As the Monitoring Committee became a central point for union to Government dialogue, all participants noted the strengthening and generation through internal dialogue, of one collective position and the strength of a unified front by the union movement in negotiations. Also highlighted were dimensions of an apparent cessation in union rivalry, in an effort to derive a unified stance in negotiations and meetings with the Government, which suggests, that this was absent in previous MOU arrangements. There was an observed deepening and widening of internal consultations and problem solving, within the membership of the union movement, including non JCTU members, suggesting a diminishing in importance of the elements that composed the union divide. The demonstration of this unified collective position conveyed that there was an increase in strength, or an empowerment that suggested a renewal but also a change in the way they saw themselves 'ideationally' and their role.

It was noted that prior to the MOU there were waves of industrial action and there was no functional collective body that could speak with one voice. Further, that there was now engendered a better working relationship, as issues previously affecting one union, was now resolved multilaterally and the matter of rivalry, that was seen in other social partnership efforts, had subsided in this arrangement. This conveyed a growing prominence to the Jamaica Confederation of Trade Unions, enhancing its validity and existence. Influential decisions were brokered and advice was extended to any union seeking it, broadening its remit, whether or not the union was part of the JCTU. The practice of rivalry as an outcome of the contestation of power positions and relations within the JCTU and trade unions diminished in the context of being part of the MOU actor network and subscribing to its discourse, reflecting

'...how a discourse is positioned and relates within a network of discourses, the power relations between them all, the factors that have influenced the position of the discourse, the reciprocal interaction and influence with those discourses in the network and the very relationship between these discourses themselves.' (Fairclough, 2003)

This is exemplified within trade union discursive practice, for as social actors, they have been situated within the broader context of national political discursive practices, from which it has emerged. These associated practices have been incorporated or recontextualized into their own practice reflexively, dominating the heart of trade union discourse to the extent that it has been termed 'political unionism' (Cowell, 2006; Stone, 1989) due to the incursion of the political. One could argue that the political practices and divisiveness along party lines effective in the society had been represented and inculcated in the Bustamante Industrial Trade Union (BITU) aligned to the Jamaica Labour Party and the National Workers' Union (NWU) aligned to the Peoples' National Party (PNP) interdiscursively within the trade unions' genre and order of discourse, exerting a level of control over their behaviour and decision making. This interdiscursivity with the rivalry, displayed in the political genre and practice of Jamaica, encroaching into union practice, contributed to how trade unions were represented and identified in the semiotic mode, by the establishment of certain expected behaviour patterns and characteristics which conveyed a certain outward perception of them discoursally. These incorporated practices have been represented in the shaping of the social practices of the unions who from experience, were expected to align with political partisan concerns. It was noticeable that for the first time the BITU and the NWU worked closely together. Before, everyone was seeking their own turf and territorial border but now, they were a united front which made a difference.

In accounting for the change in the discursive practice of the unions, it was purported that through the MOU, the unions had been able to assert themselves, demonstrating the capability to reassert and revive its own 'raison d'etre', identity and representation, realigning themselves ideationally and prioritizing a worker- welfare centered ontology, which sidelined the political partisan concerns, which formerly, had a tendency to dominate union discourse and practice. Further, the change in social practice reflected an acceptance of their position as unions within the MOU network whereby the MOU Agreement therefore had the authority to '...speak on behalf of those translated elements...' (De Jong, 2007, p. 10).

There were also interdiscursive linkages of the traditional trade union discourse and practice to a wider global context of social dialogue. Parallels were drawn in discussions to synergies and events in the power struggle involving the trade union culture and practice in the United Kingdom (UK) under the aegis of the Conservative Party Government of Margaret Thatcher, who was the Prime Minister, leading to the eventual transformation of the UK trade union culture and movement. Regulations (Willman & Bryson, 2007) (Martinez Lucio & Stuart, 2004), were devised in an effort to limit the power of the labour unions (Gough et al., 2008), and reduce the ability of the unions to act as a collective political force (Pierson, 1996).

The UK Prime Minister, Margaret Thatcher after she came into office, imposed what was said to have been labelled, 'draconian laws' on the trade unions. Kreiger (1987, p. 179) describes these 'draconian' measures as follows.

Through the Employment Acts of 1980 and 1982, and the Trade Union Act of 1984, the Thatcher government has substantially reduced the rights with which British unions have been collectively endowed since 1906. Taken together, these Acts (among other things): hold union officials as individuals financially and legally accountable for a wide range of unlawful activities (including large-scale picketing, strikes to protest at government activity, and secondary strikes); severely restrict the institution of the 'closed shop'; expand the ability of owners to dismiss strikers and union officials; and remove legal immunity from unions (and officials) who authorise otherwise legal industrial action without meeting specified balloting procedures.

Regarding the issue of "wildcat" strikes, the trade unions had to notify the factory owner, giving 24 hours prior notice that a strike would be taking place and the affected plant had to be closed-down properly. There had to be prior communication. Hence, the union practice of just walking off the job or out of the factory and leaving the machines running and so on, was no longer permissible and there were legal penalties and charges if this occurred and prior communication was not given.

The UK trade unions and the Conservative UK Government became embroiled in a power struggle in their social relations, where as an outcome, the Government of Margaret Thatcher imposed legislation and removed legal immunity, imposing 'draconian measures.' This had an effect upon the genre of the UK trade unions, their culture and social practices in the semiotic mode, by making some aspects of their normal discourse and practice illegal and subject to punitive and legal measures.The UK trade unions lost elements of their militancy within their trade union culture and practice reflected by the diminished 'militaristic discourse' as well as that of the 'threat of the use of force', because they were legally bound to forewarn prior, losing the element of surprise. Negotiations became entrenched as the key vehicle to the settlement of issues and securing worker benefits, which practice grew in ascendancy, while the role of the 'threat of force' essentially became devalued within the discourse, coupled with the fall of union voice and emergence of non-union elements (Willman, et.al., 2007a).

However, it has also been argued conversely, that these measures augured good for the trade unions as they discovered that there was no need to rely upon "wild cat strikes' anymore, in that a lot more could be accomplished for the workers by social dialogue. Consequently, the onus and effort became centered upon negotiating skills and to negotiate contracts properly. Ancillary issues could now be integrated in the negotiation process such as worker welfare, training, employment, certification and health benefits and insurance, instead of a focus on monetary compensation or salaries and 'fighting for a few dollars more.'

An analogy was drawn between the trade union movement in Britain and that of Jamaica and the view that the leadership of the latter had adopted a new vision and approach in the negotiating of worker related benefits. As part of the MOU actor network there was a translation resulting in a change in the discourse and practice of the JCTU which augured more to the benefit of the workers overall, by pursuing more negotiated settlements.

There was a diminished emphasis upon negotiating for monetary salaried benefits, as against a shift towards a more comprehensive and holist one, which incorporated worker welfare concerns such as health insurance, which, in essence, embraced a broader concept of benefits.

The unions changed their discourse practice, inculcating or emphasizing a mixture of other discourses, genres and styles semiotically into their trade union practices thereby, integrating aspects of the genre of training and health benefits. The unions therefore began to give equal, if not greater weight in terms of value, to these parameters of social discourse, holding them commensurate with the normal direct monetary salaried benefits, which was the focal point of wage negotiations.

These international 'moments' related interdiscursively, to how the unions in Jamaica have altered their discourse practice, highlighted in terms of 'ways of interacting, ways of representing and ways of being' Fairclough (2003). There has been a heightening of the role of dialogue and a reduction in the use of the threat of force, in union management bargaining, locally and in contrast, there has been an enrolment into the logic of a discourse of dialogue as a function of being inscribed by the MOU network of relations.

Members of the union movement were of the view that what was being purported and being visualized by union leadership, was similar to the changes propelled under Thatcherism in terms of trending towards a discourse of dialogue and a different model of industrial relations than that pursued in the past.

Outsiders Looking On

When the MOU was brokered there were notable reactions from Jamaica's international financial and development partners to the MOU Agreement. The international partners used language such as 'stroke of genius' and 'occasion of luck' to describe the achievement of an MOU between the Government of Jamaica and the JCTU. Further they were 'shocked' by the role played by the unions in facilitating fiscal stability which was a departure from the role customarily played by them in their traditional discoursal mode. Literature emanating from the engagement of the multilateral institutions with Jamaica over the years, has recorded and noted the instability of the labour relations climate. But in this case, there was an irony, where it was observed that labour leaders were taking credit for the MOU, the commensurate industrial peace, as well as fiscal stability, which was not the norm and was unknown for them in the past

Secondly, the unlikelihood of such an outcome, given Jamaica's socio political, historical legacy (Johnson 1980: Acosta & Alleyne, 2006: Stephens & Stephens, 1986) and that it would have resided in and involved such unlikely bedfellows, (Mulvey, et.al., 2003; Goolsarran, 2006; Cowell, 2006) as Government and the trade unions. Given Jamaica's tempestuous, historical relationship between unions and government, there were many who felt that it was not possible for this arrangement to have occurred and for it to be applauded as a model agreement between Government and trade unions. Thirdly, from the historical context of traditional trade union discourse and practice discussed earlier, the culture of intense, fractious, political rivalry internally had engendered a divisiveness, which had infiltrated the culture, discourse and practice of the union movement, deeming it unlikely that unity within the trade union movement would have predicated a wider accord to have been reached with an external partner. Overall, these reflections infer the uniqueness of the accord as given historical precedence it was unexpected and highly unlikely that the trade union movement would have facilitated and give support to efforts of fiscal stability.

Relations With the Monitoring Committee

Several participants noted the ability of union leaders to make the transition, through their behaviour within the context of the Monitoring Committee, to the new 'genre' and modalities of procedures and practice that MOU discourse required which was more policy oriented in focus. In the MOU actor network, the JCTU was essentially 'pulled the under the tent', or had "access or a place at the table' in terms of their membership on the Monitoring Committee (MC), thereby bringing them into the MOU process at a leadership level together with the Government, engendering their ownership of the process and garnering joint efforts in sustaining, implementing and fulfilling the MOU agreement and its enactments. The use of the language, 'pulled under the tent' or 'place at the table' signifies exclusivity, benefits accessible for a special group, given special access as the elite or chosen ones, but conversely, access or favour has been extended to you to pull you from a former position to special access or a better or higher position or status. Further, as joint and equal partners to the Agreement and members of the MC this resulted in the unions being given access to and afforded audiences with Government stakeholders and participating in dialogue with the multilateral development partners and international financial institutions.

Sufficient to say, the relationship between the Government and the unions had not been one which enabled the latter to be 'at the table' as participants in policy fora and development dialogue, in comparison to the private sector. Hence, there were union consultations with these entities which were, in retrospect unusual, and formerly very limited in scope and frequency. But under the MOU agreement the interaction of the unions with the development partners were also encouraged by Government, which again, was not the norm. One could argue that involving the trade unions in the leadership and decision-making functions of the MOU on the MC was strategic.

The equitable status, and elevated power position, with access to special knowledge and greater intimacy within the inner circle as well as being privy to elite discourses from which they were previously excluded, would be of valued by the unions and would hence diminish the likelihood of them engaging in language that would undermine or jeopardize their new status.

To a large extent, the owners of capital and such institutions as the Private Sector Organization of Jamaica (PSOJ), have always been 'at the table,' in dialogue with Government and its associates. It has also been argued, wittingly or unwittingly, that it has always been Government and the owners of capital wondering how to control 'labour' or the unions, given the historical context and traditional discourse and social practices of the latter. The alignment of the trade union network within the MOU network of relations and their inscription, led to visible changes in the traditional discursive practices and behaviour of the unions, noticed as being departures from the norm by other external networks. Furthermore, the repositioning of the unions altered the relative power position and image of them as perceived by external networks.

The unions were also empowered by being afforded an equity and opportunity of access to 'the table' by an increased standing in their relationships with local societal stakeholders of Government and private sector capital. This reflects an increase in the power status of the unions, conferred upon them by the MOU and its network of relations, repositioning them and increasing their standing, commensurately, also with regards to other external networks of influence. Attributes of the 'new MOU discourse', were now being demonstrated by the unions in their relationships within the MOU network of social partnership and the practice of industrial relations generally. The following text reflected the view held by several of the senior union partners to the process, acknowledging a change in the approach taken by the unions and the industrial relations climate, under the MOU agreement.

There was no need for dislocation. There was no need for strikes. There was no need for lockouts. There was no need for aggression and hostility, you know between partners. You can sit down and have dialogue and come out with an understanding. And I think of the MOU had this national impact in industrial relations." Now from the MOU I am hearing 'let us talk… discuss… let us see how we can manage. (Union 5)

The unions did not engage in the customary militaristic, aggressive and hostile, 'disruptive' behaviour that characterized and represented the traditional trade union discourse in the past, replacing it with practices that were more dialogue-oriented and engendering settlements by peaceful negotiation, as against recourse to the threat of use of force. The change in the customary social practice stabilized the sector and contributed to the durability of the social partnership and the network of relations around the MOU. Hence the MOU network of relations and discourse being inscribed, extended into the 'space of flows' (Jessop, 2007, p. 184) of adjoining networks to which the TUN was associated.

Centralized Collective Bargaining

Another outcome was the deepening of the inculcation of centralized collective bargaining practices as a part of the social practices within trade union discourse. The change from exercising individual union bargaining practices as aforementioned, to that of a centralized collective bargaining practice, had direct effects upon the genre and relationships within the associated industrial relations practice and stability of the trade union network itself. Fairclough (1992) notes that there are 'socio cognitive 'dimensions of text production and interpretation, which are constrained by available resources – internalized social structures, norms, orders of discourse, conventions, etc., constituted through past social practice as well as by the specific nature of the social practice itself. Prior discussions reflect, briefly contrasts and describes the difficulty in managing numerous bargaining units and the benefit of a collective bargaining arrangement operationally, in the process of arriving at the MOU agreement.

The MOU agreement instituted a "joint bargaining" arrangement whereby once a major bargaining accord was struck and was 'out of the way', it influenced other bargaining entities, which regarded themselves as being outside of the MOU for example, the police force. The Government used the MOU as a major policy document in determining its Wages Policy despite other unions not joining in because of various rivalries. In cases, there were those who wanted to stay outside the MOU arrangement but had to come on board, while other unions outside the Confederation, were influenced by it, nevertheless.

The 'playing field was levelled' as information on bargaining positions became more transparent and there was an equity in positions taken supported by how budgetary ceilings were allocated by the Government. There was the tendency for rumours or '*sus*,' to be circulated and used to fuel internal union rivalry and create inter group competition in the quest for each to obtain a better wage settlement than the other. Several participants opined that the change in how post MOU industrial relations was conducted was 'a paradigm shift', comparing the former, to a 'crab dance', being 'adversarial', 'time wasting' and 'uncivilized behaviour', which all persons were reluctant to return to. The change in terms of how bargaining in the public sector was practiced, was deemed a higher level of operation and it was felt that this should remain and there should be no reversion to the old ways

However, what also emerged from the data were suggestions of a 'psychological ripple effect' that the MOU had on the industrial relations decision making of other bargaining groups, who were influenced interdiscursively, whether they were attached to the MOU trade union network or not. Noticeably, the industrial relations climate before the MOU agreement was somewhat volatile as intimated by the proliferation of bargaining units which were becoming more and more difficult to manage. This included the process of negotiations, given the many bargaining units.

Several outcomes precipitated in the pursuit of centralized collective bargaining practices in terms of influencing the internal distribution of power within the union movement. The MOU discourse afforded the opportunity for the unions to exercise centralized collective bargaining practices, however, this would have implications for the distribution and exercise of power within the network of relations within the trade union movement itself. The corollary of this and the diminishing of the multiple bargaining units led to some perceived internal challenges in trade union social relations generally, triggered by the transitioning towards and the exercise of, a centralized collective bargaining approach to wage negotiations.

The characteristics of the governance of the multiple bargaining units were such that most of them were often singly represented in that, no one union represented more than one. The union functionaries and representatives had the opportunity to develop, present and negotiate a claim.

This provided for some union functionaries and representatives a level of recognition, acceptance as well as the opportunity to be at the table in the industrial relations practice. The imagery surrounding being at the table conveys, a privilege and access to information, being able to participate in policy making and development forums nationally or otherwise. It was a position of power and access.

The individual representation of the many bargaining units held a special value for those union representatives in terms of their identity, worth, relevance and being essential to the process. There was the recognition that an established status, position of authority or power was afforded each representative within their respective union grouping, that would be reduced or removed under centralized collective bargaining. The practice of centralized collective bargaining resulted in the unions selecting a small central group, representative of the entire body, to negotiate and make decisions on their behalf, negating individual union group representation.Collective bargaining represented an effort to employ a mechanism that would allow better utilization of limited human and material resources in the bargaining process and also to allow the negotiations to be conducted in a timely way, in terms of the early accrual of benefit to the workers, than normally would have occurred on an individually negotiated basis.

Discussions suggests that there was a genuine fear, (recognized by the leadership of larger unions) on the part of the smaller unions, that their small voices and uniqueness would be smothered by the larger unions, becoming 'ostracized' or 'emasculated' in the process. This recognition would infer that the larger unions had to consistently exert an effort to translate, through *interessement*, by convincing, negotiating, with small unions, appealing to the greater good on a consistent 'circular' (Shaikh & Cordello, 2006, p. 4) basis to lobby and assuage those fears and affirm that the smaller unions' interests would be served.

To address the concerns of these smaller union functionaries, attempts were made to convince them that the mechanism of centralized collective bargaining was not seeking to ostracize or emasculate them but had its benefits.

The persistence of so many individual unions, as referred to earlier, would suggest a general unwillingness to relinquish such positions of status, to being subsumed within a small negotiating umbrella group. There were efforts at engendering *interessment*, in the form of an appeal to the logic of the smaller unions and presenting a rationale as well as justification for using centralized collective bargaining, in terms of improving the efficiency the bargaining process and deployment of resources. Additionally, there were appeals made to the 'raison d'être' or core philosophy of the unions which was to ultimately seek the welfare of workers and obtain benefits. Actual settlements were customarily delayed for years and 'backed up' in terms of delivery, becoming retroactive, due to the nature of the bargaining process which was time consuming and lengthy in its cycle, extending the time it took for workers to actually receive the benefits that were negotiated years prior. What was also incorporated as a tool to solicit *interessement*, was the benefit of faster delivery of the gains after settlement. The removal of the individual representative status and the perceived downgrading of the function under collective bargaining signalled growing divergence within the TUN, weakening alliances and fractured *interessement*

Trade Unions and the MOU Compromise in Industrial Relations Practice

Within the trade union movement, there was resistance to the institutionalization of social dialogue or non-adversarial approaches and inculcating a discourse of dialogue and consensus as compared to traditional trade union practice. The nature of the industrial relations climate reflected a 'clash of civilizations' between the traditional, confrontational school and style of industrial relations bargaining, as against a more consultative, conciliatory partnership approach. Other forms of resistance emerged from the smaller unions whose voice was being curtailed by larger union constituencies through centralized collective bargaining mechanisms.

The participation 'at the table' with equity with other stakeholders, relationally facilitated the unions to 'box and dance' (Huzzard et al., 2004) from the MOU standpoint becoming equal partners, being privy to transparent disclosures of information, seeking to negotiate amicably, and consensually, through consultation, affording them a degree of reciprocity and mutual benefit from within the agreed arrangements. Contests arose within the union constituency regarding the perception of a compromise in credibility by unions' leaders (Martinez-Lucio & Stuart, 2004; Taylor & Ramsay, 1998; Kelly, 1996) by their adoption of a more managerial stance and conciliatory dialogue (Iankova &Turner, 2004) with management.

The MOU strengthened the shift in the modus operandi within the Trade Union Movement, with respect to the institutionalization of collective bargaining. The inculcation within union discourse of collective bargaining and the streamlining of the bargaining process has altered the traditional constructs within the bargaining process. There has been the shift in the emphasis on monetary salary in the negotiations mix, commensurate with an increase in importance of a distinct concept of equitable 'benefit' within the context and construct of bargaining and wage negotiation.

The reconceptualization of benefit resulted in a departure from being monetary in nature to a new equivalence to include benefits, such as access to education, training and investment in the human resource capacity of the individual as an element, which has allowed it to be used as a similar and at times an equal bargaining instrument, with regard to substituting or compensating for the reduction in direct monetary gains or wage increases. The culture of rivalry, that subsumed the union movement, became degraded as a discursive practice, as the union captured and retained a more 'independent' discourse which favoured internal unity and the brokering of new power relations and 'enrolment' within the MOU network. Internally, the centralized collective bargaining practice and the challenges of exclusion for the smaller unions required new alignments in power relations.

All participants acknowledged or recognized that there had been an unanticipated and unexpected change in the behaviour of the trade unions, which was demonstrated in the interaction between them and the Government. The diverse ways of acting for trade unions in Jamaica, focused on the welfare and treatment of workers and types of related labour, identificational, social activity with networks of social practices reflected in the discourse, genres and styles

You may recall that trade union practice forms part of and is influenced by a broader network of practices globally and order of discourse through adherence to labour conventions and other interdiscursive representations of international hegemony. These have ideological linkages with the ILO, in terms of 'ways of believing', demonstrated through specific types of social activities and values associated with and reinforcing the labour genre and practice. Further, that as part of the nationalist political movement in Jamaica, Goolsaran (2006) argued that trade unions were integrally involved in the political movement, which still affects the contemporary dynamics of labour management network relations. This was reflected in the alignments with and fluctuations between practices of political unionism within network practices of industrial unionism, retaining elements of the practices of the former, in the latter and in labour relations practice.

The MOU dialogue and discourse challenged these modalities, evidenced by the leadership demonstrating realignment, independence and a new preference by their accession to the more 'consensus based' MOU discourse model' and social dialogue as espoused in MOU text, seen as being contrary to traditional discourse and culture. Industrial relations practice as a discipline of study can reassert its relevance within the constructs of productivity and national competitiveness dialogue. Labour productivity as an outcome, is a function of the dynamics of and capacity within the labour force and the social relations between management and worker, which is its foundation, undergirding the nature of the interactions.

CONCLUSION

The trade unions, traditionally participating as external actors to the public sector network of relations, were afforded powers through the new MOU discourse, that in cases, seemed to supersede and subordinate that of public sector managers, reflected in the positive results of union advocacy in the areas of appointments and following up on infringements regarding employment issues and human resources management practices. Several of the union participants inferred that the MOU became a tool of governance and advocacy for compliance with respect to relations with public sector management. Public sector managers were, as a result, called upon to account for their stewardship, particularly as it related to human resource management. Moreso, they were resentful of the unions making representation for remedies, their advocacy energised by the MOU institution of the Monitoring Committee (MC). Commensurately, the MOU also became a tool of empowerment and a means for employees to advocate for the benefits as contained in the text of the MOU, as well as those left in abeyance by management complacency over the years and the public sector establishment's structural limitations under operations of a traditional public sector discourse and culture. Relevance remains in certain dimensions of the discourse between management and worker to address competencies, participation in decision making, equitable partnership, established standards of quality and performance assessment within a framework of trust, a 'mutual coincidence of need' and reward. Considering these, the role of industrial relations remains relevant and essential to create the social infrastructure and parameters for the dialogue within discourses concerning productivity and competitiveness. The role of trade unions and industrial relations practice to facilitate cultural change within networks of social relations, especially within the public sector is dialectic, being influenced by dialogue on productivity and enhancing same.

REFERENCES

Acosta, A., & Alleyne, D. (2006). *The policymaking process in Jamaica.* Inter-American Development Bank.

Cowell, N. M. (2006). Industrial Relations-Theory and Practice with reference to Jamaica. *Industrial Relations in the Caribbean*, 281.

Daniel, G. T. (1957). Labour and Nationalism in the British Caribbean. *The Annals of the American Academy of Political and Social Science, 310*(1), 162–171. doi:10.1177/000271625731000117

De Jong, B. (2007). Shedding Light on the darkness: Using the Actor-Network theory to analyse the distribution of power. Paper for the 47th Europe Regional Science Association, Paris, France.

Downes, A. (2003). *Productivity and competitiveness in the Jamaican economy.* Economic and Sector Studies Series. Washington, DC: InterAmerican Development Bank. (RE3/OD6)

Fairclough, N. (1992). *Discourse and social change*. Cambridge, UK: Polity Press.

Fairclough, N. (2003). *Analysing discourse: Textual analysis for social research.* London: Routledge. doi:10.4324/9780203697078

Farnham, D., Horton, S., White, G., & Dennison, P. (2003, September). *The search for industrial democracy in British Public Services*. European Group of Public Administration. Retrieved from http://soc.kuleuven.be/io/egpa/HRM/lisbon/Farnham_et_al.pdf

Goolsarran, S. J. (2006). *Industrial Relations in the Caribbean, Issues and Perspectives*. International Labour Organization.

Gough, R., & Ogden, M. (2008). Partnership, Bargaining and Production in 'Liberal Market' and 'Co-ordinated Market 'Economies. *Varieties of Capitalism, Corporate Governance and Employment Systems*, 39.

Huzzard, T., Gregory, D., & Scott, R. (2004). Strategic unionism and partnership: boxing or dancing? In Book of Abstracts (p. 135). Academic Press.

Iankova, E., & Turner, L. (2004). Building the New Europe: Western and eastern roads to social partnership. *Industrial Relations Journal, 35*(1), 76–92. doi:10.1111/j.1468-2338.2004.00301.x

Jessop, D. (2007). *State power: a strategic relational approach.* Cambridge, UK: Polity Press.

Johnson, C. L. (1980). Emergence of Political Unionism in Economies of British Colonial Origin: The Cases of Jamaica and Trinidad. *American Journal of Economics and Sociology, 39*(2), 151–164. doi:10.1111/j.1536-7150.1980.tb01624.x

Kelly, J. (1996). Union militancy and social partnership. *The New Workplace and Trade Unionism, 3*, 77-109.

Krieger, J. (1987). Social policy in the age of Reagan and Thatcher. *Socialist Register, 23*(23).

Lincoln, Y. S., & Guba, E. G. (1985). *Naturalistic inquiry* (Vol. 75). Sage.

Martinez-Lucio, M., & Stuart, M. (2004). Swimming against the tide: Social partnership, mutual gains and the revival of "tired' HRM. *International Journal of Human Resource Management, 15*(2), 410–424. doi:10.1080/0958519032000158581

Mulvey, M., Goolsarran, S. J., & Gomes, P. I. (2003). *Strategic Visions for Labour Administration in the Caribbean.* International Labour Organisation: ILO Sub-regional Office for the Caribbean.

Munroe, T. (1992). *The industrial relations culture: perspectives and change.* Paper presented at the Conference: Planning Institute of Jamaica, 30th Anniversary, Kingston, Jamaica.

Munroe, T. (2000). *Voice participation and governance in a changing environment: the case of Jamaica. Caribbean Group for Cooperation in Economic Development (CGCED).* Washington, DC: World Bank.

Patton, M. Q. (2002). *Qualitative Research and Evaluation Methods.* London: Sage Publications Inc.

Pierson, P. (1996). The new politics of the welfare state. *World Politics*, *48*(2), 143–179. doi:10.1353/wp.1996.0004

Shaikh, M., & Cordello, A. (2006). *From epistemology to ontology: challenging the constructed truth of ANT*. London: London School of Economics and Political Science.

Stephens, E. H., & Stephens, J. D. (1986). *The Political movement and social transformation in dependent capitalism*. London: Macmillan. doi:10.1515/9781400886074

Stone, C. (1985). *Class State and Democracy in Jamaica*. Kingston: Blackett Publishers.

Stone, C. (1989). Power, policy and politics independent Jamaica. In R. Nettleford (Ed.), *Jamaica in Independence. Heineman: Caribbean.*

Taylor, P., & Ramsay, H. (1998). Unions, partnership and HRM: Sleeping with the enemy? *International Journal of Employment Studies*, *6*(2), 115.

Willman, P., & Bryson, A. (2007a). Union organization in Great Britain. *Journal of Labor Research*, *28*(1), 93–115.

Willman, P., Bryson, A., & Gomez, R. (2007). The long goodbye: New establishments and the fall of union voice in Britain. *International Journal of Human Resource Management*, *18*(7), 1318–1334. doi:10.1080/09585190701393863

Chapter 9
MOU Convergence:
Governance, Institutions, and Discourse

ABSTRACT

The Monitoring Committee (MC), consisting of both government and union officials institutionalized dialogue as a practice in the governance of the implementation of the MOU. The MC demonstrated value by becoming a responsive mechanism and sounding board for preventative, dispute resolution, and for engaging in joint decision making. The unions rejuvenated their own discourse practice and acquired new avenues of influence in relation to public administration policy decisions. While the private sector occupied a position of self-exclusion, leadership engendered collaborative governance obfuscating the political divide, enabling the Monitoring Committee to consolidate the accord. The inclusion of discourse as a moment in actor networks is advocated as a means to reveal the inner operations and network interactions within the "black box," rendering the impenetrable, penetrable.

THE INSTITUTION OF THE MONITORING COMMITTEE (MC)

The Monitoring Committee was valued as a tool to oversee the process of social dialogue and became an effective mechanism for public sector problem solving, promoting a shared responsibility (Ballantyne, 2004) and authority by the Partners, within a framework of engendering transparency, fact and information sharing. As a structured forum, the Committee was valued for

DOI: 10.4018/978-1-5225-8961-7.ch009

allowing freedom of expression, the resolution of issues and by being an avenue that facilitated greater inclusion by the unions. As an established forum for joint decision making at the highest level, this inclusion by the unions was exploited in the form of influencing government decision making at the policy level. The Partners successfully managed to militate against and avoid long incidences of social and labour unrest, which assisted in maintaining fiscal stability and stymieing a mass separation of employment in the public service.

Viewed as a new territory of learning in partnership interaction, the MC's institutional legitimacy has been retained and endorsed by Cabinet, with its role consolidated and integrated within the existing bureaucracy of government and union partially due to its value in stemming potential industrial disputes. The Committee promoted an operational framework and standard conduct in supporting partnership arrangements– involving respect, honesty, mutual respect, collaborative, frankness and consensus building.

The regularizing of and increased dialogue and equal participation at the highest level' through the mechanism of the MC, could represent a template for such arrangements at the bureaucratic level between managers and staff through the replicated mechanism of the CSCs meetings and the increased union interface at the lower levels of the organization.

The MC demonstrated in part, the institutional framework of what could be a working model of good internal governance, which is consistent with the overarching good governance discourse of Government and the larger role of the involvement of stakeholders as joint partners in public sector development. Legge (2002, p. 78) argues that a central actor is always in danger of being taken over by a potential ally and as "such networks are never completely fixed and stable, but rather fragile and transient and, hence, require hard work on the part of those who seek …to develop and maintain [them]".

As a partner to the MOU Agreement mention has to be made of specific dimensions of the Government as an actor. You may recall the circumstances, socio economic environment and structural context foregrounded in the MOU negotiations leading to its formation. These issues were discussed pertaining to the state in chapter 1 and the political culture with low social capital (Brewster, 2007; Brown, 2002; CAPRI, 2009; Fashoyin, 2001) which is further reflected upon by Schoburgh (2006) who notes that:

The development of the island's political system was marked by divisions and confrontations between groups … suspicions which were to have lasting effects on the ability of Jamaicans to trust each other and to work together

Of note also, which also contribute to contextualize the investigation, are the type of government and governance modalities remaining from the vestiges of the Westminsterial constructs of colonialism, as explored in chapter 7, having undergone several structural and institutional modifications, in relation to public sector reform initiatives, such as the Administrative Reform Programme (ARP I and II) (Isaacs, 2002; Tindigarukayo & Chadwick, 1999), New Public Management, (Hood, 1986; Bissessar, 2002) and the recent Public Sector Modernization Programme (PSMP).

These dimensions together arguably, establish the context from within which the discourse of Government emerges with a role prescribed by the text of the MOU Agreement in terms of its responsibility for the broad macroeconomic and fiscal outcomes, the management of public sector expenditures through wage, employment and expenditure restraints and the development of the public sector. However, in relation to the influence of discourse on the network of relations, the institution of the MC, in which the Government was represented, provided a key forum through which the practice of MOU discourse and the power in the MOU social partnership was demonstrated.

THE MONITORING COMMITTEE (MC)

The membership of the trade unions within the institution of the MC as joint partners with Government in the MOU social partnership, suggests a level of "symmetry" (Law & Hassard, 1999, p. 40) in the social relations and equality in the MOU actor network provided for in the mechanism of joint decision making through the operations of the Monitoring Committee (MC).

The MC consisted of persons at the "highest level" in the Government of the day namely ministers, policymakers, public sector bureaucrats etc., The trade unions' membership in this forum was described in the text as analogous to them gaining entry to the "Great House".'

It's suggested ... for the unions are ... they were in the 'Great House', for the Government its suggesting that you know... we would be willing to listen and do with them on an equal footing yes. (Respondent 3)

The choice of language to use the term "Great House" links intertextually and graphically across time, with the language of the plantation and the historical legacy of plantocracy and slavery in Jamaica. The "Great House" conveys the socio-cultural imagery within slavery and plantation culture as the home of the plantation owner, symbolic and representative of the nexus of authority and power over the economy of the plantation and top of the social order, being the centre of economic governance and decision making.

The unions, in the analogy were equated to the slaves on the plantation, or those positioned peripherally in terms of power and authority, relegated to being subordinate in plantation society. The MC, institutionalized as a mechanism to facilitate dialogue between the Partners, repositioned and enabled the unions to be become equal partners with the Government in the MOU network of relations, elevating their status to be joint decision makers, gaining entry to a the "Great House' of power. Which suggests, that under normal circumstances they would have been excluded. What is also mirrored is the MC with plantation governance hierarchies, compared and contextualised across time and space.

The term interdiscursively links to the unions being repositioned and also being given access to enter and interface within the "Great House," as an outcome of inculcating the new MOU discourse, "representationally," "ideationally" and "relationally" (Fairclough, 1992) within the power constructs of MOU network relations. This extends into their acquisition of new discursive practices as decision makers signifying their new power status.

PROBLEM SOLVING CAPACITY

The Monitoring Committee, partly because of the composition of its membership had acquired value as a quick responsive mechanism and interlocutor with respect to industrial relations dispute resolution within the public sector, having a broader sphere of influence even outside the Committee. The MOU discourse afforded the unions special access, which began to be exploited for problem solving purposes. This was made possible as the unions were afforded direct access to persons holding bureaucratic positions, power and status on the Committee who also had commitment authority, which provided the opportunity for issues to be agreed and dealt with directly with persons at the top, instead of tunnelling through bureaucratic tiers for solutions. Monitoring committee members could actually sit down and discuss critical issues directly with for example, a member of Government at a senior level who had the authority to make commitments to address the issues. The type of interface resulted in the reduction in the time taken to solve issues with the avoidance of time-consuming bureaucratic processes, which were avoided. The MC provided avenues for the unions to pursue and articulate their concerns linked to core traditional trade union discourse practice issues, which could be aligned and accommodated within the new MOU discourse as common overlapping interests.

Being a forum and facility for trade union advocacy and voice, the MC was important as a vehicle for trade unions to, reassert their core discourse and practice maximizing opportunities to express their perspectives, articulate their views and be heard by relevant actors with authority, who had the power to act and effect change to resolve their problems. This suggests that under normal circumstances the unions would not have been afforded such an opportunity, more so, on a regular basis for their views to be taken into account with a heightened assurance of the possibility that they would be acted upon, because of the nature of the MC and its positioning with MOU discourse and practice.

From the literature, Jones (1996) notes that within the reform efforts of Jamaica that the non-public actors such as the trade unions, appeared to behave and were often regarded as 'junior' members in multilateral interactions. He also notes that socio political partnerships have been effective in systemic problem solving where formal and informal mechanisms for consultation have been employed for decision making and implementation. Once they are based upon consensus about action programmes, have a clear division of labour and dominant operating norms have been oriented to preserving the identities of those involved, the arrangements have been effective. The MC, as a vehicle for the unions to reassert themselves has become valuable, in that within the forum they are able to retain their identities and have not become subordinated or emasculated as an outcome of the MOU dialogue or appropriating MOU discourse.

INSTITUTIONALIZATION OF SOCIAL DIALOGUE AND PARTICIPATORY DECISION MAKING

Dialogue as a practice was institutionalized and consolidated in the MC providing the unions with a mechanism and avenue to exert power by influencing policy and by increased participation in joint decision making on public sector policy and development issues. You may recall in that according to Stone (1993) wages policy in the 1990s was in effect being manipulated by union militancy, support from trade union Prime Ministers (Mills, 1990) and policymakers. Consequently, wage increases during the nineties and the gains made, had been higher than inflation and at the expense of productivity.

Furthermore, that in the 2000's, Acosta and Alleyne (2006) explained that the trade unions have had a diminishing influence on the policy making process, attributing this to weak union membership, membership benefits and the reduction in the contribution of unions to party financing. They also account for the reduced policy influence and a waning of the power of the labour lobby, by the growing presence of non-unionized Government employees who are appointed at the recommendation of Government officials' and a reduction in the number of effective veto players in the policymaking process which serve to derail the practice of good governance. However, the inclusion of the Unions on the MC accentuated change in the traditional trade union discourse, moving away from stereotypical expectations of them resorting to 'strikes and mashing up the place' as described by participants towards dialogue and resolution, which had broader implications for societal expectations.

INDUSTRIAL RELATIONS PRACTICE: THE MC RESOLUTION ECHANISM

In terms of industrial relations practice in the public sector, the MC played a positive role to address issues that would threaten the achievement of black box equilibrium in the operations of the MOU network. The MC was valued by being an early "sounding board" for potential disputes and a forum where issues that would derail the MOU could be recognized and addressed quickly before they became a full-blown crisis with contagion effects. This led to a degree of responsive and members being proactive to curtail any labour crisis that had the potential to escalate. The Committee prevented the escalation of potential industrial disputes and became a valuable arbitrator and mechanism for conflict resolution by resolving issues quickly through dialogue, hence "nipping them in the bud," by;

1. creating an atmosphere where the problems could be discussed;
2. good working relations between parties on the monitoring committee;
3. the recognition and support of the Government of the role of the MC as an early detection mechanism; and

Table 1. Industrial action: pre MOU and post MOU

Date		Industrial action #
2001	Pre MOU-period	7
2002		12
2003-2004		18
MOU 2004-2006		5

Source: Industrial Relations Unit, Ministry of Finance & Planning 27/11/2007

4. recognition that such a mechanism was absent from the Industrial Relations landscape.

Statistics supported the perspective that there was a reduction in the number of incidences of industrial action which declined over the MOU period as a result of the interventions of the Committee. See Table 1.

Initiating traditional industrial relations mechanisms such as the three-tier system, referred to in Chapter 8, would have been the traditional protocol to follow for redress. However, the MC, by error, inadvertently or by design, began to seemingly displace existing mechanisms in the industrial relations conciliatory framework by becoming an avenue for grievances and for conflict resolution. The normal system or process for redress would be abrogated in favour of the MC being an avenue that didn't exist before, but now afforded issues to be dealt without them actually reaching to the dispute stage.

There were cases where breaches were highlighted in the media i.e., the Air Jamaica redundancies of May 2005, where the management of Air Jamaica management were making redundant 180 pilots following the redundancy of 40 pilots, less than a month earlier, which was resolved through the intervention of the MC.

The MC etched out a place for itself as an additional governance mechanism within state industrial relations bureaucracy, by being a quicker, more responsive dispute resolution mechanism, dissolving tension and stemming the incidence of industrial action and disruptions in employer employee relations.

The effectiveness of the MC in problem solving, from the texts, suggests a supplanting of the existing mechanisms already existing and operable in the sector. The revealed deficiencies in the local conciliatory process led to the questioning of the effectiveness of these existing procedures and institutions, embedded in the traditional industrial relations discourse, to the point of their

Table 2. Estimates of percentage wage increases in the private sector

	Pre-MOU	2004	2004/5	2005
General	10	9		11-12
Finance			22	
Manufacturing			5-12	
Security			5	
Telecommunications (Media)			7-8	
Janitorial Services			<10	

Source: PIOJ, September 2005, citing Jamaica Employers' Federation (JEF) PIOJ, *Memorandum to MOU Monitoring Committee- unpublished correspondence*, September 2005

role being contested by some participants. However, several participants still supported the existing dispute resolution mechanisms and their relevance despite acknowledging the deficiencies.

THE TRADE UNIONS AND THE PRIVATE SECTOR

The scope of the MOU's effect extended beyond the public sector into the practice of industrial relations in the private sector, in terms of the influence of a negotiated approach and dialogue by the unions, which had repercussions on the industrial relations practice in two dimensions. One inference was that the private sector benchmarked their salary increases to the wage restraint component of the MOU. Essentially, they incorporated them into their own practice, with different social actors representing them differently according to how they are positioned within the practice (Chouliaraki & Fairclough, 1999). The private sector recontextualized the practice of wage restraint in the MOU incorporating low salary increases into their own industrial relations practice as a benchmark. The private sector offered low wage increases to their workers consonant with that of the public sector, which drew resentment from the workers in the private sector. See Table 2.

Figure 1 displays the negative perceptions of the private sector which were held by the public sector, some in response to the unresponsiveness of the private sector which was solicited to become a part of the cooperation and sacrifice for national benefit. This alluded to the motivations behind the Barbados social partnership whereby the unions, government and private sector came together in patriotic and mutual accord to prevent the devaluation of the Barbadian dollar. The centre of the figure identifies the 'deficits' of the private sector and links them to the reactions, perceptions and emotions held by participants to them.

The non-participation of the private sector was viewed as being unpatriotic and rationalized as being due to them possessing diverse institutional objectives, with egocentric and fractured leadership, held together by a *raison d'etre,* labelled as being neoliberal in origin and profit seeking. Union participants alleged that other entities sought to establish MOU type arrangements to guide relations between staff and management than those traditionally used, as popular outcome of the MOU, due to the flexibility of its design to reflect parameters not strictly limited to wages.

Historically, efforts have been made towards building a social contract in the dimension of the exertion of political capacity, which has been controversial. This could arguably be an indication of the inability to obtain consensus and also to mediate effectively with the private sector. In that, there could be an anomaly or recognition that the interests or "discourse' at the very heart of private business and the market is towards capital accumulation and profit. To solicit them to be part of the network of relations as an actor, the private sector would be asked 'buy in' to the concerns of *interessement* and also act and behave contrary to their traditional discourse and practice.

Texts suggest that the MOU was being institutionalized further, being accepted as a viable accord within private sector industrial relations practice, especially in the case of benchmarking the percentage increase in salaries of the private sector with that of the public sector. Other dimensions of the MOU/ industrial relations practice relationship especially with respect to the core practice of dispute resolution was influences within the practice with the Monitoring Committee which function had a direct correlation with it.

MOU initiative. Their non-involvement was interpreted negatively by the public sector and unions alike as the MOU was interpreted as being a 'patriotic' initiative and a demonstration of mutual co-operation and

LEADERSHIP

In chapter 1 it was highlighted that three aspects namely dimensions of the globalization process, a weak state and crisis conditions have interacted in various country contexts, with differing historical, cultural socio economic, institutional and political backgrounds, to yield different forms of social partnership, albeit with these three elements being constant.

Figure 1. Perceptions of the private sector by the public sector in the MOU process

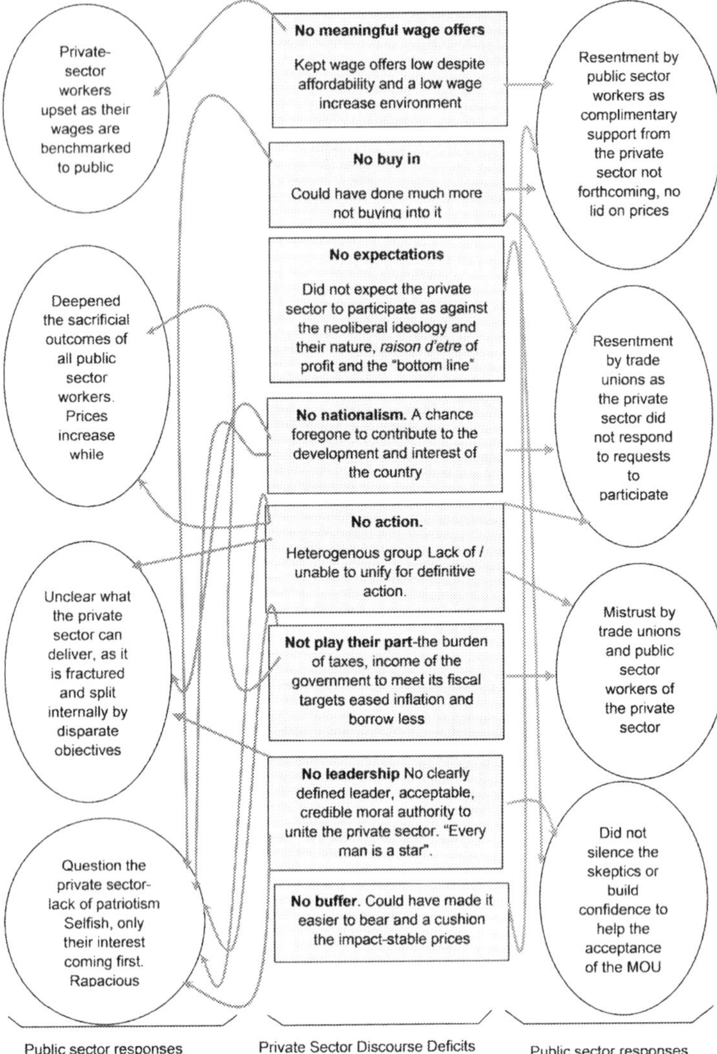

There is the suggestion that these three elements are interdependent, but it is recognized that perhaps more intangible dimensions such as trust, leadership, social capital and mutual need, may play a subtly greater role in the formation and duration of partnerships. There is therefore a role for leadership, leadership personalities and attributes as put forward by Djuric (2002) and others (Ghellab & Vylitova, 2005) with respect to the development of social partnerships.

The role of leadership in power relations and with respect to governance, as discussed by Hyden (1996), considers particular types of relationships among political actors which are socially sanctioned. He posits from the perspective of governance, that leaders can move society forward in new productive directions, once, they have the ability to intervene creatively, change ordinary structures by rising above them, to inspire and change the rules of the game. One may recall that attitudes to dialogue (Boyd, 2002), such as unwillingness, as well as a lack of knowledge and information, are mentioned by Djuric (2002) including issues of past legacies and leadership that contribute to weaknesses in the institutionalization of social partnerships. Leadership that can mitigate contending and diverse interests were signalled in the case of the Barbados Social Partnership and the Bauxite Memorandum of Understanding of Jamaica. One could argue that the successes of the work of the MC and the maintenance of the MOU cannot be divorced from the leadership and personalities composing the MC members. Several participants emphasized the role of

The leadership represented "new ways of acting and being" in seeking to maintain the network enrolment within the context of the institution of the MC. What was observed by participants was the ability of both leaders to unify or translate their constituencies around the MOU discourse and practice through *interessement* to *enrolment* demonstrated in their efforts at governance and problem solving. Given their origins, there was observed a setting aside of political, rivalry and vestiges of their traditional partisan political discourses in order to appropriate the new discourse of the MOU Agreement as reflected in the texts.

Participants made the distinction that the leadership of the unions chose to undertake a more collaborative approach than before and adopted a discourse of dialogue that operated within the MC. They were also an appreciation in the discourse as texts, that the parties recognized that there was worth in a more collaborative approach yielding benefits, compared to the outcomes from using the normative 'hard-nosed bargaining' practices of the past.

Associated with this issue is the dimension of how the unions in turn, are perceived (Martinez-Lucio & Stuart, 2004) by their constituents and the possible resistance and tension internal to the trade union constituency relationships according to Hyman (1975, p. 90) described as being "between power for and power over." The demonstration of a more "managerial" union discourse could trigger suspicions of compromise (Iankova & Turner, 2004) and the questioning of union legitimacy (Taylor & Ramsay, 1998) amongst

Figure 2. Leadership personality traits: monitoring committee

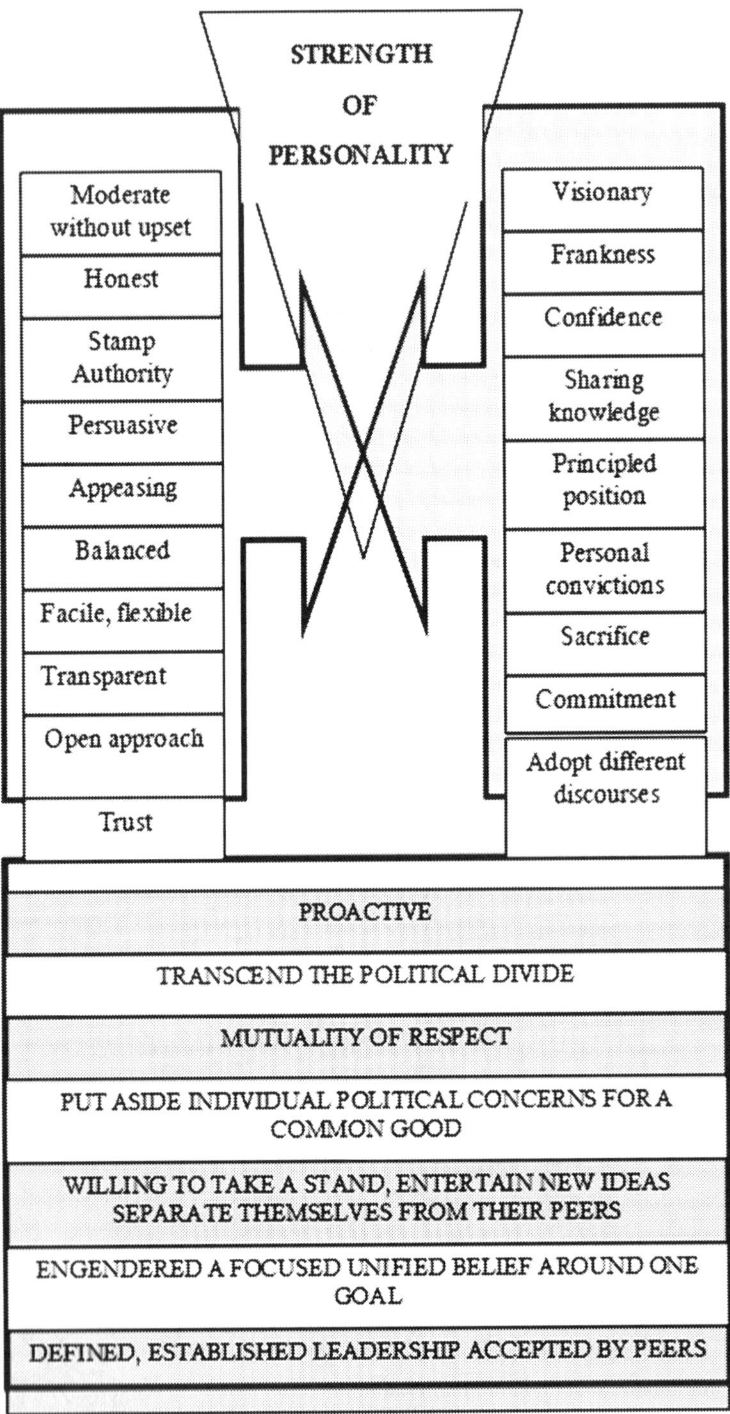

union constituents, as the language of partnership engenders a more conciliatory process within organized labour (Martinez-Lucio & Stuart, 2004).

The equitable status, and elevated power position, with access to special knowledge and greater intimacy within the inner circle as well as being privy to elite discourses from which they were previously excluded, would be of valued by the unions and would hence diminish the likelihood of them engaging in language that would undermine or jeopardize their new status.

To a large extent, the owners of capital and such institutions as the Private Sector Organization of Jamaica (PSOJ), have always been 'at the table, as mentioned in Chapter 8.

POWER PLAYS

A concern in the network of relations was the task of maintaining the black box status achieved and a balanced equilibrium, in the nature of deliberations, and to subtly enforce "informal' and "formal" power boundaries which had to be implicitly and or explicitly recognized and delicately upheld. The practice of power was reflected in the nature and the manner in which;

- the process of translation was operationalized within the MC;
- the circularity (Shaikh & Cordello, 2006, p. 4) in the practices of *interessemen*t, negotiation, joint decision making and conciliation towards *enrollment* being effective;
- the process of inscription, inculcation and the dissemination of the new philosophies, text and discourse through operationalization within the network of relations.
- MOU imaginaries, social practices and modalities of MOU discourse led to the recession of dimensions and institutions of the traditional discourses by members;
- Leadership was accepted and guidance received 'as a given' in the black box that enabled a direct focus, that was continually maintained, centred directly on the issues in translation, towards deriving consensus and the encouragement of the convergence of actors in concert with MOU text and discourse.

The participants noted that the MC and the MOU process afforded the unions increased opportunities for empowerment which were exercised. However, there were struggles with respect to the maintenance of a balance, to prevent the MC from overreaching itself and thereby abrogating powers unto itself beyond the remit given. The nature of the problem solving that the Committee was engaged in traversed into conflict resolution and operations with respect to industrial relations practice. There was an implicit acceptance that the MOU network had definitive institutional boundaries and a context within which its function had limits.

The issue of abrogation could reflect the fluidity of the network whereby power although not possessed and shared within the ANT construct, is still contested between the actors in an effort to hold relative positions and leverage their own interests in the midst of the tenuous black box stability that existed. So, translation exists as balancing circularity (Shaikh & Cordello, 2006, p.4) with the set of moments whereby the alignment within the MOU actor network can adjust, giving rise to convergence or divergence according to individual issues.

Both partners exercised and leveraged elements of their traditional discourses within the institution of the MC, while acceding to the 'new' MOU discourse and modalities of operation, identity and relationships. This accession brings adjustments and compromise in the modus operandi of each, to maintain a black box stability, sufficient also to further the MOU discourse within the 'space of flows' (Jessop, 2007, p. 184).

One of the weaknesses exhibited was the tendency for entities within the public sector to traverse the principles and provisions contained within the MOU, suggesting that their *enrollment* had not been complete or adequate, or fluctuated in terms of following through on responsibilities that were conferred upon them as a result of the MOU. Lapses such as these can be viewed as depicting power struggles, exhibited in unilateral action by entities which further demonstrated the need for greater *interessement* and *enrollment* of leadership in respect of their actor networks.

Representing an institutional image of MOU solidarity and cohesion, the MC demonstrated the ability to intervene with timely responses to conflicts or breaches that emerged. In effect, the MC strengthened the existing governmental/ industrial relations machineries in spite of tendencies to side-line the existing mechanisms, such as the three-tier system, for a more rapid response and resolution of issues by some parties. One could argue that these lapses could reflect a function of the dissemination of information, culture, (Jones, 1974; Mills, 1990; Schobergh, 2006; St Hill, 1970) reaction to exclusion, (Hood, 1986) threat of power loss, or ego resistance in the transference of wills.

The MC obtained its raison d'être as a valuable interface, arbitrator and mechanism of conflict resolution with respect to industrial relations issues, performing an important function and role within the existing conciliatory discourse infrastructure, but maintained its own identity, being distinct from it.

There was also an opportunity for the Committee's role to be sustained and or be diversified into other areas, i.e., to examine the human resources and industrial relations policies operating within the public sector, or to overhaul the associated machinery with a view to increase performance and greater coherence. Strengthening the human resources within the context of labour relations could militate conflict resolution efforts over the long term and avert the recurrence of crises. Another role could be with respect to formalizing methodologies of an industrial relations dispute settlement policy to become operational and focused on internal agency issues within the public sector and an overhaul of the existing measures with a view to strengthening them to perform at a higher level. Especially alongside efforts aimed at enhancing worker productivity and joint accountability for performance between management and worker.

Strengthening these aspects at the ground level by creating an interface between the conjunctures of human resources and industrial relations could mitigate deterrents to productivity over the long term.

ACTOR NETWORK THEORY: GOING BEYOND TEXT

The practice of power proceeded within the framework of the network interactions within the black box, which determined how seamless the diffusion or inculcation of the new discourse within the sector proceeded, networks diverged or converged and the durability and consistency of MOU network outputs and outcomes.

The MOU Agreement as an actor within a network of relations is therefore endowed with the capacity, as animate objects, to possess its own discourse as a participant in the network towards forming the black box. The inherent flexibility within the network construct has helped to understand and explain change, the mobility of actors within the dynamics of interaction, the ebb and flow of the mechanics of translation in changing power relations, as revealed in discourse as a moment leading to the subversion of other discourses.

Hegemonic relations of power born out of tradition and precedence within the public sector and union movement contested and resisted the tenets of the MOU Agreement and discourse and the empowerment sought by those previously excluded. Within the formation of the MOU network of relations, translation and network strategies for change required a 'new' discourse and narratives that would be operationalized, enacted or inscribed as new ways of being, new identities and materialized as new ways in space and time (Fairclough, 2005).

Enactment of discourses included new forms of communicative interaction with new genres, dialogue and relations between genres and new communicative styles. Issues of discourse arise for partnership governance strategies and leadership as facilitators in the implementation of policy. As the MOU discourse is constituted, it is being influenced dialectically by existing discourses and networks, as well as articulating elements of existing discourses and recontextualizing them (across structural boundaries, locales, scales, within differing fields etc., (Fairclough, 1992) within the MOU network of relations.

It is, at the same time, establishing itself as the dominant discourse as the black box becomes stabilized and inscription permeates discourse and is inculcated.

DISCOURSE AND THE "SOCIOLOGY OF TRANSLATION"

You may recall that ongoing translation or the sociology of translation in the network of relations involves four moments- *problematization, interessement, enrollment and mobilization*. Given that the network is a shifting open alliance system, (Williams-Jones & Graham, 2003) consisting of social groups, people, artefacts, devices and objects, each play a role in influencing one another (Shaikh & Cordello, 2006; Law, 2007) in the alignment and networking of interests. ANT indicates that in the incorporation of a new actor into a network, or convergence, there is a taking over of the alignment that the newcomer had with other networks and there is the transference of wills (Callon & Latour, 1981, p. 279).

The networking of interests (*problematization* and *interessement*) alignment (*enrollment*) and the transference of wills (*mobilization)* presumes "negotiations, intrigues, calculations and acts of persuasion and violence ... to which an actor or force takes or causes to be conferred to itself.' (De Jong, 2007, p. 7). This is part of the process towards alignment where the characteristics of actors are exercised towards determining relative power positions with respect to other actors in the actor-network. Translation, therefore, would require discourse and implies discursive properties of the actors.

The 'Discourse' Moment

Fairclough (2003) describes network relations as involving – representation, social practice, enactments, discourses and inculcation processes which are characterized as dialectical. The network of relations, therefore, reflects discourse in all its dimensions, which necessitates going beyond text and language considerations, to include other elements and social processes including discourses within discourse and discourse in context, into actor networks.

Discourse shapes society and culture dialectically, from the perspective that every single instance of language use reproduces shapes or transforms society and culture, including power relations. Hence, discourse as a moment affords an exploration of transformations, inscription activities within the context of actor networks. The concomitant effect is seen in network dynamics of convergence, divergence and reflexivity at the point of interaction and concomitantly reflect the relations of power over time.

Table 3 is a comparison of the moments in translation and the discourse moment indicating the synergies with specific dimensions of discourse highlighting the moments in translation and synergies for strengthening the inclusion of discourse as a moment in actor- networks within it. This opens up new avenues of exploration, such as the nature of power relations as "power in discourse is to do with powerful participants controlling and constraining the contributions of non-powerful participants" (Fairclough 2001, p. 38).

ACTOR NETWORK THEORY: GOING BEYOND TEXT

Actor Network Theory, acknowledges the use of text as a means of inscription, as one of the many material forms which includes artefacts, work routines, legal documents, prevailing norms and habits, written manuals, institutional and organizational arrangements and procedures, within which patterns can be inscribed (Montiero, 2000). Text in the process of heterogeneous engineering (Law, 1992, p. 2) is also seen as one of the pieces to be fitted or translated and can be considered an actor or actant.

ANT goes as far as to allow the conceptualization of legal text, such as the law, as being a collection of black boxes, which influences the social, forging of consensus between various interests and alliances (Stadler, 1997). ANT also notes the importance of the text intermediary (Bijker & Law, 1992)

Table 3. Equal partners: discourse moment and moments in "translation"

MOMENTS IN *TRANSLATION*	ANT ACTIVITY	DISCOURSE MOMENT ACTIVITY
Problematization	The focal actor's dialogue and work to form an alliance around the OPP or problem to address it, as all sides have a vested interest and interests that must be satisfied.	Discourse in terms of representation by actors – how things are or have been. Forming the alliance around the OPP, involves social practices and networks of social practices. Synthesis of activities, subjects, social relations, instruments, objects, space-time, values, forms of consciousness around it. Imaginaries enacted as actual networks of practices becoming real activities, subjects, social relations etc.,
Interessement	Locking actors into position' or stabilizing their identities in the network. It involves all the "negotiations, intrigues, calculations and acts of persuasion and violence to which an actor or force takes or causes to be conferred to itself." (De Jong, 2007, p. 7).	Discourse and language is used to position and identify oneself with and within a "socially meaningful group", (MacKay, 2007), or actor discourse network. There is the merging of "ways of talking, listening, writing, and reading," with "acting, interacting, believing, valuing, and feeling" into patterns associated with a recognizable social network, or affinity group (Gee 1996, p. 131).
Enrollment	There is ongoing inscription as inter related roles are defined and attributes accepted by the actors, building upon the moment of interessement This continuous process allows other actors the option of exercising choice, to either reject or accept them which include the acceptance of roles, identities and position in the network of relations.	Discourse involves inculcation by actors- material aspects, in genres, styles, ways of using language, materialized in bodies, postures, gestures ways of moving (Fairclough, 2001). Accommodates language/ communication between human agents, between inanimate objects and between both human and inanimate actors, considering the heterogeneity and precariousness of actor networks.
Mobilization		Discourse as representation. This suggest new ways of being, new identities, people coming into their "own" discourses to position themselves inside them, to act and think and talk and see themselves in terms of 'new discourses' (Fairclough, 2001)

such as in this study, the text of the MOU which assists to inscribe the actors into the processes of the MOU network. The MOU Agreement provisions encapsulated and provided the text and new language for inscription by the actors in MOU network relations and became an actor in its own right.

Text, text production, consumption and distribution, as one element of discursive practice emerge from a specific context and a combination of multi-dimensional social processes in production. By the inclusion of the discourse moment one is able consider dynamism, time and context issues within actor networks, which was one of the criticisms made by Johnston (2001). Each actor goes beyond text, by bringing to the actor network other factors and discursive practices and these too, influence the interpretation, production, distribution, transformation and consumption of texts (Fairclough, 1992).

As discussed, discourse goes beyond text, to include talk and language (Yates et. al., 2001), as well as other elements of social practices, including semiosis, where social life is seen as an interconnected network of diverse social practices where each one is an articulation of diverse social elements which always includes a discourse (Fairclough, 2001).

The role of discourse within the processes of change and shifts in the network relations between other social elements within the network of practices (Fairclough, 2000) provides data and affords the theorizations of that data, to interpret, explain and analyze social behaviour in actor networks in discoursal terms.

Discourse and the Black Box

Discourse as a unit of analysis, has value in usage to reveal, deconstruct and examine the practice of power in the connectivity or linkages of interface of the MOU network and within the black box that are brought to light and by which the nature of the inner fabric of social partnership power relationships can be observed.

The nature of the struggle between the different discursive practices and discursive endowments of the actors, interface and are contested in the derivation of consensus, modulated and encapsulated within the black box of network interactions. CDA methodology was insightful in deconstructing these inner operations, deriving the themes and discoursal roots that on analysis help further an understanding of the innermost interactions and implications for outcomes materially, institutionally, relationally and discoursally. The methodology also brought to the fore discourses hidden within and below discourses and explained the contests and the changing power relations evidenced in social practices and the material.

Actors in the black box become "punctualized actors" according to Law (1992, p. 385) to the point of having one voice by means of accession to, (what I posit) the dominant discourse, whereby authority is given for the macro social focal actor to "speak or act on behalf of another actor or force" (Law 1991, p. 151). The term 'black box', in either technical or social sciences, relates to being impenetrable, with its internal operations and activities being hidden, understood and viewed solely in terms of its inputs and outputs which are described.' The MOU network of relations, has through translation, achieved a black box equilibrium, however the precariousness of the actors, their heterogeneity, be it human beings, text, or an artefact (Garson, 2008, p. 2), are all trying to translate other wills into their own, (Callon & Latour (1981, p. 279) which causes the network to be in a continuous state of mutation.

The inclusion of the discourse moment in these precarious actor networks or in the black box, allows for the deconstruction and understanding of the dynamics within the black box itself, which could be considered as being a "discourse box" or in keeping with the French descriptors of the moments "*boîte de discours*" within it. (Nelson, 2016)

The inclusion of the discourse moment captures deconstructs and explains the nature of this precariousness inside the black box in discourse terms and the inner struggle between traditional discourses and the MOU discourse. Further, what is also facilitated is the inner exploration of the connectivity of power, which is shared in the network but also augmented by the MC in the "boîte de discours" at the institutional nexus of the macro social actor. Additionally, the power differentials between actors are revealed in multi level outplays of social processes through the lens of competing discourses and discursive practices.

This "*boîte de discours*" represents the fluid nexus of discourse integrated as a moment, which allows us to answer the "who," "what," "why" and "where" and the deeper exploration of the mechanics of power, as it is exhibited in and over discourse in the effort of the macro social actor to maintain dominance through discourse in the actor discourse network and the ongoing translation processes in the network. Discourse allows the power relations in actor networks that are said to be impermeable to social analysis by Mutch (2002) to now become permeable through the inclusion of the discourse moment.

REFERENCES

Acosta, A. M., & Alleyne, D. (2006). *The policymaking process in Jamaica*. Washington, DC: Inter-American Development Bank.

Bijker, W. E., & Law, J. (1992). *Shaping technology/building society: Studies in sociotechnical change*. MIT Press.

Bissessar, A. (2002). The introduction of new public management in small states. In Governance in the Caribbean. Social and Economic Studies, Jamaica, University of the West Indies.

Boyd, S. (2002). *Partnership Working: European Social Partnership Models. Scottish Trade Union Congress (STUC).* Social and Economic Partnership Project.

Brewster, H. (2007). *Understanding development challenges of the Caribbean.* Prepared for World Bank Forum for parliamentarians on *'Shaping A Trade Agenda to Promote Regional Integration and Competitiveness for CARICOM.* St. Lucia, May 2007.

Brown, D. (2002). The private sector as a social partnership: the Barbados model. In R. D. Selwyn & A. M. Bissessar (Eds.), *Governance in the Caribbean. Sir Arthur Lewis Institute of Social and Economic Studies (SALISES).* University of the West Indies.

Caribbean Policy Research Institute (CaPRI). (2009). *A new social partnership for Jamaica.* Kingston, Jamaica: Author.

Chouliaraki, L., & Fairclough, N. (1999). *Discourse in late modernity-rethinking CDA.* Edinburgh, UK: Edinburgh University Press.

Djuric, D. (2002). Social dialogue, tripartism and social partnership in the South East European countries, including recommendations for Serbia and Montenegro. *Europe Revie for Labour and Social Affairs, 3,* 87-100. Retrieved from www.ceeol.com

Fairclough, N. (1992). *Discourse and Social Change.* Cambridge, UK: Polity Press.

Fashoyin, T. (2001). *Fostering economic development through social dialogue.* Geneva: ILO.

Ghellab, Y., & Vylitova, M. (2005). *Tripartite social dialogue on employment in the countries of South Eastern Europe.* International Labour Organization.

Hood, C. (1986). *Administrative Analysis: An introduction to rules, enforcement and organizations.* Brighton, UK: Wheatsheaf Books.

Hyden, G. (1996). African studies in the mid-1990s: Between Afro-pessimism and Amero-scepticism. *African Studies Review, 39*(2), 1–17. doi:10.2307/525433

Hyman, R. (1975). What is Industrial Relations? In *Industrial Relations* (pp. 9–31). London: Palgrave Macmillan. doi:10.1007/978-1-349-15623-8_2

Iankova, E., & Turner, L. (2004). Building the New Europe: Western and eastern roads to social partnership. *Industrial Relations Journal*, *35*(1), 76–92. doi:10.1111/j.1468-2338.2004.00301.x

Isaacs, H. (2002). *Evaluations of civil service systems: case study Jamaica*. Washington, DC: Inter-American Development Bank.

Johnston, R. B. (2001). Situated action, structuration and actor-network theory: an integrative theoretical perspective. *ECIS 2001 Proceedings*, 73.

Jones, E. (1996). Jamaica: a framework for managing the reform process. In M. Garrity & L. A. Picard (Eds.), *Policy reform for sustainable development in the Caribbean*. IOS Press.

Law, J., & Hassard, J. (1999). *Actor network theory and after*. Oxford, UK: Blackwell.

Legge, K. (2002). *On knowledge, business consultants and the selling of total quality management. In Critical Consulting: New Perspectives on the Management Advice Industry* (pp. 74–90). Oxford, UK: Blackwell.

Martinez-Lucio, M., & Stuart, M. (2004). Swimming against the tide: Social partnership, mutual gains and the revival of "tired' HRM. *International Journal of Human Resource Management*, *15*(2), 410–424. doi:10.1080/0958519032000158581

Mills, G. E. (1990). *A Reader in Public Policy and Administration*. Institute of Social and Economic Research, University of the West Indies.

Mutch, A. (2002). Actors and networks or agents and structures: Towards a realist view of information systems. *Organization*, *9*(3), 477–496.

Nelson, C. (2016). Beyond Actor Network Theory to the Marriage of Moments. *International Journal of Actor-Network Theory and Technological Innovation*, *8*(3), 48–63.

Schoburgh, E. (2006). *Taking Responsibility; The Jamaican Economy Since Independence Institutional and Administrative Capacity*. Presentation.

Shaikh, M., & Cordello, A. (2006). *From epistemology to ontology: challenging the constructed truth of ANT*. London: London School of Economics and Political Science.

St Hill, C. A. P. (1970). Reform of the Public Services. *Social and Economic Studies*, *19*(1).

Stone C. (1993) Wages policy and the social contract. *Caribbean Labour Journal*, 3.

Taylor, P., & Ramsay, H. (1998). Unions, partnership and HRM: Sleeping with the enemy? *International Journal of Employment Studies*, *6*(2), 115.

Tindigarukayo, J. K., & Chadwick, S. (1999). *Synopses of ten best practices in Jamaican Civil Service reforms, Project on "Case studies in best practices in civil service reforms," Millennium Development Goals project*. New York: UNDP.

Chapter 10
Reflections:
Social Partnership and Governance Under Crisis

ABSTRACT

This chapter contemplates governance and condenses salient themes operable from the perspective of the implementation of the MOU social partnership agreement, its discoursal effect, and governance effect upon the relations of the partners in the network. Reflections are made on the implications of the MOU social partnership agreement as a governance mechanism for the partners—the public sector, the trade unions, and industrial relations practice—and their discourses in all their dimensions, which encourages change engendering the deepening of governance.

BACKGROUND

The shift from government to governance represents one of the important theoretical developments in political science and sociology during the past two decades (Pierre, 2000). Governance is theorized as the creation of structure or order not externally imposed but results in the interaction of a multiplicity of governing actors (Kooiman,1993) while O'Brien, et al., (2000) indicates that the phenomenon of governance, is broadly, the sum of ways which individuals and institutions manage their collective affairs. According to (Hertin J, et.al., 2000).

DOI: 10.4018/978-1-5225-8961-7.ch010

governments have become nodes for communication and decision-making, constantly interacting with concerned groups. Policymakers must acknowledge the need for complex and simultaneous processes of bargaining involving several policy areas, in order to improve efficiency between levels. Barriers to co-operation and questions of competency, transparency and legitimacy need to be recognized and overcome.'

Emerging in significance to deal with the traditional state's inability to cope with a range of contemporary social problems and crisis, a governance approach is adopted to solve issues collectively through the sharing of tasks and co-managing responsibilities between political and social actors (Jones,1998).

The concept of governance has evolved to identify and explain new modes of problem solving and decision making that fill gaps created by the failure of traditional forms. The process infers participation, where policies and institutions are redesigned in the national interest, within an environment of trust, towards mutually satisfying ends. Governance is also seen as interactive between the governed and the governor (Nettleford, 2002) intrinsically connoting shared, meaningful dialogue and changing relationships between government and the rest of society. The decline in the state capabilities propelled by financial crises and diminishing financial resources in the 1980s and 1990s and later macroeconomic challenges due to increases in public expenditures, economic restructuring and efforts to stem falling state revenues have created limitations resulting in the co-opting of private interests into public service delivery and the blurring of the public private divide.

Memorandum of Understanding (MOU): A New Discourse—A New Governance?

Pending crisis resulted in the MOU being created between the Partners, which reconstructed relations between the public sector and labour. These were driven by the economic imperatives and fiscal concerns of the Government vis-a-vis the labour concerns for the preservation of employment and continued efforts of developing the public sector by the JCTU. The Government and the JCTU responded consensually to the logic of the dialogue and consultation in an effort to avert further macroeconomic decay and to minimize the risk of loss. The arrangement brokered, the Public Sector Memorandum of Understanding (MOU) or social partnership agreement linked intertextually with the discourse of the ILO as a global institution and purveyor of the global discourses on social dialogue. On the part of the Government and their interaction with international financial institutions, there is value placed on inclusive dialogue and joint consultation with societal stakeholders as a condition for engagement and governance. Correspondingly, the trade unions linked to the hegemonic discourse of the ILO and labour relations genre maintained their consistency with ILO accords. Hence, consonant with ILO's social dialogue discourse, social dialogue and partnership in effect become a mode of governance, (Kuruvilla, 2003; Minet, 2008) that served to manage the crisis of a weakened state within the context of globalization (Bangs, 2006).

Discourse also has constructive effects in relation to social identities and subject positions, relationships between people and the construction of systems of knowledge and belief. The operationalization in the enactments of the 'new' discourse created new institutions, new relations and resulted in new identities, representations and ways of being to be inculcated within existing institutions and established practices and processes, resulting in their modification, eradication, transformation or them becoming obsolete. According to Fairclough (2003; 2005) 'operationalization' also involves the 'enactment' of discourses in new forms of communicative interaction, new genres, new forms of dialogue – and new relations between genres, with inculcation involving new communicative styles, with one such distinction being the reflection of government as a 'facilitator' in partnership governance. Consequently, discourse has a place both for strategies of partnership governance and implementation of actual forms of partnership governance. There were discursive elements in the Agreement in terms of imaginaries -- solving problems negotiating a solution and by constructing a logic, a governance modality which gives solutions their legitimacy.

Legitimizing narratives draw upon other discourses interdiscursivity and intertextuality as well as genres and styles which are articulated together in the formulation of the strategic interventions. These elements are reconceptualized into complementary relationships which are articulated within the context of existing discourses, social processes, structures and institutions which create tension, contention and contestation within the established 'status quo' of the public sector, government and their governance discourses.

Thus, the new governance of MOU discourse begins to erode the established discourses through hegemonic struggle between itself and the accepted, established practices and cultural effects within industrial relations practice, public sector practices and human resource management.

Traditional hegemonic discourses of the public sector were overturned, compelled to accept, accommodate or assimilate the new MOU discourse and governance, resulting in a dialectic relationship operating and semiotic differences. The responses to the MOU's 'new discourse'- institutional and operational demands on the part of the public sector management, workers, trade unions, and government -were diverse as well as their responses to the logic of the process and their acceptance of a 'new governance' - the MOU. The scales of responses varied according to the representation of each within the social ordering of practices within the public sector and at its interface with the MOU, as well as the articulation within genres of knowledge and ability to practically fulfil the obligations.

The 'Governance' of Discourse

Within ANT constructs, the MOU Agreement became an actor seeking to build its own network by incorporating other actors and those in the public sector that converged to create the MOU network of relations towards attaining governance through the black box stability. The text of the MOU Agreement, was inscribed, being the connectivity between the actors in the construction of the network through the process of the sociology of translation (Callon, 1986; Latour 1996; Law & Hassard 1999) – *problematization, interessement, enrollment and mobilization.* The incorporation of discourse as a moment within the actor network, introduces an analysis of the connectivity between and within the actors in the network and their associated networks. The MOU Agreement text provides for an MOU discourse with a view to permeate the network, in the establishment of MOU discourse, to become the dominant discourse, expressing governance through the moments of *enrollment* and *mobilization* and processes of alignment and inscription of the actors.

However, actors also bring their corresponding traditional discourses into network relations of shifting open reliance systems (Williams-Jones & Graham, 2003) through this connectivity of the discourse moment in relational interplay (Shaikh & Cordello, 2006). The nature of and power relations underlying the connectivity explored through the discourse moment and deconstructed using the CDA methodology) concomitantly provides for the deconstruction of the power relations and governance dimensions within the 'black box' of the MOU network relations using discourse and text as data and units of analysis.

Discourse triangulates between society/culture/situation/ cognition and discourse and language (Wodak & Meyer, 2009) and from the analyses of the 'black box', the discourses evidenced the stimulation of contraventions and multilevel 'clashes' within and between the constituencies of all the actors within the MOU actor network being translated. Discourse as a moment in the network deconstructs, enabling the exploration of the innards of social phenomenon and the power relations underlying networks, materialized as discourse in social processes and institutions. Contests occurred within the domain of discourse and text. Contests occurred between MOU discourse and practice vis a vis the traditional discourses and cultural norms and practices entrenched as identifiers within the network of relations of the actors externally and internally within the MOU network which served as a governance mechanism seeking to manage these human relations and social interactions between and amongst the actors, aligned to itself.

In the MOU network, there were discoursal power contests, at various levels within the hierarchy of the social and institutional structures of the actor networks. Furthermore, within the 'culture' is the broad articulation of different genre, discourses and inter discursive practices between groups which in contest, reflect power struggles that are internalized in discourse and between discursive practices, but externalized in terms of governance effects. Kelly (2004) you may recall, that social partnerships are a special kind of labour cooperative agreement which varies in the balance of power between parties existing along a continuum. These were displayed within the hierarchy of relations in and between networks.

Governance Within the Trade Unions

Within the trade union movement, there was resistance to the institutionalization of social dialogue or and inculcating non-adversarial approaches towards a consensus as compared to traditional trade union practice. The nature of the industrial relations climate reflected a 'clash' between the traditional, confrontational school and style of industrial relations bargaining, as against a more consultative, conciliatory partnership approach. Other forms of resistance emerged from the smaller unions whose voice was being curtailed by larger union constituencies through centralized collective bargaining mechanisms.

Internal to the TUN, issues arose within the union constituency regarding the perception of a compromise in credibility by the Unions' leaders (Martinez-Lucio & Stuart, 2004; Kelly, 2004) by them adopting a more managerial stance in practice and conciliatory dialogue (Iankova & Turner, 2004) with management. The participation 'at the table' with equity with other stakeholders, relationally facilitated the unions to 'box and dance' (Huzzard et al., 2004) from the MOU standpoint becoming equal partners, being privy to transparent disclosures of information, seeking to negotiate amicably, and consensually, through consultation, affording them a degree of reciprocity and mutual benefit from within the agreed arrangements. Contests arose within the union constituency regarding the perception of a compromise in credibility by unions' leaders (Martinez-Lucio & Stuart, 2004; Kelly, 1996) by their adoption of a more managerial stance and conciliatory dialogue (Iankova &Turner, 2004) with management. Concerns included how the power relations of trade union leadership were altered in the new network alignment within the MOU network, in the pursuit of centralized collective bargaining practices. The new alignments dialectic to each other, (within the TUN and in the TUN's alignment in the MOU network), resulted in reconfigurations to the perceived detriment of the smaller unions, in terms of the loss of an individual voice, representativeness and direct participation.

However, it can be posited that the unions, having gained access to dialogue in the context of the Monitoring Committee, were given the opportunity to influence policy, participate in decision making with implications for how the overall governance process of the Agreement was conducted and executed. Further, that they had avenues to affect and address issues jointly being 'seated at the table'.

The MOU strengthened the shift in the modus operandi within the Trade Union Movement, with respect to the institutionalization of collective bargaining. The inculcation within union discourse of collective bargaining and the streamlining of the bargaining process has altered the traditional constructs within the bargaining process. There has been the shift in the emphasis on monetary salary in the negotiations mix, commensurate with an increase in importance of a distinct concept of equitable 'benefit' within the context and construct of bargaining and wage negotiation. The concept of benefit and its reconceptualization, has its equivalence in benefits, such as access to education, training and investment in the human resource capacity of the individual as an element, which has allowed it to be used as a similar and at times an equal bargaining instrument, with regard to substituting or compensating for the reduction in direct monetary gains or wage increases.

The culture of rivalry, that subsumed the union movement, became degraded as a discursive practice, as the union captured and retained a more 'independent' discourse which favoured internal unity and the brokering of new power relations and 'enrolment' within the MOU network. Internally, the centralized collective bargaining practice and the challenges of exclusion for the smaller unions required new alignments in power relations.

The Government and the JCTU responded consensually to the logic of the dialogue and consultation which has links intertextually with the discourse of global institutions. On the part of the Government and their interaction with international financial institutions, there is value placed on 'inclusive dialogue and joint consultation with societal stakeholders' as a condition for engagement. This logic of dialogue between parties of different orders of discourse is becoming more pervasive within the institutions of Government and Labour in operational procedures and is reflected in varying dominance.

Alignment with the MOU network and commensurate inscription repositioned and strengthened the union movement institutionally within the construct of power in the network. As an equitable focal actor, participating in the governance of the network of relations with the Government, evidence of being less marginalized and gaining entry to joint governance, decision making and public policy making as well as the exercising of the shared power in the new network alignment, allowed the unions to influence the development of the public sector. The equal participation 'at the table' relationally, facilitated the unions to 'box and dance' (Huzzard et al., 2004) and become privy to transparent disclosures of information and repositioning in the new MOU network of flows.

Union advocacy was empowered by the MOU discourse in the governance of the public sector in relation to their agitation for worker benefits that were received above and beyond that of the traditional discourse practice which was acknowledged and recognized as an improvement over the existing modality of operation. Regarding the trade unions, their alignment in the MOU network and inscription with MOU discourse, influenced their traditional trade union discourse and practice in several dimensions. By appropriating a more consensus-based dialogue, akin to global discourses on social dialogue, rather than the traditional, militaristic discourse, had the effect of altering the image of the trade unions in the eyes of society and to the international community, which was recognized and acknowledged by the unions themselves and fostered internal unity and consensus building.

With respect to governance, interdiscursive links had been drawn between the traditional trade unions discourse and global discourses, using the example how the edicts of Prime Minister Margaret Thatcher reined in the powers of the UK trade unions and similarly, the concomitant effect the MOU Agreement and discourse had on the TUN. The imposition of legislative changes by Prime

Minister Margaret Thatcher, 'outlawed' tenets of UK trade unions' militaristic practices which prompted movements and the direction of efforts towards negotiated settlements and the reconstruction of labour relations around partnership and consensus (Martinez-Lucio & Stuart, 2002). The institution of the Monitoring Committee, provided access, gave voice and opportunities for the JCTU to participate in decision making in the context of the MOU Agreement resulted in fewer disputes and the resolution of issues before they became disruptive resulting in a calmer industrial relations climate.

Industrial Relations Practice

You may recall that as part of the nationalist political movement in Jamaica, that Goolsarran (2006) argued that trade unions were integrally involved in the political movement, which still affects the contemporary dynamics of labour management network relations. This was reflected in the alignments with and fluctuations between practices of political unionism within network practices of industrial unionism, retaining elements of the practices of the former, in the latter and in labour relations practice. The MOU dialogue and discourse challenged these modalities, evidenced by the leadership demonstrating realignment, independence and a new preference by their accession to the more 'consensus based' MOU discourse model' and social dialogue as espoused in MOU text, seen as being contrary to traditional discourse and culture.

Industrial relations practice as a discipline of study can reassert its relevance within the constructs of productivity and national competitiveness dialogue. Labour productivity as an outcome, is a function of the dynamics of and capacity within the labour force and the social relations between management and worker, which is its foundation, undergirding the nature of the interactions.

Certain dimensions of the discourse between management and worker must address competencies, participation in decision making, equitable partnership, established standards of quality and performance assessment within a framework of trust, a 'mutual coincidence of need' and reward. Considering these, the role of industrial relations remains relevant and essential to create the social infrastructure and parameters for the dialogue within discourses concerning productivity and competitiveness. The role of industrial relations practice to facilitate cultural change within networks of social relations is dialectic, being influenced by dialogue on productivity and enhancing same.

Governance Within the Public Sector

The alignment of the public sector in the MOU actor network, diminished management's authority, position and 'practice of power' with respect to their position within the traditional public sector discourse, (in terms of their representativeness to their constituents/ employees) and to the degree to which they felt that their relative power positions had been altered or superseded by the new governance institutions operable through MOU discourse. Elements of an entrenched traditional public sector discourse and the governance of the public sector conceptualized, 'ideationally' and 'relationally' (Fairclough, 1992) within a Westminster construct, had pre-conditioned attitudes and responses to the new discourse with resultant modalities of resistance. Analogies of the MOU being a threat, for example, 'noose around our necks', in terms of force being exerted in an attempt to modify traditional behaviour (although accepted) and unseat norms, reflect how management perceived the MOU and resisted the mutual shaping (Stadler, 1997) of new governance in the network.

In the development of the public sector, MOU discourse influenced modalities of how workers were treated with respect to pending retrenchment and by the institutionalization of training as a preparatory measure. The inculcation of tenets of the discourse of entrepreneurialism which contends with traditional public sector discourse reflects a mixing of traditional trade union discourse philosophy which supports and focuses upon addressing wider labour market concerns rather than that of the public sector only.The governance of MOU discourse, had differential effects within the constituency of the public sector network, in terms of multilevel contests which played out in processes seeking alterations of traditional social practices and behaviour of the actors, towards new governance modalities being inscribed through the MOU network, deep within the black box of network relations.

Overall, the inscription process of MOU discourse within the MOU network, led to contests with and within the discourses of the public sector (Downes, 2003; Bissessar, 2002; Mills & Robertson, 1990; Stone, 1989; Schoberg, 2006; Taylor, 2001) and union movement within the 'black box'. The strength, stability and governance of the MOU network became a function of:

- Intermediation in relationships with the focal actors;

- How effectively, dimensions of the traditional discourses and social practices (commensurate with relations of power between the actors, in and between their constituencies in the network), were militated; and
- The nature of the supporting mechanisms for the inscription of MOU discourse in the network and processes of inculcation within the actors' discourses.

Within the public sector, stereotypical traditional "discourse, the management style, or genre was depicted as being unresponsiveness, which conflicted with that of the staff seeking to be emancipated and empowered or being 'enrolled' and 'mobilized'. By inculcating and being empowered by knowledge concerning the discourse of the MOU, staff agitated for benefits that were withheld or not delivered, although they were afforded some benefits through the MOU text, such as, an improved speed of appointment to vacant posts. The revelations concerning the challenges of the unresolved human resource functions within the service brought into focus, presents the possibility that the success in part of institutional reforms and structural change efforts, may be compromised by the lack of a similar, concomitant emphasis on the human resource component within the service.

There was a perceived diminishing of the scope of authority of some managers who felt that their autonomy to manage and make unilateral decisions was being eroded. There was resistance to the increased democratization of decision within the construct of the CSCs, which threatened the 'status quo' or norms underlying existing power relations and institutional hierarchy of the traditional public sector discourse practice. The reluctance of management to become aligned through translation and resistance to inscription was reflected in their response to the MOU institution of the MC which, apart from curtailing the remit of management in certain dimensions, also relegated their position in the traditional hierarchical network as well as, within the MOU network of relations.

Government and the Public Sector

The political capacity of the state must be used via distinct mechanisms, to mobilize private sector and societal associations equitably to enhance the redistribution of growth. According to Jessop (1990, p.270),

..the state as such has no power – it is merely an institutional ensemble. It has only a set of institutional capacities and liabilities that mediates that power. The power of the state is the power of the forces acting in and through the state.

Consequently, issues of governance, political leadership and institutional reform would need to operate to support an internal self-perpetuating network within a framework of long-term commitment. There is a rational choice assumption that entities only collaborate when it is in their interests to do so hence collaboration and the 'mutual coincidence of need'' must outweigh costs or risks in terms of the loss of elements of power or autonomy. Other intangible factors would have to be brought to bear such as the quality of communication, common values and leadership attributes that can engender partnerships beyond self-interest.

Since the successful implementation of government policies and programmes are dependent upon public-sector management, it may be necessary to reconceptualize public sector management and its role under 'good governance' models, towards being more consistent with increasingly accepted standards of democratization and a modern public sector being pursued. It may be necessary therefore, to apply more introspection towards public sector management and its alignment in networks of governance and policy making to:

- Contemporize or re-conceptualize public-sector management Stone (1985) and Bissessar (2002) identity, genre and discourse differently from that construed under a Westminster model paradigm, in concert with modernization;
- Be consistent with increasingly accepted standards of democratization, participation and good governance being pursued externally, which may need to be applied internally through new modalities or mechanisms of governance of the service;
- Government would have to treat, possibly requiring separation and differential treatment, to engender greater *enrollment* in governance and policy implementing processes;
- Reconstruct existing power distributions, relationships and the hierarchical ordering of governance structures and relationships within the public sector;
- Promote and adopt a new paradigmatic base through the independent strengthening of the rigor of communication networks, accountability,

performance and governance frameworks at the management and technical policymaking levels; and
- Institute mechanisms for effective communication and the mandatory inclusion of management in policy dialogue.

The MOU has exacerbated the need for good governance practices and tenets of democratizations and inclusiveness to be extended within operations and functions of the public sector and the stability of the network of alliances created, becomes a function of the commitment (Law, 2007) of the actors to it.

THE MOU: A DISCOURSE OF DIALOGUE

The MOU network of relations served to order human activity, namely that of the public sector and trade unions as actors as reflected through the lens of discourse as a moment in the network, operating through the intermediation, inscription and inculcation of MOU text. Using the chronologies of events from the discourses of participants and by 'following the actors' (Latour, 1987, p. 176).

The application of ANT to the MOU chronology provides a network perspective useful for understanding the development of the MOU partnership. Further it, exhibits the value of ANT towards explaining the mechanics of the interactions and as a "lens" through which even as an emerging network and mode of governance.

This process would be repeated with respect to garnering and inscribing the other actors being co-opted into the MOU network, with mobilization being attained once a certain level of stability has been achieved, to black box status, even if the arrangement is tenuous, given the dynamics and heterogeneity of the actors and their alliances.

The MOU Agreement can be viewed as founded upon a discourse of dialogue, which became the dominant discourse to the subverting of tenets of the traditional public sector and trade union discourse and practice, demonstrating 'the practice of power in and over discourse' within the MOU network of relations.

As discussed, there were contests within the network of relations internally between the modus operandi of the traditional public sector and trade discourses and practices, as against MOU discourse, which determined externally, the extent and nature of the stability and sustainability of the network.

The resolution of these contests or successes at ordering the power relations in the network would reflect how seamlessly, the actors have accepted their new positions and alignment in the MOU network of flows. The equilibrium or stability derived would be as an outcome of how successful the diffusion/ inculcation/ inscription of the new discourse underlying the network had proceeded. There would be a concomitant outcome of stability reflected in the MOU discourse becoming black boxed and the dominant discourse over and against the traditional discourses and practices modified in some form, alongside their associated networks, in the process of translation and inscription with MOU discourse and practice.

Within the agreed arrangements, the unions appropriated an MOU discourse of dialogue and social practices that pursued amicable negotiations and consensus through consultation, to engender a degree of reciprocity and mutual benefit from within.

THE 'MOU': A NEW DISCOURSE—A NEW GOVERNANCE?

The MOU Agreement forged a 'socially ordered network of practices', subsuming genres and discourses from various fields in the text such as industrial relations practice, economics, human resource management, which all possess their own 'language' which have influenced the MOU discourse, which in turn interacts reciprocally with them within the MOU network of relations.

According to Fairclough (2003, 2005) 'operationalization' involves the 'enactment' of discourses in new forms of communicative interaction, new genres, new forms of dialogue – and new relations between genres, with inculcation involving new communicative styles, with one such distinction being the reflection of government as a 'facilitator' in partnership governanc. Consequently, discourse has a place both for strategies of partnership governance and implementation of actual forms of partnership governance.

The operationalization in the enactments of the 'new' discourse created new institutions, new relations and resulted in new identities, representations and ways of being to be inculcated within existing institutions and established practices and processes, resulting in their modification, eradication, transformation or them becoming obsolete. There were discursive elements in the agreement in terms of imaginaries -- solving problems negotiating a solution and by constructing a logic which gives solutions their legitimacy.

Legitimizing narratives draw upon other discourses interdiscursivity and intertextuality as well as genres and styles which are articulated together in the formulation of the strategic interventions. These elements are reconceptualized into complementary relationships which are articulated within the context of existing discourses, which social processes, structures institutions which creates tensions and contention and contestation within established 'staus quo' public sector, government and the governance discourses.

Thus, the MOU discourse begins to erode the established discourses through hegemonic struggle between the accepted, established practices and culture effects on industrial relations practices, the public sector practices and human resource management. Existing hegemonic discourses of the public sector overturned, were compelled to accommodate or assimilate the new MOU discourse, resulting in a dialectic relationship operating and semiotic differences.

Other factors impinge on the modalities of decisionmaking and the nature of the engagement, such as, the quality of communication, leadership modalities, common values, principles and factors that engender partnerships. The MOU has exacerbated the need for good governance practices and tenets of democratization and inclusiveness to be extended and intensified within the operations of the civil service, with the view to dismantling paradigms of precedence, structures and vestiges of top down governance Rhodes (1997) towards engendering ownership.

The clear revelations concerning the challenges of the human resource functions within the service, brings home, that the success in part of institutional reforms and structural transformation have been stymied, despite increasing education levels and capacity, by possible compromise by the absence of a similar emphasis on the operations of the human resource component on the ground and management's conduct and accountability mechanisms in this regard, which the MOU brought into focus. The growth and convergence of the MOU network was conditioned by the placement within the existing hierarchy of network relations within institutions and between the partners within the network and their associated discourses.

The dynamics of globalization and the interdependence of decision making has influenced growth and development to be achieved and defined in the context of 'the national interest' being interpreted, prioritized and accepted beyond the state's perception of such, to one that has to become compatible with that of collective and group interests of domestic sub actors who are now included in the policy process in social partnership governance models. Efforts that have been made towards building a social contract via the dimension of exerting political capacity has been controversial, with challenges to obtaining a consensus and also to mediate effectively with issues agreed. The Partners to the accord embraced the elements of it, resulting in compromises between them in adjusting traditional discoursal behaviour and practice to enable the network of relations to hold. Different facets of their relationship for example, trade unions' unilateral action -options to strike and labour unrest, and on the part of government, redundancies for fiscal expediency, have both been reined in and replaced by joint decision making and consultation along an agreed path created by an MOU discourse and institutional framework of operations.

It is within this sphere that the state and partners, such as the trade unions, have had to redefine themselves and negotiate their interests from within policy dialogue constructs and governance as a development strategy (Jones & Cruickshank, 2004) which can be viewed as a "self-organizing and inter organizational network' (Rhodes, 1997) consisting of state and non-state actors, resting upon relations of exchange and trust rather than on informal institutional roles and boundaries Jones (1998).

The application of ANT to the MOU chronology exhibits the utility of ANT towards explaining the mechanics of the interactions and as a "lens" through which to provide a network perspective useful for understanding the development of the MOU partnership, even as an emerging network and mode of governance.

CONCLUSION

The commitment to the principle of consultation and negotiation is in itself as important as the Agreement that had been negotiated and signed. The acknowledgement by the Partners of the strategic value of dialogue in responding to serious national economic crises is an important outcome. The Partners believed that social dialogue has served a useful role in helping to reconcile and resolve differences, providing a response over the nature and direction of the economy at a time of crisis.

The responses to the MOU's 'new discourse' - institutional and operational demands on the part of the public sector management, workers, trade unions, and government -were diverse as well as their responses to the logic of the process and their acceptance of the 'new governance' of the MOU. The scales of responses varied according to the representation of each within the social ordering of practices within the public sector and at its interface with the MOU, as well as the articulation within genres of their knowledge and ability to practically fulfil the obligations.

It is proposed that the commitment to the principle of consultation and negotiation is important as a precursor to agreements and sustained dialogue and consultation. The acknowledgement by the partners of the strategic value of dialogue in resolving serious national economic crises is an important outcome which has served to help reconcile and resolve sectoral differences over the nature and direction of the economy. Nonetheless, what is also underscored is the critical role of effective, sustained multilevel communication as a foundation to ensuring translation, stakeholder awareness and education of principles, provisions and policies with regard to social partnership and expectations. Issues of exclusion, non-participation, lack of transparency and non-compliance are capable of bringing about discord in social partnership arrangements as inhibitors, preventing effective inscription and inculcation to deform black box equilibriums achieved in the process of stabilizing network convergence as against divergence.

The MOU social partnership process has implications for state autonomy domestic sovereignty and policy development as issues of governance, political leadership and institutional reform implicit in these accords, require a framework of long-term commitment to operate and support, through ongoing translation and communicative inscription, an internal self-perpetuating dynamic or network. There is a assumption that actors only collaborate when it is in their interests to do so hence collaboration must outweigh costs, in terms of the loss of autonomy or minimize the potential risk of loss. Implicit in this is the assumption, that there must reside an openness and willingness for inter actor collaboration to be negotiated and negotiable, in the determination of self-interest and degrees of sacrifice entertained.

It is proposed that the commitment to the principle of consultation and negotiation is important as a precursor to agreements and sustained dialogue and consultation. The acknowledgement by the partners of the strategic value of dialogue in resolving serious national economic crises is an important outcome which has served to help reconcile and resolve sectoral differences over the nature and direction of the economy

The dynamics of globalization and the interdependence of decision making has influenced governance and development to be achieved and defined in the context of 'the national interest'. However, this is being interpreted, prioritized and accepted beyond the state's unitary perception of such, to become inclusive of collective and group interests of domestic sub actors who are now included in the policy process in social partnership governance models. It is within this sphere that the state and partners, such as the trade unions, have had to redefine themselves and negotiate their interests from within policy dialogue constructs and governance as a development strategy (Jones & Cruickshank, 2004) which can be viewed as a 'self-organizing and inter organizational network' (Rhodes, 1997) consisting of state and non-state actors, resting upon relations of exchange and trust rather than on informal institutional roles and boundaries (Jones, 1974).

REFERENCES

Bangs, J. (2006). Social Partnership: The Wider Context. In *FORUM: for promoting 3-19 comprehensive education* (Vol. 48; No. 2, pp. 201-208). Symposium Journals.

Bissessar, A. (2002). The introduction of new public management in small states. In Governance in the Caribbean. Social and Economic Studies, Jamaica, University of the West Indies.

Callon, M. (1986). Some elements of a sociology of translation: domestication of the scallops and the fishermen of St Brieuc Bay. In Power, Action and Belief (pp. 196-223). London: Routledge.

Downes, A. (2003). *Productivity and competitiveness in the Jamaican economy.* Economic and Sector Studies Series. Washington, DC: InterAmerican Development Bank. (RE3/OD6)

Environmental Change Programme. (2000). Brighton, UK: University of Sussex.

Fairclough, N. (1992). *Discourse and Social Change.* Cambridge, UK: Polity Press.

Fairclough, N. (2003). *Analysing discourse: Textual analysis for social research.* London: Routledge. doi:10.4324/9780203697078

Fairclough, N. (2005). Peripheral vision: Discourse analysis in organization studies: The case for critical realism. *Organization Studies*, *26*(6), 915–939. doi:10.1177/0170840605054610

Goolsarran, S. J. (Ed.). (2006). *Industrial relations in the Caribbean: issues and perspectives.* International Labour Office-Caribbean.

Hertin, J., Ian, S., & Frans, B. (2000). *Who governs the global environment?* ESRC Global.

Huzzard, T., Gregory, D., & Scott, R. (2004). Strategic unionism and partnership: boxing or dancing? In Book of Abstracts (p. 135). Academic Press.

Iankova, E., & Turner, L. (2004). Building the New Europe: Western and eastern roads to social partnership. *Industrial Relations Journal*, *35*(1), 76–92. doi:10.1111/j.1468-2338.2004.00301.x

Jessop, B. (1990). *State theory: Putting the capitalist state in its place*. Penn State Press.

Jones, E. (1974). Some Notes on Decision-Making and Change in Caribbean Administrative Systems. *Social and Economic Studies*, *23*(2).

Jones, E. (1998, June). *Caribbean Local Governance: Re-examining the building blocks*. OAS/ISER/UWI Workshop on Local Government.

Jones, E., & Cruickshank, I. (2004). Forging Institutional Convergence Between Labour Policy & Public Sector Reform: The Case of The Ministry of Labour and Social Security, Jamaica. *Social and Economic Studies*, 89–124.

Kelly, J. (1996). Union militancy and social partnership. *The New Workplace and Trade Unionism, 3*, 77-109.

Kelly, J. (2004). Social partnership agreements in Britain: Labour cooperation and compliance. *Industrial Relations*, *43*(1), 267–292. doi:10.1111/j.0019-8676.2004.00326.x

Kooiman, J. (Ed.). (1993). *Modern governance: new government-society interactions*. Sage.

Kuruvilla, S. (2003). *Social Dialogue for Decent Work, Education Outreach Programme, International Institute for Labour Studies*. Geneva: International Labour Organisation.

Kuruvilla, S., & Erickson, C. L. (2002). Change and transformation in Asian industrial relations. *Industrial Relations*, *41*(2), 171–227. doi:10.1111/1468-232X.00243

Latour, B. (1987). *Science in action: How to follow scientists and engineers through society*. Cambridge, MA: Harvard University Press.

Latour, B. (1996). *Aramis, or, The love of technology*. Cambridge, MA: Harvard University Press.

Law, J. (2007). *Actor Network Theory and Material Semiotics.* Centre for Science Studies and Department of Sociology. Retrieved from www.heterogeneities.net/publications/Law-ANTandMaterialSemiotics.pdf

Law, J., & Hassard, J. (1999). *Actor network theory and after*. Oxford, UK: Blackwell.

Martinez-Lucio, M., & Stuart, M. (2002). Assessing the principles of partnership, workplace trade union representatives' attitudes and experiences. *Employee Relations*, *24*(3), 305–320. doi:10.1108/01425450210428462

Martinez-Lucio, M., & Stuart, M. (2004). Swimming against the tide: Social partnership, mutual gains and the revival of "tired' HRM. *International Journal of Human Resource Management*, *15*(2), 410–424. doi:10.1080/0958519032000158581

Mills, G. E., & Robertson, P. (1990). The attitudes and behavior of senior civil servants in Jamaica. In *A Reader in Public Policy and Administration*. St Augustine, Trinidad: Sir Arthur Lewis Institute of Social and Economic Studies, University of the West Indies.

Minet, G. (2008, July). Some aspects of social dialogue from an ILO standpoint. In *Expert Group Meeting on Economic and Social Councils* (pp. 24–25). Academic Press.

Nettleford, R. (2002). Governance in the contemporary Caribbean: Towards a political culture of partnership. Governance in the Caribbean, 11-22.

O'Brien, R., Goetz, A. M., Scholte, J. A., & Williams, M. (2000). *Contesting global governance: Multilateral economic institutions and global social movements* (Vol. 71). Cambridge University Press. doi:10.1017/CBO9780511491603

Pierre, J. (Ed.). (2000). *Debating governance: Authority, steering, and democracy*. OUP.

Rhodes, R. A. W. (1997). *Understanding governance: policy networks, governance, reflexivity and accountability*. Buckingham, UK: Open University Press.

Schoburgh, E. (2006). *Taking Responsibility; The Jamaican Economy Since Independence Institutional and Administrative Capacity*. Presentation.

Shaikh, M., & Cordello, A. (2006). *From epistemology to ontology: challenging the constructed truth of ANT*. London: London School of Economics and Political Science.

Stalder, F. (1997). *Latour and actor-network theory*. Available online at http:// amsterdam. nettime. org/Lists-Archives/nettime-l-9709/msg00012. html

Stone, C. (1985). *Class State and Democracy in Jamaica*. Kingston: Blackett Publishers.

Stone, C. (1989). Power, policy and politics in independent Jamaica. *Jamaica in Independence: Essays on the early years*, 19-53.

Taylor, O. W. (2001). *The Employment Relationship (Scope) National Study 2001 (Jamaica)*. Retrieved from http://www-ilo-mirror.cornell.edu/public/ english/dialogue/ifpdial/downloads/wpnr/jamaica.pdf

Taylor, P., & Ramsay, H. (1998). Unions, partnership and HRM: Sleeping with the enemy? *International Journal of Employment Studies*, *6*(2), 115.

Williams-Jones, B., & Graham, J. E. (2003). Actor-network theory: A tool to support ethical analysis of commercial genetic testing. *New Genetics & Society*, *22*(3), 271–296. doi:10.1080/1463677032000147225 PMID:15115034

Wodak, R., & Meyer, M. (Eds.). (2009). *Methods for critical discourse analysis*. Sage.

Appendix 1

INNER WORKINGS OF RELATIONSHIPS: CRITICAL DISCOURSE ANALYSIS AND THE TEXT OF THE MOU

Introduction

The diverse perspectives which converge within the conceptualizations of critical discourse analysis (CDA), as espoused by Norman Fairclough, holding to the Foucauldian tradition and steeped within critical theory are contemplated. Tenets of CDA, related themes—text, language, and discourse—are discussed and utilized to traverse the Provisions within the text of the MOU Agreement itself. The exploration of its text and language brings to the fore the dialectical influences of existing discourses, networks articulated and recontextualized across diverse domains within differing fields, etc. in the creation of the text, undergirding the discourse of the MOU Agreement and operations within the macro social network of relations. The inclusion of discourse as a moment in the actor network facilitates a multi-dimensional analysis of the nature of the connections in discourse and texts between actors within the context of MOU network relations.

CDA Analysis: Text of the MOU Agreement (2004-2006)

One may recall that pending crisis resulted in the MOU being created between the Partners, which reconstructed relations between the public sector and labour driven by the economic imperatives and fiscal concerns of the Government, as against the labour concerns for the preservation of employment and continued efforts of developing the public sector. This relationship was demonstrated in the discourse of the text of the MOU, through certain words, such as "dialogue, social partnership', "The Partners' and consultation'. Discourse also has constructive effects in relation to social identities and subject positions, relationships between people and the construction of systems of knowledge and belief.

The MOU encapsulated the commitment of both Partners to the:

- Sustained growth and development of the public sector
- Establishment of a mechanism for collaboration and consensus building in the public sector through social dialogue.
- Development of a framework for the conduct of good industrial relations in the public sector

In applying the CDA approach, focusing mainly on the text of the MOU Agreement, a number of themes emerge that would inform the nature of the interface on implementation.

MOU Agreement Provisions Numbers 1-4

Provisions Number 1-4, seen in Table 1 below, are statements that speak to the legitimacy of a course of action based upon facts, hopes and beliefs. There is cognitive recognition of the macroeconomic state of affairs in No.2, where there is an acknowledgement of fact in relation to the negative macroeconomic conditions which are specified, such as the debt to GDP ratio, the fiscal deficit, economic growth and employment.

The macroeconomic information and terms in Provision 2, reflect an economic genre. There is a hopeful imperative that all sectors will cooperate in the 'National Interest' and the belief that the 'Government will in good faith pursue the appropriate macroeconomic policies' to turn around the negatives. In terms of Fairclough's discourse definition, the language is seen to be oscillating between fact (what is represented) and hopes or 'imaginaries' (what things might or could be). It is noted that the text links the negative macroeconomic conditions together and this is a 'fact' which is represented. Additionally, with respect to the 'imperative that all sectors,' should cooperate, it is an 'imaginarie' as the Agreement is between the Government and the JCTU specifically, and it is only a hope that all sectors would be included which is an expression of what would be the ideal.

The text has also labelled the macroeconomic negatives as a group, calling it 'the path' which is a nominalization conveying agentless, as it would appear that the 'path' was created by itself, hence having a power in and of itself. There is a distinction made between 'halting' and 'correcting' which suggests that they are independent and are not mutually exclusive.

With regard to the 'National Interest' around which the cooperation of all sectors should coalesce, this has not been defined, but one could assume that this relates to the macroeconomic challenges aforementioned. However, there is an agreement by the Partners, that 'the Government in 'good faith' is to pursue the appropriate macroeconomic policies which provide a stable economic environment and encourage GDP growth and create employment' which relates to a) c) and d) specifically less item a).

The idiom of 'good faith' has several connotations to it and is used in many agreements specifying contractual legal obligations by parties. It implies honourable intentions, and the avoidance of any attempt to deceive in assuming and performing contractual relations. It also implies that in fulfilling obligations there is no intention of malice and covers consequences made in the mistaken belief that you were doing the right thing at the time. There is an element of trust and expectancy on the part of the Government's "good faith' commitment in areas represented which they have direct responsibility for - namely the management of the economy.

There is no concomitant agreement in "good faith' for the Jamaica Confederation of Trade Unions (JCTU) as the other Partner to pursue. The commitment to pursue 'the appropriate macro-economic policies which provide a stable economic environment and encourage GDP growth and employment creation,' would imply that the current policies being followed were not 'appropriate' or lacked effectiveness, that adjustments were needed or a probable change of policies altogether would be required, to achieve the desired end. There are other elements to this which will be discussed at Section II Macroeconomic Management.

In terms of social level of analysis concerning the dynamics of how the text was produced, consumed, distributed and transformed, situating 'discourse-as text' within 'discourse–as-discursive practice' (Waller 2006), Chapter 1 detailed the macroeconomic context of Jamaica which explained how the state became so macroeconomically challenged, and these indicators in text (Low Economic Growth etc.) included in the Agreement provide an appreciation of what contributed to the issues and the inability of the Government to pay public sector salaries.

The text of Provisions Numbers 3 and 4 reflect labour relations genres and foregrounds the development of the public sector and industrial relations concerns. Provision Number 3 essentially summarizes two needs that underlie any Agreement of this nature, which is the cooperation by all sectors to a common agreed agenda which is the development of the Public sector, (that is assumed as being accepted by both Partners). Secondly the development of a foundation of trust and confidence to a satisfactory level, so that commitments to deliverables can be made and followed through to completion. The mention of 'developing and maintaining a satisfactory level of trust and confidence' suggests two things.

Firstly, that the JCTU is being realistic in terms of the extent of the level of trust and confidence that could be developed between the Partners, thereby aiming at a 'satisfactory level....' This may be based upon their previous experience with Governments in dialogues of this kind and the levels of suspicion and lack of trust that has prevailed in those discourses, so there would be little over optimism.

Provisions Number 4 (i) and 4(ii) are linked by the objective of 'harmonious labour management relations' which under certain conditions can contribute to growth and development in the national economy and the public sector. In 4 (i), the condition is the conformity to good industrial practices and in 4(ii) by the acceptance of bipartisan agreements as an effective strategy to achieve the same end. The aspect of peace and harmony in relations through bipartism is noted especially against the background of Provision Number "3". At the interdiscursive level, there is a possibility that the experiences of other countries which have had successful social partnerships and achieved economic growth, such as Ireland and Barbados (not bipartite agreements) are alluded to here, and the value obtained from those arrangements can give assurances of positive outcomes in the Jamaican context. However, Provision Number 4(ii) also mentions 'the acceptance of bipartisan agreement as an effective strategy through which growth and development may be realized'.

The JCTU has over the years pursued a strategy of forging sectoral agreements with the view to realize a national social partnership and have engineered several "MOU's" (which was also highlighted by several interviewees) that have had degrees of success and have also provided lessons of experience, brought to bear upon consecutive MOU's forged. Mention was made by interviewees of several MOUs in the mid-90's such as the Jamaica Public Service MOU which preceded the Bauxite and Alumina MOU and the National Water Commission MOU.

At the discursive level, **Number 4 (iii)** exhibits intertexuality, by drawing upon the dialogue and language of the ILO, which is reflected in the Conventions, which subsumes certain orders of discourse. There are associated discourses and socially ordered networks of social practices in the field of labour relations with its own genres, language and terminologies associated with industrial relations globally. These associations can be viewed as hegemonic as there is 'organizational control of linguistic variation and their elements....' (Fairclough, 2003, p. 24). The manifest intertexuality in the text and the expected social practices associated with commitments to the Conventions by states- e.g. freedom to associate, right to organize, etc., carry their own protocols and standards of best practices to which the discourse is aligned and similarly, states who are signatory will have concomitant social practices and regulations to legislate, implement and effect.

The latter line of **Provision 4(iii)** speaks to the Convention relating to Social Dialogue, Labour Relations Codes of Jamaica which represent how the Jamaican state has become embedded and subscribed to ILO discourse and practice through the legislation it has effected, as well as entrenching within the local labour relations practices, standards, conduct and modus operandi of employers, the language of ILO discourse, terminologies, meanings and ideological precepts. The affirmation that sound industrial relations 'may be maintained' by the commitment to the MOU principles and ILO Conventions, to which Jamaica is already signatory, suggests that the commitment to principles is not enough but there is no indication of anything else as other things that need to be included or what has been excluded.

The framing of the text for the Agreement also draws upon elements of the Social Partnership of Barbados as well as that of the Bauxite MOU, which are articulated together as other voices (Fairclough, 2003) in the text.

MOU Agreement Provisions Numbers 5-6

A number of principles were agreed at Provisions Number 5, A to G, which form part of a strategy for the sustained growth and development of the public sector which is a theme carried from Provisions Number 4 (i) and 4 (ii), with 4(ii) specifying bipartism agreement as also being a strategy to the same end. It is noted that provisions 5A-5D relate specifically to the public sector and highlight the commitments of the Partners to labour related indices such as;

- pursuing strategies designed to achieve a reduction in the cost of salary/salary related and ancillary benefits granted to all public sector employees for an agreed period of time.
- the establishment of a mechanism for collaboration and consensus building in the public sector through social dialogue.
- the development of a framework for the conduct of good Industrial relations in the public sector.

- A commitment to work together to preserve employment, improve the quality of the labour force through training, retraining and education and the maintenance of core labour standards in the public sector.
- An acceptance by both PARTNERS of the potential societal and economic benefits to be derived from such a Memorandum of Understanding.
- An acceptance by both PARTNERS that voluntarism applied to industrial relations practice in the public sector remains critical to the success of any endeavour.
- The recognition of both PARTNERS that the success of the Memorandum of Understanding is dependent on the other sectors of society restraining prices

In **5A**, strategies were mentioned to reduce the cost of salaries and benefits for an agreed time, in consideration of Government's concern for the fiscal agenda. In 5B establishing a mechanism for social dialogue to build consensus and collaboration within the sector, would be the Union's agenda in terms of greater voice and involvement in decisions for the sector at the national level, substantiated in Provision Number 6, by the formation of a Monitoring and Evaluation Committee. This was also a feature of the Bauxite MOU which was allegedly not very effective.

The inclusion of **Provision 5C** would imply that there was no framework for the conduct of good industrial relations in the public sector, or that if there was such a mechanism, it was weak and dysfunctional, as there are mechanisms and institutions that exist that have oversight over this area. One Participant described a 'three tier' system with a local level, ministry level reconciliation mechanisms and the Industrial Disputes Tribunal being the third tier. The Industrial Relations Unit, at the Ministry of Finance and Planning, also has a mandate that includes creating harmonious relationships within the public sector.

Provision Number 5D, states a commitment to work jointly to 'preserve employment ', 'improve the quality of the labour force through training and retraining and education' and the ''maintenance of core labour standards' in the public sector. This provision indicates the trade-off to 5A, as the implications are that there will be no retrenchment and efforts will be made to improve the quality of the labour force and adherence to practices that maintain the core labour standards, despite the wage restraint.

Putting aside the list of commitments, there is acceptance of the potential benefits to be derived from the Agreement **in 5E.** In terms of societal benefit, there would not be the effect on the society of making redundant 15,000 persons, especially within the context of very limited job market opportunities for them.

Additionally, the effect of 5D, would be to the benefit to the public sector, service delivery and implementation of Government policy as well as contribute qualitatively to the growth and development of the sector as the strategies intended. Economically, the Government would have been afforded a fiscal 'breathing space' and not have to expend political capital in retrenchment exercises as well as separation costs to the fiscal budget of related processes.

The importance of voluntarism to industrial relations practice in the sector has been valued as being 'critical to success'. The weight placed on voluntarism here, differs in scale from that of the other principles in terms of being labelled 'critical to success', without which there is none.

What is noteworthy, is that all the Provisions from 5A to 5F contain activities within the capacity of the Partners to perform, except 5G. The success of the Agreement has been recognized as depending upon "other sectors of society restraining prices', over which neither Partner has explicit control over. It can be speculated that it may have been a means of prompting a contribution from of the involvement of the 'other sectors' to commit to the effort that the Partners were making, for although the 'other sectors' are not named, it clearly includes the private sector, with the ability to restrain prices. This inclusion can be linked intertexually to the dialogue and discourse pertaining to the 'Partnership for Progress Initiative' that started November 2003. Intertextuality looks at how texts draw upon and incorporate, 're-work', re-contextualize, transform and dialogue with other texts, which is inextricably linked to what is made 'explicit', signaling what is left 'implicit' (Fairclough 2003).

The Partnership for Progress Initiative

This Initiative consisted of a number of societal stakeholders- trade unions, private sector organizations, academia, key NGOs etc., who met with Government representatives with the view to create a social partnership. This initiative was fuelled by a desire to see Jamaica regain position in the ranking of developing countries in terms of growth and development indices as against the general disappointment in its post-independence economic performance (Collister, 2005). The goals of the Initiative were to develop a social dialogue and partnership agreement which would build trust, seek consensus on issues of national importance, and promote a climate which would sustain economic growth, equity and justice that would benefit the widest cross section of Jamaican people (Collister, 2005). Strands of this intent are reflected within the text, which could be partly attributed to the involvement of some of the same union representatives in the dialogue concerning that Initiative, as who developed the MOU Agreement.

The discourse concerning the Partnership for Progress Initiative, which was an attempt at collaboration between labour and the private sector, are also echoed within this provision of the MOU, which calls for price restraint, acknowledging a dependence on private sector collaboration from the outset, to achieve success with the MOU. More so, that the collaboration between the sectors, despite the Initiative not materializing, was still desirable even in this framework that excluded the private sector from the initial dialogue. Implicit in this, is the notion that the success of the MOU resided with the ability of the Government and or the Trade Unions to negotiate, 'coerce, cajole, appeal to the patriotism, exercise some leverage or finally persuade the private sector, without the formality of signing an Agreement, to garner their "buy in' or *interessement* in the prescribed fashion of restraining prices. This would have proven a challenge, on the part of the Partners, given that the Partnership for Progress Initiative which had preceded that of the MOU discussions resulted in no accord between themselves and the private sector, on similar issues.

This position according to Fairclough (1992) the implicit recognition and need for the private sectors involvement and how valuable their contribution was to the MOU's success also highlights the relationship of intertextuality with hegemony on the part of the private sector. The Partners were prepared to commit to the MOU regardless, as there was a 'mutual coincidence of need' which was valued higher than achieving a 'successful' MOU, being reconciled to have an MOU which was not as 'successful' but would be sufficient in terms of the immediate 'needs' of the Partners and the potential benefits.

The texts from the participants signaled implicit understandings through intertextuality and the drawing upon other texts incorporating them within their discourse. The discourse of the Government which represented an economic genre and discourse with respect to the economic state of affairs, and the use of economic language by several participants in their discourses, is a case in point, being worked into their own Trade union discourses, as represented by its own socially ordered network of social practices and genres within the field of labour relations and language terms epitomized globally by the institution of the ILO.

In text production they have drawn on language, discourse, discursive practices, orders of discourse as well as social practices from their associations with the ILO, and its network. The genres associated with the ILO relate to social practices which regulate and control (a form of governance) other networks of practices. These elements have been brought into the trade union dialogue hinged to their "raison d'etre', all being articulated together in discourse.

From the perspective of the Unions, the cutting of public sector jobs had other implications, leading them to negotiate employment preservation, given Government's economic imperatives and the social implications. There was also the need, as represented by respondents, for the unions to preserve their membership and financial base which would prevent the further weakening of the trade union movement affected prior by layoffs as aforementioned by participants. Furthermore, the weakening of the union movement has reflected itself in their growing marginalization at the workplace and their limited inclusion into the processes of public policy making by other stakeholders.

Cumulatively, retrenchment would diminish the membership and financial base of the trade unions and weaken the labour movement already grappling with previous layoffs and globalization effects.

From the Government's perspective there was the need to avoid the loss of political capital before the next national election, by having to carry out public sector layoffs and if not this option, to have to implement a seemingly 'horrendous' tax package in order to address the recurrent growing expenditure of public sector salaries. Both options would have yielded severe political challenges. The Partners had agreed to the formation of the 'Monitoring and Evaluation Committee' (MC), (Provision 6) to ensure that the 'spirit and intent' of the MOU was adhered to, with representation from both sides. Interdiscursively, a similar committee had been set up under the Bauxite MOU with similar responsibilities. Multiple references to the experience of the Unions with the performance of such Committees within the context of previous MOUs may indicate inter discursivity, that the lessons learned and social practices from previous engagements would be used to frame and operate this Committee successfully. Three areas were designated that would achieve the objectives of the Agreement, namely- Restraint, Macroeconomic Management and Development of the Public Sector, of which 'Restraint' was operationalized from three dimension- namely Wage Restraint, Expenditure Restraint and Employment Restraint.

MOU Agreement Provisions Numbers 7-I Restraint A

Wage Restraint

The text in Table 3 is instructional, establishing parameters and giving guidelines to effect the policy of Wage Restraint. In 7 I A (i), it communicates the types of compensation arrangements to which the restraint will apply throughout the public sector and the employment status of the persons involved. It is interesting to note, that where increases are derived from promotion or increments that these are excluded, which would have been interpreted as possible punishment for performance and be a disincentive. The Health Sector is specifically mentioned as payments for sessions and emergency duty were usually paid to officers on duty, whether they were physically present or not, so a distinction had to be made, which is separate from 'on-call' allowances. Items 7 IA (iv) and 7 IA (vi), relate to the effecting of contracts on April 1, 2002 – March 31, 2004 whereby (iv) is to be settled at or below 3% wage increase, if no arrangement has been put in place, while in the latter 7 IA (vi) whatever has been arranged if above 3%, if the offer is on the table it is deemed the final offer to conclude the contract. Item 7 IA (v) indicates the same but relates to contracts coming into effect April 1, 2003 to March 31, 2005.

The type of genre appears to be that of the field of employee compensation and contract arrangements for remuneration between employee and employer, which is shown by the focus on how variations are to be treated through instructions and policy guidelines. In **7 IA (vii)** and **7 IA (viii),** the issue of 'retroactive payments' arise which is a consequence of the nature of the wage negotiation process. The tendency was for agreements for salary increases to take several years to be finalized before payment could be effected, sometimes falling in another negotiation cycle, so payment was after the fact, according to the status of the Government's cash flow. **Number 7 IA (ix),** is an attempt to prevent an inadvertent increase in the wage bill, through reclassifications which usually result in salary increases or an expansion of benefits with associated costs, without the approval or knowledge of the Monitoring Committee.

MOU Agreement Provisions Numbers 7- I B. Employment Constraint

Employment Restraint

The language of the text in this section relating to Employment Restraint is similar to the previous one, but the instructions seem to allow for greater flexibility. This is displayed in the use of phrases such as 'should be', 'with a view to', 'as far as possible', and 'there will be no', instead of more definitive language such as' there must be'. There is the endorsement of Circular 21 which was received negatively by the unions when it was initially promulgated. However, there is also the acknowledgement of the need for special treatment for certain groups, for which shortages were well recognized – teachers, correctional officers, the Constabulary Force, fire services and health professionals.

This would suggest that there was a mutual acceptance of the positions of both Partners to – curtail the growing wage bill but increasing employment, balanced against the special treatment required for certain groups which was justified due to existing staff shortages such as, the Correctional Services. **Number 7 B (iii),** is the conditional acceptance of no redundancies for public sector workers except through dismissals, restructuring and mergers, and with the prior knowledge of the Monitoring Committee. It is clear from **7 B (iv)** that it is coherent with the policy position of the Office of the Services Commission, and through the discourse of the MOU, it gives strength to its mandate.

But there is the acknowledgement in the use of language that there will be cases where officers act in clear vacancies beyond six months, but there is also an implicit plea to curtail this 'as far as possible'. This situation can, among others, be attributed to a number of issues, such as the establishment and or cadre not configured to accommodate the addition, budgetary constraint, the qualifications of the individual not being at the level required etc. This challenge speaks also to systemic or even cultural features of the public service, with respect to the non-enforcement this aspect. There was the tendency for staff to be acting indefinitely in vacant posts which has resulted in 7 B (iv)'s inclusion in the MOU.

Other reasons could be that the posts of the establishment was limited or the human resource manager, deficient in terms of a responsiveness to realities of service and demand on the ground. It is customary that an evaluation of employee performance be carried out, but there has been the trend for this evaluation to be stymied in objective (ignored systemically) and subjective (discriminatory) ways leading to the MOU being used as a tool to deliver security of tenure and access to benefits, such as pension, for workers who for years have been deemed "temporary' and excluded from certain benefits.

Number 7 B (v) pushes the 'dictatorial' theme of the MOU in relation to appointments for persons already acting over six months in a post, to be appointed within six months of the MOU being signed, unless valid reasons are given. With **Number 7 B (vi),** there is the call for Senior Management positions to be competitively tendered internally and externally, again with flexible language, cognizant of the realities on the ground in the public service which is inconsistent with regards to this approach. With respect to **Number 7 B (vii)** this would appear to be the weakest in terms of commitment as there is no concise joint agreement on the use of contractors and outsourcing of jobs. Both Partners agree 'to support the principle' only which is not fully committal to prevention or stoppage of the practice, likewise the practice of outsourcing jobs.

Government has a policy which allows the contracting out of particular services, after which the contractor then employs persons for the task. Concerns relate to the view that without more transparency, the practice of issuing fixed term contracts was being used to obtain cheaper labour, exclude a certain level of benefits and protection for the workers, which fosters the potential for employee abuse which undermines the spirit and intent of the MOU.

The Unions have expressed the view that fixed term /non-permanent contract workers are routinely excluded from the same contractual terms as permanent employees for example exclusion from employer's pension and sick pay schemes and contractual redundancy schemes. Yet in reality many fixed term contract workers may have a long employment history with the same employer than those permanently employed. One issue here has been that some contractors tender low bids for the contracts and employ persons who are paid very badly and in cases contravenes the labour laws. Secondly, other concerns relate to unfair dismissals and potentially unscrupulous employers who will use fixed term/non-permanent contracts rather than permanent contracts as a way of excluding employee's rights. The employers themselves may also become vulnerable to unfair dismissal claims. In the fostering of good labour relations, the manner in which outsourcing procedures and practices have been integrated within procurement policy and operations of the Government service, needs to be comprehensively revisited. This is in relation to the strengthening of the degree of inclusion of ILO Conventions and practices that the Government of Jamaica has already ratified, within contracts, agreements and arrangements.

Given that under such arrangements the Government, as the original agent, retains overall responsibility for the activity, there needs to be a renewed initiative to ensure compliance with ILO commitments and the relevant labour laws and standards, making them intrinsic but explicit to the contract arrangement, further strengthened by the development of regulatory norms within the context of procurement policy. Hence there is a need for the requisite labour standards to be explicitly contained as a conditionality for the contract to be accepted. The MOU has further exposed the need for a structured approach to outsourcing from the perspective of human resource management within the Government Service, which would avert the view that the process is being carried out in an ad hoc manner, inconsistent with overall strategic objectives. Without some guidance on approaches, ripples will inevitably be created within the context of GOJ/Union industrial relations which may undermine the 'spirit and intent' of the MOU.

Expenditure Restraint

With respect to discursive practice and what factors would influence how this Provision would be interpreted, this text (See Table 5) of the Agreement has been influenced by previous discourses concerned with reducing public expenditure, which has been reworked into the text production. This Provision also relates discursively to previous attempts at reducing waste within the public service. There was acknowledgment, at the highest levels of government, that a reduction in public expenditure was necessary, as well improvements in the efficiency of the public service' (1998).

A task force created from both private and public sectors and appointed by Cabinet produced a report called the 'Orane Report,' named after the Chairman of the Task Force, Mr. Douglas Orane, the CEO of Grace Kennedy Ltd at that time, which provided recommendations with regard to what could be done to reduce waste in the public service. The Report highlighted that the incidence of waste was widely known in the sector and partially attributed this to a lack of accountability at every level of the service, the absence of a culture of economy accompanied by deficient management practices which could not ensure compliance despite the presence of the necessary regulatory framework.

The Report made recommendations on the following areas to reduce waste, which are very similar to those expressed within the text of 7 I C (i), as follows:

1. Rental and Space Utilization
2. High Utility Costs
3. Use of Consultants
4. Domestic and Overseas Travel
5. Government Overseas Missions & Agencies
6. Abuse of Government Vehicles
7. Waste: Unnecessary Expenditure for Stationery, Furniture and Newspapers

It is useful to note that the call for reduced expenditure is consonant with that of the Orane Report, where some of the recommendations are being carried out by Cabinet Office which is in support of them. The Orane Report makes mention of other reports that have studied and made recommendations of the matter of waste in public expenditure to which its own text pays recognition.

The request for the implementation of systems to monitor expenditure patterns and the use of assets, to reduce abuse and expenditure, fall within the same frame of reference. However, there are certain power relations that are drawn upon which also motivated the inclusion of this Provision to engender equity and justice. The union leadership who wished to ensure that expenditures were carried out with moderation, with due consideration to costs and expenditure controls, mindful of the sacrifices the workers were making. The provision sought to cause those in authority at the upper levels of the service who had the power to authorize 'spending for aesthetics,' to by choice, exercise pragmatism and a sense of equity, and demonstrate a similar 'buy in' of sacrifice, similar to that being undertaken by the workers.

Given the context, the provision sought to compel a 'toeing of the line' by senior management as well as the Government having the responsibility to issue the necessary policy advice and framework on expenditure restraint within the service. The MOU, through this provision, seeks to institutionalize a cost savings programme throughout the public sector requiring the creation of committees in each entity with appropriate quarterly reporting procedures. There are immediate implications internal to the delegation of functions within ministries with respect to the allocation of staff and resources to ensure thoroughness, continuity and implanting the process within public sector operations.

Given the human resource constraints experienced by entities the required information for the creation of the reports would prove challenging. From the statement, one could assume that entities have not been carrying out cost saving measures at all. However, in discussions with several managers, in their creation of cost savings committees, it was acknowledged that cost savings has been a 'way of life' for many of them given the fiscal constraints and limited resources with which they had to operate, so this effort in the MOU served to formalize the effort. From the issuance of the Orane Report, several initiatives had begun which resulted in ministries adopting cost saving measures, but with a focus upon energy related consumption. It was noted from the outset that certain synergies could be built between the objectives and information emanating from these Energy Committees that were formed from this initiative and the MOU Cost Savings Committees.

The language of the text is instructional and policy oriented but seeks to engender a greater buy in from staff through the introduction of an incentive for worker welfare, from the cost savings effort.

The issue of procurement arises in **Provision 7 I D (iii)** and **(iv)** as this area cannot be overstressed, as the vehicle through which cases of over expenditures and breaches occur. However, with respect to procurement reform, the Procurement Policy Implementation Unit (PPIU), and the Public Expenditure Policy Coordination Division (PXPC) began a review of the framework in 1999 and represented ongoing work, with the present structural and procedural framework being launched in 2001, which preceded the MOU. There is also highlighted a weakness in the procurement guidelines which was the absence of sanctions for enforcement that would require the enactment of provisions that were legally binding, under the instruction to act from the highest level.

II. Macroeconomic Management Provisions

The Provision relating to the macroeconomic parameters for the MOU utilises the use of the word 'occasioned', conveying a lesser weighting and omitting causality, in the phrase.

There is a weakening in emphasis, in terms of the language with the terms, 'will commit to', being different from, 'will pursue', and the 'complimentary fiscal and monetary policies. Stronger emphasis is demonstrated in the latter elements of the Provision, in Table 5, which relays a definitive commitment to 'pursue the appropriate macro-economic policies which provide a stable economic environment and encourage GDP growth and employment creation,' but this could also suggest that policies being followed are not 'appropriate' or lacked effectiveness, with respect to the outcomes, hence reframed.

Regardless, a change of policy direction etc., could be argued based on the statements which are implicit. Fiscal and Monetary Provisions (i) to (iii) register predictive authority and purpose in the use of the language, "will manage,' will implement', and 'will pursue'. This belies the complexity of processes, resources, inputs and networking that would have to obtain to achieve the policy deliverables and targets, considering the context and the current background.

III. Development of the Public Sector so as to Produce a Sector That Is Modern, Efficient and of the Optimum Size, Properly Equipped and Suitably Rewarded

With respect to Provision III, the text begins with a statement possessing an intrinsic value which 'covertly' invites (Chouliaraki & Fairclough, 1999) action and is motivational. Further it relays commitment to tasks on the part of the Partners as well as reflecting the new role of government in governance discourse as being a 'facilitator'. The Provision has purposive and consequential relations which is to "explore possibilities of partnering', 'to provide', with the consequence being 'an expanded training programme in nursing'. The Ministry of Health (MOH) is seen as having the agency to 'partner' which is consistent with the ethos of social dialogue intrinsic to the new MOU discourse. Regarding (i) for the Ministry of Health (MOH), there are relationships between the clauses with 'are committed' and 'realizing the full' which are representative of relationships between processes which are both additive and elaborative.

In III (ii) there can be described a 'texturing of the text' as an explanation is given as to the conditions giving rise to the Provision, which is 'the severe shortage of nurses'. For III (i), (iv) and (vii) it is noted that the Partners are committed to facilitate training programmes or to 'make contacts', as against the direct responsibilities being delegated by the Partner's themselves to the Government which would in turn act through or delegate the responsibility to one of its agents- Ministry of Health, the Ministry of Education, Youth & Culture (MOEYC), or Ministry of Local Government Community Development & Sport (MLGCDS) to "explore', 'to carry out', 'to examine' and to 'report back' on specific tasks.

In a wider context the issue of training has been a factor in the Public Service whereby due to fiscal constraints, the level of training activities undertaken in the public sector had generally waned. The MOU was used as a vehicle to bring to the fore pending training needs left in abeyance by the unions, with the Agreement providing an imperative to reinvigorate the activity.

With respect to provisions (v) and (vi) the Cabinet Office would be the agency through which the training plan for the Public Sector work force would be developed for the needs of the 'modern labour market, as well as the exchange programme between ministries. Consequently, the operations and functions of the Cabinet Office to engineer and effect elements of Provision III is also brought to the fore as a key actor in the development of the Public Sector and aspects of its modernization.

The Cabinet Office provides the Prime Minister and his Cabinet with high quality information and policy advisory services leading to sound and timely Cabinet decisions which are effectively implemented by line Ministries. It is also responsible for the reform of the Public Service, to one that is more efficient, effective, accountable, and that treats the public as valuable customers. Other functions of the Cabinet Office apart from the operations of the business of Government, includes the management and direction of the various public sector reform programmes, improving the quality of customer service, training for public servants that are relevant to needs and assisting in developing and approving organizational structures in the Civil Service, as well as determining the appropriate classification of staff.

The Cabinet Office has led and participated in several phases of trying to develop and modernize the Public Sector through various programmes with the assistance of several multilateral development partners, such as the Administrative Reform Programme (ARP I, 11, 111) and currently the Public Sector Modernization Programme (PSMP). There has also been systemic changes, whereby the Human Resource Management Information System (HRMIS) has been transferred to Cabinet Office from the Office of the Prime Minister, as well as "Policy Coordination and Analysis" functions. In 1993, the Cabinet Secretary was designated as Head of the Civil Service as well as Chairman of the Permanent Secretaries' Board with attendant responsibilities. In 1995, restructuring of government ministries, resulted in Cabinet receiving some functions of the former Ministry of the Public Service.

These changes over the years could partly be attributed to attempts to address the perception of fragmentation and alleged lack of coherence between the Ministry of Finance and Cabinet Office with respect to the human resource management functions and the absence of a human resource policy for government. Furthermore, these perceptions were further alluded to by participants in terms of part of the human resource management responsibilities residing with the Ministry of Finance which seemed more preoccupied with macroeconomic, debt and fiscal concerns, vis-à-vis the human resource management responsibilities.

Contextually, one may recall that one of the concerns that the Unions had with the promulgation of 'Circular 21', which triggered the formation of the MOU Agreement to begin with, was the cap on employment when shortages of staff existed in certain areas, such as nursing, teaching and the fire services. Consequently, employment in these professional areas were exempt from the Employment Restraint and Section III (i) to (iv) sought to strengthen these areas which indicates a 'meeting of the minds' with the Unions' position.

The MOU was positioned as a tool to stem the decline of training activities the sector, under the rubric of the theme of Provision III, where training is emphasized using different mediums- cross training, intra governmental exchanges and the development of a comprehensive plan for the service- as well as throughout the text of the MOU, in the references to "the growth and development of the public sector'.

Some participant's texts noted that, the policy of Expenditure Restraint as pursued through the MOU could provide an excuse for managers to use budgetary funds allocated to them differently.

However, it was opined that the direct inclusion of training as an imperative and explicit obligation in the text of MOU Agreement would mitigate this effect.

With respect to (v) there is an acknowledgement of the need for managers and supervisors to receive training in human resource management, particularly the industrial relations aspect of interaction between management and staff within the sector. Implicitly suggested is the possibility that difficulties between management and staff within the sector could be attributed to the need to revise or update their existing knowledge base, to inform, due to a lack of knowledge or reinforce the need to apply techniques given the new imperatives of the MOU and its relationship to existing labour and industrial relations practice.

The MOU has also provided a vehicle whereby specific training to strengthen industrial relations practice within the sector, especially in cases where entities have human resource managers who also 'double up' to address industrial relations matters, while in some entities you have individuals to address these functions separately. One could opine that this indicates the challenge in that the industrial relations aspect of managing staff relations has been sidelined by the focus on human resource management, without due recognition to the former as a distinctive discipline, within staff management relations in the sector, which may not be seen as being 'glamorous' given the direct interface with the traditional trade union culture and industrial relations practice.

Special Items

The Provisions covering 'Special Items', as portrayed in Table 7, includes the treatment of pensions and the commitment to review the income tax threshold. With respect to pension payments, the instructions exempt payments already due to be paid as under normal circumstances according to existing contract terms. This seeks to assure recipients and establish level of security with regard to pre-existing commitments, moreover to include the public sector groups afforded special emphasis under the MOU.

The scope of application of the Agreement, as in **Provisions 10, 11, and 12,** seeks to engender some equity in implementation, delivery and streamline expectations on the part of the public sector on implementation, in that, the sector would be required to cooperate and collaborate with a sense of fairness. Rank or position in the sector would not make anyone exempt from any of the obligations compelling a multipartite contribution towards fulfilling the terms of the Agreement.

Concerning delivery, wherever benefits were being derived, equity would infer that the sector holistically would partake of them and in terms of expectations, that there would be distributive justice. No exclusions and no preferential treatment afforded certain groups more than others.

These latter Provisions highlight the institutional inclusiveness and the individual inclusiveness at the Executive level specifically, who would under normal circumstances be afforded special treatment in certain respects. Furthermore, the specific reference to these persons at the executive and political representative levels of the Public Service conveys an implicit expectation that it would be required and expected that they would 'lead by example' and demonstrate responsible leadership in the areas within their frame of reference.

With respect to **Provision 13,** one could contend that the flexibility of the Agreement is demonstrated by 'breaches', being referred to the Monitoring Committee for joint adjudication.

One could also posit that the contractual status of the Agreement is 'watered down' or diminished because there is no clear, hard and fast application of sanctions or immediate repercussions or penalties, with none being defined in the text. This suggests that the Monitoring Committee would adjudicate on what would be a 'breach' and how it would interprete whether a provision was being 'violated or not. There is the suggestion that breaches could occur that the Monitoring Committee would not be aware of and there is a dependency upon issues being reported to them for a response to be determined and also an assumption that '*any breach will be reported*' to them.

With respect to the MOU Agreement a 'socially ordered network of practices', was created subsuming genres and discourses from various fields in the text such as industrial relations practice, economics, human resource management, which all possess their own 'language' which influenced the character of the MOU discourse and practice emerging in the context of the MOU network of relations.

FUTURE RESEARCH DIRECTION

In exploring the MOU construed as an actor network, ANT provided an explanation as to the MOU network's mechanism and relations, being 'a social construction of social relations' (Lowe, 2001) and the dynamics operable within it. The MOU Agreement, given ANT's ontology is enabled to represent its own discourse as an actor, with the intermediary of text as the discourse of the MOU, seeking to inscribe other actor-networks into the MOU network, to achieve black box and macro social status.

The MOU actor network emerged as black box consisting of "punctualized actors" according to Law (1992, p. 385) to the point of having one voice by means of accession to the dominant discourse, whereby authority is given for the macro social focal actor to "speak or act on behalf of another actor or force" (Law, 1991, p. 151). Winner (1993, p. 365) indicates that the term black box 'in both technical and social science parlance is a device or system that, for convenience, is described solely in terms of its inputs and outputs, and one need not understand anything about what goes on inside such black boxes'.

Discourse as a unit of analysis, has value by its use to reveal, deconstruct and examine the practice of power in the connectivity of the MOU network and within the black box that are now brought to light and by which the nature of the inner fabric of social partnership power relationships can be observed. The nature of the struggle between the different discursive practices and discursive endowments of the actors, have to become engaged in the derivation of consensus, modulated and encapsulated within the 'black box' of network interactions. The positioning of discourse as a moment in the actor network provides for the use of discourse as text, as a unit of analysis and CDA methodology, to explore in depth the nature of the actor network interactions and connectivities during the process of translation, portrayed in dimensions of discourse and text.

CONCLUSION

The ongoing process of translation of the MOU actor network within the 'black box involves negotiating actor networks towards convergence and alignment. The MOU "black box' of actor network of relations created reflect Foucauldian discourse tenets in all its dimensions, which necessitates going beyond text and language considerations, to include other elements and social processes including discourses within discourse and discourse in context, into actor networks. With the inclusion of the discourse moment there is an avenue or lens to deconstruct and understand this dynamism within the black box itself.

Hence, discourse as a moment affords an exploration of transformations, inscription activities within the context of actor networks, the concomitant effect as seen in network dynamics of convergence, divergence and reflexivity at the point of interaction and concomitantly, the relations of power over time.

REFERENCES

Alvesson, M., & Deetz, S. (2000). Doing critical management research. *Sage (Atlanta, Ga.).*

Chouliaraki, L., & Fairclough, N. (1999). *Discourse in late modernity-rethinking CDA*. Edinburgh, UK: Edinburgh University Press.

Collister, J (2005, August 28). Looking for a better Jamaica. *The Sunday Gleaner,* p. 8.

Denzin, N. K., & Lincoln, Y. S. (Eds.). (2011). *The Sage handbook of qualitative research*. Sage.

Fairclough, N. (1989). *Language and power*. London: Longman.

Fairclough, N. (1992). *Discourse and Social Change*. Cambridge, UK: Polity Press.

Fairclough, N. (2000). *New Labour, New Language?* London: Routledge.

Fairclough, N. (2001). The dialectics of discourse. *Textus*, *14*(2), 231-242. Retrieved from http://www.ling.lancs.ac.uk/staff/norman/2001a.doc

Fairclough, N. (2003). *Analysing discourse: Textual analysis for social research*. Psychology Press. doi:10.4324/9780203697078

Fairclough, N. (2003a). Critical discourse analysis and change in management discourse and ideology: a transdisciplinary approach. In *II Congreso Internacional sobre Discurso, Comunicación ea Empresa, Vigo*. Universidad de Vigo.

Fairclough, N. (2005). Peripheral vision: Discourse analysis in organization studies: The case for critical realism. *Organization Studies*, *26*(6), 915–939. doi:10.1177/0170840605054610

Foucault, M. (1980). *Power/knowledge: Selected interviews and other writings, 1972-1977*. Pantheon.

Frow, J. (1985). Discourse and power. *Economy and Society*, *14*(2), 193–214. doi:10.1080/03085148500000010

Gee, J. P. (1996). *Social linguistics and literacies: Ideology in discourses*. Taylor & Francis.

Gee, J. P. (2004). *An introduction to discourse analysis: Theory and method*. Routledge.

Habermas, J. (1984). *The theory of communicative action* (Vol. 2). Beacon Press.

Halliday, M. A. (1978). *K (1978). Language as social semiotic: The social interpretation of language and meaning*. London: Arnold.

Harvey, D., & Braun, B. (1996). *Justice, nature and the geography of difference* (Vol. 468). Oxford, UK: Blackwell.

Janks, H. (1999). Critical discourse analysis as a research tool. In J. Marshall & M. Peters (Eds.), *Education Policy* (pp. 49–62). Cheltenham, UK: Edward Elgar.

Jørgensen, M. W., & Phillips, L. J. (2002). Discourse analysis as theory and method. *Sage (Atlanta, Ga.)*.

Kress, G. R., & Van Leeuwen, T. (1996). *Reading images: The grammar of visual design*. Psychology Press.

Law, J. (1991). *A sociology of monsters: essays on power, technology and domination*. London: Routledge.

Law, J. (1992). Notes on the theory of the actor-network: Ordering, strategy, and heterogeneity. *Systems Practice*, *5*(4), 379–393. doi:10.1007/BF01059830

Lowe, A. (2001). After ANT: An illustrative discussion of the implications for qualitative accounting case research. *Accounting, Auditing & Accountability Journal*, *14*(3), 327–351. doi:10.1108/EUM0000000005519

MacKay, T. (2007). Gee's theory of D/discourse and ESL research in teaching English as a second language: Implications for the mainstream. University of Manitoba.

Nowlan, B. (2001). *Introduction: What is critical theory and why study it.* Academic Press.

Richardson, T., & Jensen, O. B. (2003). Linking discourse and space: Towards a cultural sociology of space in analysing spatial policy discourses. *Urban Studies (Edinburgh, Scotland)*, *40*(1), 7–22. doi:10.1080/0042098022008013 1

Roderick, R. (1983). *The Idea of a Critical Theory*. Habermas and the Frankfurt School.

Thompson, J. B. (1984). *Studies in the Theory of Ideology*. University of California Press.

Titscher, S., Meyer, M., Wodak, R., & Vetter, E. (2000). Methods of text and discourse analysis: In search of meaning. *Sage (Atlanta, Ga.).*

Toolan, M. J. (Ed.). (2002). *Critical Discourse Analysis: Current debates and new directions* (Vol. 4). Walter de Gruyter.

Van Dijk, T. A. (1993). Principles of critical discourse analysis. *Discourse & Society*, *4*(2), 249–283. doi:10.1177/0957926593004002006

Van Dijk, T. A. (2001). Multidisciplinary CDA: A plea for diversity. *Methods of Critical Discourse Analysis*, *1*, 95-120.

Volosinov, V. N. (1973). *MM Bakhtin*. Marxism and the Philosophy of Language.

Waller, L. G. (2006). Introducing Fairclough's critical discourse analysis methodology for analyzing Caribbean social problems: Going beyond systems, resources, social action, social practices and forces of structure or lack thereof as units of analysis. *The Journal of Diplomatic Language*, *3*(1), 5.

Waller, L. G. (2009). *The role of discourse in ICT for development: Lessons from Jamaica*. VDM Publishing.

Wetherell, M., Taylor, S., & Yates, S. J. (2001). Discourse theory and practice: A reader. *Sage (Atlanta, Ga.)*.

Wickham, G., & Kendall, G. (2008). Critical discourse analysis, description, explanation, causes: Foucault's inspiration versus Weber's perspiration. *Historical Social Research. Historische Sozialforschung*, 142–161.

Winner, L. (1993). Upon opening the black box and finding it empty: Social constructivism and the philosophy of technology. *Science, Technology & Human Values*, *18*(3), 362–378. doi:10.1177/016224399301800306

Wodak, R. (Ed.). (1989). *Language, power and ideology: Studies in political discourse* (Vol. 7). John Benjamins Publishing Company. doi:10.1075/ct.7.11wod

Wodak, R., & Fairclough, N. (1997). Critical Discourse Analysis. In T. A. van Dijk (Ed.), *Discourse as Social Interaction* (pp. 258–284). London: Sage.

Wodak, R., & Meyer, M. (Eds.). (2009). *Methods for critical discourse analysis*. Sage.

Appendix 2

THE MEMORANDUM OF UNDERSTANDING 2004-2006

Figure 1.

Memorandum of Understanding for The Public Sector

1. The Memorandum of Understanding arrived at on the 16th day of February, 2004 between the Government of Jamaica on the one hand and The Jamaica Confederation of Trade Unions on the other hand (hereinafter called the PARTNERS):

2. Acknowledging that the country faces
   (a) A High Debt to Gross Domestic Product (GDP) ratio
   (b) A large Fiscal Deficit
   (c) Low Economic Growth and
   (d) Low Employment Creation

the PARTNERS recognize that these combine to create a path that is unsustainable and therefore agree that in the National Interest it is imperative that all sectors should cooperate to halt and correct the situation. Consequently, the PARTNERS agree that the Government will in good faith pursue the appropriate macro-economic policies, which provide a stable economic environment and encourage GDP growth and employment creation.

3. The PARTNERS recognize the need to chart a new course of co-operation in the achievement of the common objective of the development of the Public Sector and the

Appendix 2

Figure 2.

achievement of the common objective of the development of the Public Sector and the need to develop and maintain among themselves a satisfactory level of trust and confidence;

4. In recognition of the above the PARTNERS

(i) Acknowledge that peaceful and harmonious labour-management relations contribute to growth and development in the National Economy and the Public Sector and that these relations must be characterised by conformity to good industrial relations practices.

(ii) Recognise that such relationships emanate from the acceptance that bi-partisan agreement is an effective strategy through which this commitment to growth and development may be realised.

(iii) Affirm that sound industrial relations may be maintained by a commitment to the principles expressed in this Memorandum of Understanding and the principles laid down in the International Labour Organisation' Convention No. 87 (Freedom of Association and the Right to Organise) Convention No. 98 (The Right to Organise and to Collective Bargaining), and the Convention relating Social Dialogue and the Labour Relations Code of Jamaica.

Figure 3.

5. The PARTNERS agree to the following general principles underpinning the Memorandum of Understanding for the Public Sector, which will form part of an overall strategy for the sustained growth and development of the public sector in particular and the country in general:

A. A commitment of both PARTNERS to pursuing strategies designed to achieve a reduction in the cost of salary/salary related and ancillary benefits granted to all public sector employees for an agreed period of time.

B. A commitment of both PARTNERS to the establishment of a mechanism for collaboration and consensus building in the public sector through social dialogue.

C. A commitment of both PARTNERS to the development of a framework for the conduct of good industrial relations in the public sector.

D. A commitment of both PARTNERS to work together to preserve employment, improve the quality of the labour force through training, retraining and education and the maintenance of core labour standards in the public sector.

E. An acceptance by both PARTNERS of the potential societal and economic benefits to be derived from such a Memorandum of Understanding.

F. An acceptance by both PARTNERS that voluntarism applied to industrial relations practice in the public sector remains critical to the success of any endeavour.

G. The recognition of both PARTNERS that the success of this Memorandum of Understanding is dependent on the other sectors of society restraining prices.

MONITORING COMMITTEE

6. The PARTNERS agree that there will be a Monitoring/Evaluation Committee comprised of representatives from the Government of Jamaica and the Jamaica Confederation of Trade Unions to ensure that the Partners adhere to the spirit and intent of this Memorandum of Understanding.

7. In seeking to attain the objectives of this Memorandum of Understanding, the PARTNERS agree to the following three areas: Restraint, Macroeconomic Management and the Development of the Public Sector.

I. RESTRAINT

Reduction in the growth of the Wages Bill in nominal terms through:

A. Wage Restraint

There will be a general policy of wage restraint in the public sector for the period April 1, 2004 to March 31, 2006.

Appendix 2

Figure 4.

This policy of restraint will apply to all remuneration under contracts of employment for any kind of work to be performed in the public sector of Jamaica save and except for those instances where increases are arrived at through promotion and increments.

The policy of restraint will extend to all pay, including wages and salaries at all organisational levels, allowances, payments in kind, fringe benefits, and lump sums. It will also apply to all types of employment as well as to both full time and part time work.

During the period of restraint, sessional payments and emergency duty allowances will be paid only when the officer is physically on duty. This does not include the on-call allowance paid in the Health Sector.

Wage contracts to come into effect during the period April 1, 2002 – March 31, 2004 and for which there have not yet been any arrangements are to be settled strictly within a wage bill increase of 3%.

Wage contracts to come into effect during the period April 1, 2003 – March 31, 2005 are to be settled strictly within a wage bill increase of 3% for the period April 1, 2003 – March 31, 2004 except where offers above three (3) percent are on the table, the current offers on the table are deemed to be the final offers and the contracts will be concluded on that basis.

Wage contracts to come into effect during the period April 1, 2002 – March 31, 2004 and for which offers in excess of (iv) above are on the table, the current offers on the table are deemed to be the final offers and the contracts will be concluded on that basis.

New rates due for the same period 2002/2004 will be scheduled for payment in fiscal year 2004/2005 in accordance with the Government's cash flow situation whilst retroactive payments will be made in fiscal year 2005/2006 except where a payment schedule has already been committed.

For those groups with a current contract that extends into fiscal year 2004/2005, further implementation of that contract to be delayed until 2006.

During the period of restraint, there will be no reclassifications. Any requests for special cases are to be submitted to the Monitoring Committee.

Figure 5.

This policy of restraint will apply to all remuneration under contracts of employment for any kind of work to be performed in the public sector of Jamaica save and except for those instances where increases are arrived at through promotion and increments.

The policy of restraint will extend to all pay, including wages and salaries at all organisational levels, allowances, payments in kind, fringe benefits, and lump sums. It will also apply to all types of employment as well as to both full time and part time work.

During the period of restraint, sessional payments and emergency duty allowances will be paid only when the officer is physically on duty. This does not include the on-call allowance paid in the Health Sector.

Wage contracts to come into effect during the period April 1, 2002 – March 31, 2004 and for which there have not yet been any arrangements are to be settled strictly within a wage bill increase of 3%.

Wage contracts to come into effect during the period April 1, 2003 – March 31, 2005 are to be settled strictly within a wage bill increase of 3% for the period April 1, 2003 – March 31, 2004 except where offers above three (3) percent are on the table, the current offers on the table are deemed to be the final offers and the contracts will be concluded on that basis.

Wage contracts to come into effect during the period April 1, 2002 – March 31, 2004 and for which offers in excess of (iv) above are on the table, the current offers on the table are deemed to be the final offers and the contracts will be concluded on that basis.

New rates due for the same period 2002/2004 will be scheduled for payment in fiscal year 2004/2005 in accordance with the Government's cash flow situation whilst retroactive payments will be made in fiscal year 2005/2006 except where a payment schedule has already been committed.

For those groups with a current contract that extends into fiscal year 2004/2005, further implementation of that contract to be delayed until 2006.

During the period of restraint, there will be no reclassifications. Any requests for special cases are to be submitted to the Monitoring Committee.

Appendix 2

Figure 6.

B. Employment Constraint
There will be a general policy of employment constraint in keeping with the Ministry of Finance and Planning's circular number 21 dated September 22, 2003.

(i) The PARTNERS accept that there are certain critical groups within some Ministries to which consideration/exemption would be given. These groups are:
The Health Professionals
The Jamaica Constabulary Force
The Correctional Officers
The Jamaica Fire Services and,
Teachers.

The general principles of the circular will continue to apply to ALL other groups. The Post Operation Committee will provide reports to the Monitoring Committee as requested.

During the period of restraint the PARTNERS agree that there will be no separation of employment in the public sector except for justifiable dismissals, and through restructuring and mergers of entities as agreed. All proposals for mergers and restructurings will be brought to the prior attention of the Monitoring Committee.

In keeping with the instructions/policy of the Office of the Services Commissions, as far as is possible no officer should be acting in a clear vacancy for more than six months. The PARTNERS agree that during that period, an evaluation of the officer's performance should be carried out with a view to confirmation or otherwise.

Where, at the time of signing of this agreement, persons have been employed or are acting in a clear vacancy for over six months, the PARTNERS agree that such persons are to be evaluated with a view to appointment within the first six months of the signing of this Memorandum of Understanding unless valid reasons exist why such persons should not be appointed.

The PARTNERS agree that all acting arrangements and appointments for Senior Management personnel must, as far as is possible, be subject to competition internally and then externally if necessary.

The PARTNERS agree to support the principle of filling jobs with employees rather than contractors. Also, the practice of outsourcing jobs will be curtailed.

Figure 7.

C. Expenditure Restraint
The PARTNERS agree that there will be a general policy of expenditure restraint.

(i) The PARTNERS agree that this policy is to include but will not be limited to the following areas:
Motor Vehicle Purchase (Make and Model)
Purchase of Office Equipment
Social Functions
Rental of Property
Foreign Travel
Utilities.

Additionally, Ministries will be required to implement systems to monitor expenditure patterns and the use of assets to ensure that there is a reduction in the abuse of Government assets with the aim of reducing expenditure on these items.

(ii) The PARTNERS agree that the Government through the Ministry of Finance and Planning will issue the necessary policy advice on expenditure restraint to the Ministries and Departments in respect of the agreement arrived at between the PARTNERS.

D. Cost Saving Measures

(i). The PARTNERS agree that the Government through the Ministry of Finance and Planning will circulate a general policy statement in respect of cost saving measures to be adopted in the Public Sector. Each agency will establish a Cost Saving Committee to effect general cost saving measures as well as those that are peculiar to the respective agency. Each Committee to submit through the Permanent Secretary/Head of Department/Chief Executive Officer quarterly reports to the Monitoring Committee detailing the savings achieved.

(ii) The PARTNERS agree that a proportion of the savings achieved will be available to the relevant entity as an incentive to be used for staff welfare.

The PARTNERS agree that there will be an examination of the existing procurement policy and practice so as to identify any areas of deficiency for correction.

Having achieved the aforementioned, the PARTNERS commit to the consistent application of sanctions at all levels as soon as breaches are confirmed.

II. MACROECONOMIC MANAGEMENT

In response to the fiscal constraints occasioned by the increase in expenditure over revenue the PARTNERS agree that the Government will commit to pursuing

Appendix 2

Figure 8.

complimentary fiscal and monetary policies to sustain real economic growth over the medium to long term.

Fiscal and Monetary

(i) The PARTNERS agree that the Government will manage its economic policies in order to ensure that the inflation rate remains within the Government's targeted band of 8% to 9% in 04/05 and 6% to 7% in 05/06.

(ii) The PARTNERS agree that Fiscal policy will be implemented in order to generate a fiscal deficit in the range of 3% - 4% in 04/05 and a balanced budget in 05/06.

The PARTNERS agree that the Government will pursue economic policy to deliver outcomes consistent with a medium term profile as follows:

	2004/05	2005/06
Real GDP Growth (%)	2.0 – 3.0	2.0 – 3.0
Inflation (%)	8.0 – 9.0	6.0 – 7.0
Fiscal Balance (% of GDP)	-3 to -4	0.0

III. DEVELOPMENT OF THE PUBLIC SECTOR SO AS TO PRODUCE A SECTOR THAT IS MODERN, EFFICIENT AND OF THE OPTIMUM SIZE, PROPERLY EQUIPPED AND SUITABLY REWARDED.

Training, Re-Training and Education

(i) The PARTNERS are committed to the facilitation of training programmes aimed at realising the full staff complement at the Ministry of Health in respect of the Health Professionals.

(ii) Recognising the severe shortage of nurses, The PARTNERS agree that the Government through the Ministry of Health will explore the possibility of partnering with the Northern Caribbean University and the Community Colleges to provide additional training facilities to those already provided by the University Hospital of the West Indies and the Kingston School of Nursing for an expanded training programme in Nursing.

The PARTNERS agree that the Government through the Ministry of Education, Youth and Culture will carry out a needs assessment for the training of Secondary School Principals in School administration.

Figure 9.

The PARTNERS are committed to the facilitation of training programmes aimed at realising the full staff complement at the Fire Services and the further development of the current staff.

(v) The PARTNERS agree that the Government through the Cabinet Office will examine and report back to the PARTNERS the feasibility of an "exchange programme" between Ministries that would facilitate cross training in the public sector.

The PARTNERS agree that the government through the Cabinet Office will deliver to the PARTNERS within the first year of the Memorandum of Understanding, a training plan which will have as its objective the preparation of the Public Sector work force for the needs of a modern labour market.

The PARTNERS commit to making the necessary contacts to ensure that a process of cross training with the Private Sector will be implemented during the period 2004 – 2006.

The PARTNERS agree that a programme of training in Human Resource Management with an emphasis on Industrial Relations will be implemented for Managers and Supervisors during the period of restraint.

SPECIAL ITEMS

8. The PARTNERS agree that persons who belong to those groups with a wage contract that extends into fiscal year 2004/2005 and 2005/2006 and who will proceed on retirement during the period of restraint are to be deemed to have attained the salary that would have been paid 2004/2005 or 2005/2006 (dependent on the date of retirement) for the sole purpose of pension calculations This provision will also include those persons whose salaries are derived directly from the groups stated above at the time of signing.

9. During the period of restraint the Government of Jamaica commits to reviewing the income tax threshold.

APPLICATION

10. The PARTNERS agree that the constraints contained in this memorandum of Understanding will apply to **Central and Local Government and all other Government entities, commissions, companies, corporations, institutions and statutory bodies.**

11. The PARTNERS agree that the policy of restraint will apply to all Cabinet Ministers, Ministers of State, Parliamentary Secretaries, Members of Parliament, Mayors and Councillors.

Appendix 2

Figure 10.

12. The PARTNERS agree that no sector should be treated more favourably than the groups that are represented under this Memorandum of Understanding.

BREACHES

13. The PARTNERS agree that this Memorandum of Understanding will be deemed to have been breached if either partner violates any of the provisions contained herein. Any breach will be reported to the Monitoring Committee, which will decide on an appropriate course of action.

DATE OF EFFECT

14. This agreement will come into effect on February 17, 2004.

For and on behalf of the
Jamaica Confederation of Trade Unions

For and on behalf of
The Government of Jamaica

For and on behalf of the
[illegible] Trade Unions

[illegible] behalf of
The [illegible] Jamaica

For and on behalf of
The Government of Jamaica

For and on behalf of
The Government of Jamaica

For and on behalf of
The Government of Jamaica

About the Author

Carol Nelson, as a Lecturer in the Department of Government at the University of the West Indies, Mona, holds a Doctor of Philosophy in Government and lectures in International Political Economy, International Organizations, Media and Political Opinion, Climate Change Governance & Development and Global Political Economy and Climate Change. Dr Nelson comes to the UWI with over 20 years of experience as a director in the public sector, effectively coordinating and implementing various initiatives and activities with regards to international and regional financial institutions. Dr Nelson's responsibilities for several years involved representing the Government of Jamaica in various fora, such as on the Board of the Caribbean Development Bank (CDB) and CARICOM's Council for Finance and Planning and the CARICOM Commission on the Economy, representing the Caribbean region in 2010 on the UN Committee for Programme and Co-Ordination at the United Nations. Amongst her certification, she holds a Professional Certificate in Strategic Climate Change Adaptation from the International Centre for Parliamentary Studies, UK; an MSc in International Policy Analysis from the University of Bath, in the UK as well as a BSc in Geography & Social Sciences from the University of the West Indies, Mona Campus in Jamaica.

Index

A

B

C

D

H

I

J

L

M

N

P

S

T

U

Ensure Quality Research is Introduced to the Academic Community

Become an IGI Global Reviewer for Authored Book Projects

The overall success of an authored book project is dependent on quality and timely reviews.

In this competitive age of scholarly publishing, constructive and timely feedback significantly expedites the turnaround time of manuscripts from submission to acceptance, allowing the publication and discovery of forward-thinking research at a much more expeditious rate. Several IGI Global authored book projects are currently seeking highly qualified experts in the field to fill vacancies on their respective editorial review boards:

Applications may be sent to:
development@igi-global.com

Applicants must have a doctorate (or an equivalent degree) as well as publishing and reviewing experience. Reviewers are asked to write reviews in a timely, collegial, and constructive manner. All reviewers will begin their role on an ad-hoc basis for a period of one year, and upon successful completion of this term can be considered for full editorial review board status, with the potential for a subsequent promotion to Associate Editor.

If you have a colleague that may be interested in this opportunity, we encourage you to share this information with them.